★ ★ ★

To Serve My Country,
To Serve My Race

★ ★ ★

TO SERVE MY COUNTRY, TO SERVE MY RACE

The Story of the Only African American Wacs Stationed Overseas during World War II

Brenda L. Moore

NEW YORK UNIVERSITY PRESS
New York and London

NEW YORK UNIVERSITY PRESS
New York and London

Library of Congress Cataloging-in-Publication Data

Moore, Brenda L., 1950–
To serve my country, to serve my race : the story of the only
African American WACS stationed overseas during World War II /
Brenda L. Moore.
p. cm.
Includes bibliographical references (p.   ) and index.
ISBN 0-8147-5522-4 (acid-free paper)
1. United States—Armed Forces—Afro-Americans. 2. United States—
Armed Forces—Women. 3. World War, 1939–1945—Afro-Americans.
4. World War, 1939–1945—Participation, Female. 5. United States.
Army.—Women's Army Corps. I. Title.
UB418.A47M66 1996
940.54′03—dc20   95-32467
                              CIP

New York University Press books are printed on acid-free paper,
and their binding materials are chosen for strength and durability.

Manufactured in the United States of America

10 9 8 7 6 5 4 3 2 1

*This book is dedicated to my mother
Hester W. Moore
who, from the beginning,
persevered in opening doors for me.*

★ ★ ★

Contents

All photographs appear as an insert following
page 176

★ ★ ★

Preface

This book is a result of my longtime interest in the subject of African American women in the military. While serving six years on active duty in the U.S. Army, I recognized that African American women's experiences are different from those of African American men and of Euro-American women. While completing a doctorate in sociology with a focus on military studies at the University of Chicago, I noticed the glaring absence of African American military women from all of the major studies; it was as though black women did not exist. Indeed, there has long been a need for a systematic study of African American women's role in national defense. Although a couple of books and a few articles have been written recently on the topic, research on black women's contributions in the military remains sparse.

The purpose of this book is to examine the consequences of changes in race and gender policies for the status of African American women in the Army during World War II. World War II is a logical period to study because it marked a significant turning point in the status of racial minorities and women in the U.S. armed services. During that era opportunities for women in the military expanded, as discussed at length in chapter 1. What social, political, and organizational factors influenced change in racial and gender policies in the military during World War II?

What were the unique factors associated with being African American, female, and in the armed services at that time in American history? How did these women actively shape their lives? These and other questions are explored in the following pages.

★ ★ ★

Acknowledgments

I am deeply indebted to the former members of the 6888th Central Postal Directory Battalion for their willingness to be interviewed. They were generous with their time and in some cases shared treasured scrapbooks containing photographs, official military documents with raised seals, and written memoirs. To all of them I am sincerely grateful.

Ideas for this book began to develop in spring 1991, when I received a Dr. Nuala McGann Drescher Affirmative Action Leave Award to research archival documents on women in the U.S. Army. I was able to develop those ideas further while at the University of Maryland at College Park on a postdoctoral fellowship award during academic year 1991–92. I thank Mady and David Segal for serving as my sponsors, and for their valuable feedback on my work. I researched and wrote portions of this book during the summers of 1992 and 1993, thanks to summer faculty awards from the United States Army Research Institute for the Behavioral and Social Sciences. Some of the themes in the book were reprinted from an article I wrote in 1993 titled "Serving with a Dual Mission: African American Women in World War II," with the permission of the *National Journal of Sociology*. I am also grateful to Charles C. Moskos, Cynthia Enloe, and two anonymous reviewers for their valuable comments on an earlier draft of this book.

A grant from the Julian Park Publication Fund at the State University of New York at Buffalo assisted with the duplication of some of the archival photographs. Some of my travel expenses, as well as funds for tape transcriptions, were provided by the School of Law, Baldy Center, at the State University of New York at Buffalo under the Gender and Law Project. Finally, I am thankful to Don Watkins and to Barbara Evans at the State University of New York at Buffalo's Art and Photographic Services, for preparing my figures and tables.

★ ★ ★

Abbreviations

ACWIS	Advisory Council to the Women's Interests Section
AGCT	Army General Classification Test
AWOL	Absent Without Leave
CO	Commanding Officer
ETO	European Theater of Operations
G-1	Assistant Chief of Staff for Personnel
KP	Kitchen Police
MP	Military Police
NAWSA	National American Woman Suffrage Association
NAACP	National Association for the Advancement of Colored People
NCAC	National Civilian Advisory Committee
NCO	Noncommissioned Officer
NCNW	National Council of Negro Women
OCS	Officer Candidate School
OJT	On the Job Training
POWs	Prisoners of War
SO	Special Orders
VA	Veterans Administration
WAAC	Women's Army Auxiliary Corps
Waac	A member of the WAAC

WAC   Women's Army Corps
Wac   A member of the WAC
WAVES Women Accepted for Volunteer Emergency Service
WIS   Women's Interests Section

★ ★ ★

List of Tables and Figures

★ ★ ★

Introduction

> We had classes in military organization, how to salute,
> how to march. "Take 30 steps," barked the drill ser-
> geant. "Fall in! Dress right! Fall out! Dress right dress!
> Clean the latrine! Polish the shoes! Make the cot! Police
> the area! Reveille! Retreat! Mess Call! Mail Call!
> Straighten those shoulders! Belly in! Hut two! Whatever
> made you blankety blankety women think you could be
> soldiers?"   —Gertrude LaVigne

World War II marked a turning point in the status of racial
minorities and women in the U.S. armed services. The nature of
the conflict challenged existing forms of social stratification in the
Army, as well as in other American institutions. Previous military
restrictions placed on race were lifted as a result of the Selective
Service Training Act of 1940, and African American men were
recruited for the war effort in greater numbers than in previous
wars. They also served in a greater variety of military assignments.

Opportunities for women were also expanding, beginning with
the establishment of the Women's Army Auxiliary Corps (WAAC)
in March 1942. The WAAC was converted to the WAC, or
Women's Army Corps, in 1943, giving women full military benefits. The Women Accepted for Volunteer Emergency Service
(WAVES) was instituted in July 1942, and the Marine Corps
enrolled women in February 1943. There was no separate air
force in the American military during World War II, but rather an
Army Air Corps, which was part of the War Department. Indeed,

the forties witnessed a movement launched by the U.S. War Department to recruit large numbers of women into the military to contribute to the war effort.

Until World War II African American women were virtually excluded from military service. Although several attempted to participate in World War I, only eighteen were accepted for duty in the Army Nurses Corps.[1] During World War II, by contrast, African American women were accepted into the Women's Army Auxiliary Corps as soon as it was founded, largely because of pressure placed on the War Department by black political organizations demanding racial equality. Black activists monitored closely the War Department's plans for developing a women's corps; thus, when it was revealed that a Texan, Oveta Culp Hobby, was appointed as director of the WAAC, they protested the appointment on the grounds that Hobby, because of her southern background, would discriminate against African American women. After Hobby allocated forty of the first officer trainee slots to African American women, black opposition to her appointment tapered off.[2] Independent of the efforts of black political organizations, African American women also participated in feminist ventures to gain public acceptance of a women's military corps. (Examples of these efforts are discussed at length in chapters 2 and 3.)

Most African American women who served in the military during the war joined the U.S. Army, because the other services categorically refused to admit them. The Navy, for example, did not begin accepting African American women for active duty until nearly two and one-half years after the WAVES came into existence.[3] Naval officials explained that they did not allow African American women to serve because there were no black men going on sea duty for them to replace.[4] Nobody could explain why African American women could not replace white men; obviously that was simply taken for granted. Consequently, African American women were excluded from service in the Navy until President Roosevelt ran for a fourth term of office and directly ordered the Navy to admit them.[5] Unlike African American women serving in the WAAC/WAC, the few who served in the Navy were integrated with white WAVES, largely because so few African American women were admitted.

The former director of the WAVES, Mildred McAfee Horton, revealed in a published interview that the Navy had no real problems in integrating black women at that time:

It was announced quickly that we would accept officers and we wanted officers particularly to help supervise the women—the Negro women—at Hunter [College] in the basic training school, where there was to be no segregation except that there would be a company of 250 [Negro] women, and they would have all the privileges of the station, they would eat in the same mess, everything there, which was a simply incredible achievement from the point of view of where we'd been in the Navy. . . . The 250 women to be taken into the company at Hunter were way short—I think that there were only 25. . . . The Negro girls simply went in and took their places with everyone else. . . . Captain Amsden said, "The only episode that we remember was when one white girl went down to the mate of the deck in the apartment house and said, 'I think there must be some mistake because I find that my roommate is going to be a Negro girl,' and the officer of the deck said, 'Well, we're in the Navy now, and we're all citizens.' " So, Captain Amsden said, "the white girl went upstairs and helped her roommate make her bunk."[6]

The Marine Corps did not enlist African American women until after the war, in September 1949.[7] Thus, during the war the Army offered the greatest opportunity for racial minorities in general and African American women in particular to serve on active duty. Deployment of racial minorities and women in the Army during World War II represented milestones that led in subsequent years to racial and gender integration of all the armed services.

To Serve My Country, To Serve My Race relies heavily on testimonies of women who served in the 6888th Central Postal Directory Battalion, the only group of African American Wacs (members of the Women's Army Corps) to serve overseas during the war. Because of its race and gender composition, the 6888th would have been inconceivable before World War II. An estimated 855 African American Wacs, 824 enlisted women and 31 officers, served with the 6888th. (The names, ranks, and serial numbers of 742 of these women are listed in Appendix C.) Who were these women, and where did they come from? What were their living, working, and social experiences while they served in Europe? How did military service affect their lives when they reentered the civilian world and later? What can their experiences teach us more broadly about social conflict and social change? Fifty-one women who served with the 6888th were interviewed for this book, 5 officers and 46 enlisted women. Their names and birthplaces and the places and dates of my interviews of them are listed in Appendix A. These women truly represent the diversity that characterized the unit. They entered the military from different geographical areas, from different socioeconomic backgrounds, and with different educational achievement levels, as discussed further in chapter 4.

When I embarked on this research, so little had been written about African American women in the military that I had to go out into the field to collect and consolidate information. By thoroughly examining documents at the Military Reference Branch of the National Archives, I was able to locate the names of some of the African American women who had served in England and France during World War II. I researched leads on these women and eventually obtained telephone numbers and, in some cases, addresses. After designing a questionnaire, I began conducting interviews by telephone.

When I contacted the first few interviewees, I was astounded to learn that these women lead very active lives; I had imagined them as dormant and sedentary. Much to my surprise, some of these senior citizens are still employed full time, others serve on political boards, and almost all of them do volunteer work in their communities. Many of the women travel to various organizational meetings and government functions to speak about their military experience. Several attended the Tribute to World War II Veterans held by the Black Congressional Caucus in Washington, D.C. in September 1994.

I was very pleased by the women's receptiveness to my study and by their willingness, even eagerness, to provide me with information. With each interview I acquired the names of one or two additional women who had served with the group. This snowball process continued throughout the entire interviewing period. Although I interviewed most of the women by telephone, I also traveled throughout the United States and interviewed several in person. During my travels I attended two large events for women veterans, where I was able to meet and interview some former members of the 6888th. The first event, the Fiftieth Anniversary Convention of the Women's Army Corps, was held at Fort McClellan, Alabama, in May 1992. The second event was the Black WAAC-WAC Women in the Services Eighth Biennial Reunion, held in September of the same year. Because of time constraints I interviewed some of the women during the events and made arrangements to interview others later.

This study also draws on archival documents on African Americans and women who served in the military during World War II. I obtained documents from several sources including the National Archives, Washington, D.C.; the Bethune Museum and Archives, Washington, D.C.; the Schomburg Center for Research in Black Culture, New York; the Headquarters United States Air Force Historical Research Center at Maxwell Air Force Base, Montgomery; the Historical Archives at Tuskegee University; the Center of Military History, Washington, D.C.; the National Personnel Records Center, St. Louis; the Oral History Department, U.S. Naval Institute, Annapolis; the U.S. Military History Institute, Carlisle Barracks, Pennsylvania; the Amistad Research Center, New Orleans; and the WAC Foundation at Fort McClellan, Alabama. In some instances information found in nontechnical material such as diaries and biographies helped me to formulate the data used for this study.

I first examined for content the official literature, such as military documents, and the nonofficial literature, such as biographies, diaries, documents, manuscripts, and records. Then I developed a questionnaire to survey former members of the 6888th about their lives before, during, and after military service (see Appendix B). Interviews were conducted by telephone and in person. I asked open-ended questions in an effort to encourage respondents to speak freely on a specific topic and thereby reveal unexpected insights into their military experiences. I used closed-ended questions to ascertain specific facts. All of the interviews were audiotaped; in one instance I conducted a videotaped session in Boston with a member of the 6888th. Interviewees participated voluntarily, could withdraw at any time, and were given the opportunity to review the results.

Members of the 6888th were not the only African American women to serve overseas during the war. Black nurses had served in Australia and Africa before the establishment of the 6888th. (The army nurses corps was a separate organization from the WAC.) In fact, the first African American women to serve overseas were a unit of nurses assigned to Liberia. Later, in June of 1944, a unit of sixty-three black nurses was sent to England to care for German prisoners of war. In contrast to the diverse members of the 6888th, all of these black nurses had distinguished themselves as part of the medical profession.[8]

The 6888th was more than eight times as large as the largest unit of African American nurses to be deployed overseas and was more representative of black women in the larger society; some were professionals, while others were unskilled. Members of the unit came from all walks of life. They entered the military from different regions, but the majority came from the eastern region of the United States. Some had attended elementary school in cities, others in country towns. Some went away to college and graduated before entering the military; others entered the military directly out of high school. Although they represented all levels of education, talent, and skills, most of these women were well educated and had clerical experience. They were ambitious and young and wanted to "make something" of themselves.

Moreover, they wanted to make a difference in the world. Realizing that "the eyes of the world" were upon them, members of the 6888th welcomed the opportunity to prove themselves publicly and to blaze a trail for other African American women.

Not the typical WAC unit deployed overseas, the 6888th was a microcosm of the then-current sociopolitical struggles over efforts to give black women the right to serve in all facets of the U.S. Army. Before they were assembled into the 6888th, these women worked in a variety of military occupations at a number of Army and Army Air Force installations throughout the United States. The unit was composed of women from both Army Air Force and Army Service Force units, so that all African American Wacs would have an opportunity to serve overseas. This remarkable group served in England and France from January 1945 until March 1946. The battalion's members were rotated back to the United States at different times, depending on how long they had already served.

Members of the 6888th joined the WAAC/WAC for a variety of personal, political, and economic reasons. They had no idea where they would be assigned to work once they entered the Army, but most believed that they would be treated the same as white Waacs/Wacs. African American women were told that the military would not discriminate against them because of their race, and they believed it. Deeply affected by advertisements stressing nationalistic themes, some women joined to demonstrate patriotism. Through the Office of War Information (OWI), which placed advertisements in magazines and newspapers and on the radio, the Army encouraged thousands of women to join the Women's Army Auxiliary Corps.[9] Most of these advertisements were aimed toward altering gender roles of middle-class white women by sending the message that women could retain their femininity even though they were strong enough to actively support the war effort.

A few advertisements were also placed in black newspapers. To avoid the impression of discriminating against African American women, the War Department advertised in publications such as New York's *Amsterdam News,* the *Chicago Defender,* and the magazine *The Crisis: A Record of the Darker Races* to target women in the black community. For the same purpose the Army printed a WAAC recruitment poster in 1942 on which an African American woman pointed to the caption "Women Answer America's Call." [10] Many of the 6888th members joined the military in response to Army advertisements in the black press, headlined with the now-famous slogan "Uncle Sam Needs You."

Gertrude LaVigne, supply sergeant of the 6888th, stated in an interview that the advertisements about the WAAC influenced her to join the military. Born in Jacksonville, Alabama, LaVigne lived with two brothers, four sisters, and her mother. Her father had died when she was very young; her mother supported her family by working in tobacco fields for a few years before moving to Cincinnati and starting a catering business. LaVigne left school in the eleventh grade, worked full time in her mother's catering business, and married her first husband just before going into the military. Because she placed a high premium on education, LaVigne was especially interested in the GI benefits that the military was offering: "When I saw all the advertisement about schooling and the other benefits, and the travel which would probably be involved, I thought, This is what I want." [11]

Both black and white recruiters visited black schools to encourage black women to join the WAC. Allie Davis, who served as one of the many postal clerks of the 6888th, grew up on a farm in Colbert, Oklahoma, with her parents, two brothers, and two sisters. Davis had completed three years of college; before joining the military she worked part time as a laundress to help pay her college expenses. She signed up after learning about the GI Bill from a white male recruiter who had visited her school.

Sammye Davis was born in Cottage Grove, Alabama, but grew up in Memphis with her father, stepmother, and younger twin brothers. Her biological mother had died when she was six, and her father remarried when she was eight. Davis graduated from

LeMoyne College in 1944 with a degree in education and joined the military because she was impressed by an African American Wac who visited her college. She recalls, "She looked good physically. She looked healthy and she represented the Army very well." Davis worked as a postal clerk with the 6888th.

Dorothy Johnson, another case in point, had completed four years at Spelman College before joining the military. Looking back at the reasons why she joined the military, Johnson says:

In the first place I think I joined because I was bored at Spelman. And the second reason I joined was that I wanted to travel. I wanted to go overseas. Probably the third most compelling reason was that one morning a recruiting officer was one of our speakers in the chapel convocation, and she made such an impression on a number of us that . . . we decided that was the thing that we wanted to do. And so we did.

Elaine Bennett joined the WAC "because I wanted to prove to myself, and maybe to the world, that we [African Americans] would give what we had back to the United States as a confirmation that we were full-fledged citizens." Bennett was to become the first sergeant of Company D. Born in Madison, Florida, she was one of the two children of a black businessman and his wife, who worked as a seamstress. Bennett describes her family as close-knit. Both of her parents were active in church: "My father was, of course, a trustee, my mother sang in the choir, and they were very, very religious people. You didn't play cards in my house and you didn't dance in my house, and that kind of thing." Through her church Bennett earned an academic scholarship to New York University. She completed three years of college before joining the military: "I was majoring in business administration. . . . My father and mother felt that I better major in education because during that time . . . we [African Americans] only had the opportunity to preach or teach. But teaching was really not my bag, it really wasn't."

Margaret Barbour was the youngest child in a family of three boys and four girls:

I was born in Seaford, Virginia. I lived in a white neighborhood; my family was the only Blacks there, and still is. I didn't have any racial problems. Schools were segregated. I was quite content when I came out of high school; at that time they had the National Youth Administration, and they sent me to college. I went to McKinley Union University; they had a branch in Norfolk, Virginia at that time.

When I asked her why she joined the military, Barbour responded, "My mother had passed. There was only my father and I left. So I thought it [the military] would be a good change for me, and it worked out just fine."

Some of the women joined the Army in an effort to advance occupationally. Bernice Thomas was born in Brooklyn and reared in Harlem, the only child of a musician and a domestic worker. Thomas was a single parent, working in the garment district, before entering the military in 1944:

Had I stayed in New York, I could see no advancement for me in any field. I was working in the garment district, and at one time I was working on a specialized machine where you did one little thing over and over and over all day long. And then I started pressing all of this underwear, I would just be exhausted. I wasn't really satisfied with how my life was progressing at that time, and I felt that women in the military were going to have a better opportunity when everything was over and there would be more jobs opening up, particularly for black women. Had I continued to work at the garment district, I would have been dead and gone a long time ago because I couldn't have withstood it.

Thomas, like many other African American women going into the Women's Army Corps, was willing to make the sacrifices necessary to obtain veteran's benefits in the years that would follow the war. For Thomas the sacrifice was even more demanding than it was for many others, because she left behind a 16-year-old son:

The only personal disadvantage of serving in the military was that I had to leave my son in New Jersey with some dear friends. And I kind of think I lost a lot by not being with him at the time I should have been. I tried to explain to him that I was doing this for both of our benefits. He was very unhappy when I left even though he understood my reasons because we talked it out. But he was very unhappy that he didn't have mama because I was the closest thing to him. I think that by leaving him in New Jersey with friends, I lost the friendship I once had with him.

Similarly, Blanche Scott, who was born in Boydton in Mecklenburg County, Virginia, reports:

I had one whole brother and three half-brothers and one half-sister. My parents were both teachers. My father was married before he married my mother, so I never lived around my half-sister and brothers. I went into the military from Washington, D.C. I graduated from high school in 1934 and had three years of college before the depression hit. See my mother died the year that I graduated high school. I had a scholarship and I went to Howard University in 1934. To be frank with you, the day that I was supposed to enter Howard, my mother died. She was injured in a streetcar out on Route 103; and she died, and she was buried the day I was suppose to enter Howard. But I went [to Howard] because I had a scholarship. And it was just hard and I didn't graduate and so I finally got a job after three and a half years. And I got along; there was no one but me. I remember when I had a box of crackers and a can of potted meat that would last me a couple of days, but I never thought I was poor. I think back now and I don't know how some of these people today would have made it back then. I went to work for the government as a nursing attendant at St. Elizabeth Hospital; it was a mental institution and still is. And then I was on the clerks' register; so when I came up on the clerks' register I transferred from that to the Navy Department to work as a clerk. And then I left to go into the Army.

The 1940s witnessed widespread underemployment and unemployment among African Americans. The United States at that time typified a racial-caste society, which placed African Americans at a disadvantage in relation to other racial and ethnic groups.[12] To many African American women, the military represented a glimmer of hope for realizing their dreams.

Willie Whiting joined the military because "my family could not afford to send me to college." She lived with her mother, stepfather, and brother:

My dad was a refrigerating engineer at an ice company, and my mother was a housewife and a seamstress. We lived in Chicago where Robert Taylor Homes [a housing project in Chicago, notorious for gang wars and other crime] are now erected. It was a two-story frame when I lived there. I went to elementary school in the neighborhood. My brother and I went to an integrated high school on the west side of the city, which was known as McKinley High School at the time. I graduated. My brother died [of natural causes] before he came out of high school.

Before entering the military Whiting had completed two years of college: "I had intermittently been employed. There was no money for me to go to college. The funds that were used—I guess a portion of them was a part of the insurance proceeds from my brother's death—were exhausted; and there were not the beautiful grants and those things that are available today." Whiting joined the WAC in September 1944, three months after President Roosevelt signed into law the Servicemen's Readjustment Act of 1944 (the GI Bill, which provided educational benefits for veterans). The GI Bill was a strong incentive for those who wanted to go on to higher education after their military service, and recruiters constantly mentioned it to potential recruits.

Like Bernice Thomas, Blanche Scott, and Willie Whiting, other women also joined the military as a means of upward mobility. Mary Daniels Williams, a former cook in the 6888th, was born in Cleveland and lived with her parents, two sisters, and three brothers. Her mother worked ironing shirts, and her father was a mechanic. Growing up during the depression, Williams remembers that opportunities for African American women were very scarce: "I was going nowhere fast. I was getting older and I could just see us living in the slums forever." Williams had completed the ninth grade and was cleaning houses before she joined the military. ("I had no skills.") She had an unsuccessful marriage and had given birth to a stillborn child. Williams recalls, "I could look up and see all those other [socially disadvantaged] people, and all the millions of kids. I [could see myself] living in two or three rooms for the rest of my life, and I decided for myself I wasn't going to do it." Williams spoke with a military recruiter at a post office in Cincinnati: "They promised us education, new places to go and to visit—well, just a totally new life."

Quite a few women stated that they joined the Army because they were unable to find employment in the civilian sector. Others assumed that they would increase their opportunity to obtain a good education by joining the Women's Army Auxiliary Corps. Gladys Anderson wanted to advance by acquiring the skills necessary to become a secretary. Margaret Barbour wanted a "better way of life." Still others were merely curious: they just wanted to see what military service was like.

While some of the African American women mentioned so far joined the WAAC/WAC to escape severe economic hardship, others like Davis, Johnson, Bennett, and Barbour had grown up in households where their parents made a comfortable living. Many were able to further their formal education after high school, obtaining either a vocational skill or a college degree. Some even secured stable employment. Ruth Wade, for example, was born in Jackson, Tennessee, where she grew up in a household with two sisters (one of whom was her twin) and two brothers. Her father was a barber, and her mother taught elementary school. Wade's family moved to Detroit when she was ten years old. There she completed high school and Ruby's Beauty School, "the biggest beauty school in Detroit at that particular time." In the 6888th Wade was assigned to the motor pool.

Charity E. Adams Earley, battalion commander of the 6888th, was born in Columbia, South Carolina, where she grew up with two brothers and a sister. Her mother was a former schoolteacher who had retired to be a homemaker; her father was an ordained minister in the African Methodist Episcopalian Church. After graduating from college and teaching mathematics for four years in South Carolina's public school system, Earley was invited by the War Department to apply for the Women's Army Auxiliary Corps: "Teaching was about the only thing available for you [African American women] unless you went into domestic service. . . . The Army was recommended to me and I was recommended to it, as were most of us in the first Officer's Candidate class, and I decided to take it."

A. Noel Campbell Mitchell, the executive officer of the 6888th, was born in Tuskegee, Alabama, where she grew up in a household with her parents, three brothers, and two sisters. Her father worked for the Department of Agriculture, teaching modern farming techniques to rural farmers; her mother was a homemaker. Mitchell graduated from Tuskegee Institute in 1940 with a degree in home economics and taught two years at a junior high school in Cartersville, Georgia before joining the WAAC.

However diverse their backgrounds, members of the 6888th shared the experience of being stigmatized as black women in a predominantly white male institution. African American men and (later) women of European descent were being deployed overseas, but black women were excluded from such assignments until the War Department acquiesced to political pressure specifically aimed at this omission. Challenges to the War Department's exclusionary practices surfaced in newspaper articles and were expressed in comments by black congressional representatives and leaders of such community organizations as the National Association for the Advancement of Colored People (NAACP) and the National Council of Negro Women (NCNW). (The latter group, founded by Mary McLeod Bethune in 1935, consisted of several black women's organizations.) Military officials of the European Theater of Operations (ETO) conceded and submitted a requisition for black women to set up half of a central postal directory.[13]

Dorothy Bartlett was reared in Newark, New Jersey, where she lived with her parents, two brothers, and two sisters. Her father was an elevator operator at a large hotel; her mother was a homemaker. Like many African American women of the time, she grew up in a low-income family that stressed religion and moral values: "Papa was making very little money. There was no going on picnics for us. We all belonged to Sunday school. My mother was Baptist; my father was Methodist; so we went to each church." Bartlett left school to get married in 1925. Her marriage ended in divorce in 1942, after she had given birth to one child. She lived with her oldest sister before going into the Army: "I had previously lived in Brooklyn with my husband, and then when I got divorced, I took my daughter and went to live in New York [Manhattan]."

In November 1944, two months before members of the 6888th began overseas orientation at Fort Oglethorpe, Georgia, Bartlett joined the WAC. She had been working as a silk finisher in the garment section of New York City and soon would become a postal clerk in the very unit that was at the center of much political debate:

This unit [the 6888th] was formed through a lot of persuasion and stuff. Congressman Powell from New York was complaining about the lack of black Wacs overseas, and he was able to get something passed in Congress or something. Anyhow, this [the 6888th] was the only black WAC unit overseas the whole time.

Margaret Barnes Jones, public relations officer of the 6888th, was born in Oberlin, Ohio, where she grew up with two brothers and two sisters. Her mother was a political activist, a member of the Speakers Bureau for the Republican Party in the state of Ohio, and president of the Ohio Federation of Colored Women's Clubs. Her father was a chef. Jones describes Oberlin as a pleasant area for a young African American woman: "Oberlin has quite a tradition as being very liberal. It was the first college to admit women, and the underground railroad ran right through Oberlin. As far as prejudice was concerned it never entered our lives. We had two schools and you went to the school you lived closest to."

Jones attributes the deployment of African American Wacs overseas largely to the efforts of Mary McLeod Bethune, a prominent leader and a close friend of her mother's:

I think she was one of the reasons the 6888th came into existence, and that we [African American Wacs] finally got out of the United States, because there weren't any black Wacs outside of the continental limits of the United States. She [Bethune] was very close to Eleanor Roosevelt, and Franklin Roosevelt simply asked her if it was true that there were no black Wacs outside the continental limits of the United States. He was not aware of that. He was president of the United States, and he didn't know. And she had to admit that it was true, and there were white Wacs in North Africa, and driving staff cars in Paris, and we [African American Wacs] still hadn't left the United States.

Bethune indeed played a central role in the deployment of black Wacs overseas. Her close association with Eleanor Roosevelt developed after she had been appointed by President Roosevelt as director of the Negro division of the National Youth Administration, a relief program for American youth.[14] In the spring of 1942 Bethune served as a special assistant to the secretary of war to help select black Wac officer candidates. She was also the director of the National Council of Negro Women (a nonprofit organization that works to increase opportunities and improve the quality of life for African American women, even today) and later an advisor to the director of the Women's Army Corps, Oveta Culp Hobby, on African American Wacs.[15]

Bethune knew virtually everything about African American Wacs. Ruth Wade met Bethune while she was in basic training at Fort Des Moines:

I always had small feet and when we were being fitted for clothing in Des Moines I was told that I would be issued a pair of shoes a half-size too big. When Bethune came to visit I told her that I had blisters on my feet. She said, "Go over there [to supply] and tell them that *I* said to issue you some shoes that fit."

Deeply committed to human equality, Bethune labored vigorously to get African American Wacs full participation in the Women's Army Corps.

So much controversy surrounded the deployment of African American Wacs overseas that many had lost hope of ever being deployed abroad by the time they were finally requisitioned. Some were so disillusioned that they received the news of the assignment with disbelief. Charity Adams Earley recalls:

About mid-December Colonel Mac called me into his office and asked, "How would you like to go overseas?" I smiled, assuming the question was rhetorical. I knew that the Negro press had a campaign in progress to see that Negro Wacs were assigned overseas, as white Wacs had been. To date that campaign had elicited the response that Negro Wacs would create problems in the overseas arena.[16]

Earley soon realized that African American Wacs in fact would be deployed overseas and that she would be the commander of the unit.

Noel Campbell Mitchell was stationed at Fort Oglethorpe when she received a letter from Charity Adams, a good friend of hers, informing her of the Army's plans to deploy black Wacs overseas:

We had joined the Army together and she had been my commanding officer for nine months. . . . We hadn't seen each other for over two years but had kept in touch. . . . I read the letter and was dumbfounded. Edna said that it was true that colored Wacs were to go overseas. The plans were being made at Des Moines and she had been informed that she would be commander of the troops, and if there were any women she wanted as her officers she could ask for them. She said she had thought about me, and if I was interested she would submit my name. . . . I was excited because ever since I had heard the rumors I was sure if the opportunity came, I would certainly volunteer.

(Charity Adams was called Edna by her family and friends.) Mitchell was later to become the executive officer of the 6888th.

Members of the 6888th welcomed the opportunity to serve overseas and were not likely to let anything interfere with that chance. Elsie Oliver was born in Burkeville, Virginia, where her parents were farm workers. She had completed high school and was twenty-eight years old, working in Boston as a hairdresser, before she joined the military: "My parents would have never agreed for me to go [into the Army], and I didn't say anything to them about it until I was in."

Oliver was a cook in an all-black WAC detachment at Camp Gruber, Oklahoma, when the War Department finally requisitioned African American women to serve overseas:

My company officer [a black Wac] did not want me to go; she said, "You're needed right here." I went over her head when she told me that she was going to delete my name from the list. I went to the supreme commander of the whole post, Colonel Locket. He was over everybody, both white and black. He knew me because he ate at our mess hall. That morning was so cold, but I was so provoked that I didn't even put on a coat; I went right to his office in just a white uniform. I told him that I was chosen for overseas duty and we had only a few days to get ready to leave for Fort Oglethorpe, Georgia for training, and my company officer didn't want me to go. I asked him for help so that I could go through some channel over her head. He suggested that I talk with Eleanor Roosevelt. I asked him how I could get in touch with Mrs. Roosevelt on such a short notice. He replied, "Here's my telephone." He put the call through to Washington from his office and handed the phone to me. Mrs. Roosevelt's receptionist informed me that Mrs. Roosevelt was in a meeting and that she would be in touch with me. I left my company officer's telephone number. Colonel Locket took me back down to the WAC Detachment and while he was talking with my company officer the phone rang and it was Mrs. Roosevelt. She asked my Company Officer, "Do you know Elsie Oliver?" My company officer replied, "Yes." Mrs. Roosevelt then said, "Well, have her ready for shipment at four p.m. today." That was all. I think at four p.m. I was the first one waiting for the train.

Similarly, Gladys Carter says: "When the word got out that there was going to be a group [of African American women] to go overseas, everybody wanted to go. I know I wanted to go. I think I would have climbed up a mountain to get on the list." When I asked her why there was so much excitement about serving overseas, Carter replied: "We were going to do our duty.

Despite all the bad things that happened in the country, this was our home. This [the United States] is where I was born. It was where my mother and father were. So there was a feeling of wanting to do your part."

These responses reflect those of other members of the 6888th. The United States entered World War II for the explicit purpose of making the world safe for democracy, a concept that resonated in the hearts and minds of African American women (however ironically, given their legal and societal status in pre-civil-rights-movement America). The war offered them an opportunity to demonstrate their patriotism and subsequently to reap the benefits of the country's economic and political prosperity.

Political motives alone, however, do not explain the excitement these women felt about going overseas. Many were still in their teens, young and eager to see another part of the world. Virginia Frazier recalls:

I went in when I was nineteen. We were young. We were all young then. When you're young you don't know what you're getting into. In fact who would have ever thought that a little girl from Minnesota, black at that, would go away to Europe? It was very exciting because I had never been. . . . We had a ball! We did our job, and then afterwards, we did our thing.

Born from political struggles for racial equality, the 6888th represented a victory for the NAACP, the NCNW, the black press, and all who fought for racial equality in the armed services, especially the Women's Army Corps. This book describes how change in the military was a direct result of pressure external to the institution. But even more important, it examines changes in the military that resulted from the employment of African American women. These women were not mere passive objects in an institution that had only recently opened its doors to them. They campaigned actively to change race-biased policies in the Women's Army (Auxiliary) Corps. To illustrate this point, Margaret Barnes Jones recalls an act of resistance at her permanent duty station after basic training:

[I] went to Camp Breckenridge, Kentucky. That was an experience that I'll never forget. . . . I was the executive officer, a Second Lieutenant. The company officer was a [black] first lieutenant from Boston; her name was Myrtle Anderson. She and I took 175 black women to Camp Breckenridge, Kentucky, and that was the beginning of an active experience because the commanding officer of that post was a southerner, and when he saw my records, [and] he saw those of Captain Anderson, he reminded us that although she was from Boston, which is in the north, and I was from Ohio, which is in the north, we were both then in the South. He pointed that out.

Camp Breckenridge was a predominantly white military installation in the South during World War II. The post commander whom Jones mentions was a white southerner who felt that African Americans "belonged in their place." African American Wacs in Jones's unit at Camp Breckenridge were forced to confront the obstacle of being malassigned:

Because of the assignments that those girls had, they were assigned as charwomen and they had to work in the laundry. Now those Wacs were skilled. One was a schoolteacher, they had done administrative work, they had done all kinds of things. At Camp Breckenridge they were assigned to clean the ramp, to scrub the ramp, and to work in the laundry; they rebelled. And the Post Commander heard about it. And Captain Anderson and I had a company meeting, and I told those girls that unless they carried out their assignments they would tie our hands. There wouldn't be anything we [Captain Anderson and myself] could do because the post commander was already a devout racist. I went to the motor pool that night and checked out a jeep and drove to Evansville, Indiana, and I called Fort Des Moines, Iowa (Dovey Roundtree was still out there then),[17] told the officer on duty, "I want you to listen carefully. I'm going to say this once." I said, "There's a very volatile situation here at Camp Breckenridge." And I explained to her [the duty officer] what had happened. And I said that someone needs to come here before there is more trouble than there already is. I said, "General

Faith," who was the general at Fort Des Moines, "should hear about this." [18]

Brig. Gen. Don C. Faith, the former commandant of the First WAAC Training Center at Fort Des Moines (where Jones had taken basic training), is reputed to have been a fair leader and generally was respected by African American Waacs. When Jones placed her call to Fort Des Moines, General Faith had been reassigned as commander of the WAAC Training Command, overseeing operations at three training centers (Fort Des Moines, Daytona Beach, and Fort Oglethorpe). He was also assigned as head of the Training and Field Inspection Division.

General Faith's field inspection service reported a number of malassignments of Wacs and declared that such assignments resulted in resentment and low morale. Jones continued:

Well, General Faith was told about it, and in two days he was at Camp Breckenridge. Now the Post Commander never ever knew how he [General Faith] got there. As a matter of fact I never told my commanding officer, Captain Anderson, what I had done. But I did it. So in the meantime I had all the qualifications of every woman in the organization [unit] and their assignments were changed to those commensurate with what they were qualified to do. Those assignments were changed.

Many of the 6888th members stood up relentlessly for their rights. While at Fort Oglethorpe, preparing to go overseas, Gladys Carter refused to drink out of a water fountain marked "for colored only":

I decided I wanted a drink of water and I was shocked to see two water fountains, one marked "colored" and the other marked "white." . . . I had not seen this on an Army post before. . . . It wasn't like that at Walla Walla. . . . As I was getting ready to take a sip [of water from the fountain marked "white"] a little black lady came up to me and said, "You have to drink out of this one" [pointing to the one labeled "colored"]. I remember being kind of upset about that and saying, "I'm in the United States Army, I'm not drinking out of any colored water fountain." I marched over and drank my water out of the white fountain, like Miss Jane Pittman, I guess.[19] I told some of the girls, and everybody walked over and drank out of the white fountain.

Such acts of resistance were necessary before changes were made in inequitable racial and gender policies. Struggles like these are described in further detail in chapter 3.

The women in this study were pioneers in military service during a time when racial segregation was law, and a woman's place was in the home. Consequently, African American women contributed to military service in the face of the harsh realities of racism and sexism. Their contributions too often have been omitted from historical accounts of military events and from sociological and psychological assessments of military veterans. *To Serve My Country, To Serve My Race* acknowledges such contributions by observing how the military and the lives of the African American Wacs changed as a result of World War II. Chapter 2 focuses on structural changes that were made in the military before African American women were permitted to serve. Chapter 3 discusses the uniqueness of being an African American woman in the Army during World War II; in that chapter I highlight the discrimination they faced because of their race and gender, as well as their acts of resistance to social inequality. Chapter 4 concentrates on members of the 6888th and their preparations for going overseas. Chapter 5 describes the experiences of the unit's members in England and France. Chapter 6 looks at the lives of these women when they returned to the United States and examines the military as a possible turning point and an avenue of upward mobility. Chapter 7 analyzes the 6888th in terms of three theories: social cohesion, social conflict, and phenomenology. Finally, chapter 8 looks at what some of these women are doing today.

In sum, *To Serve My Country, To Serve My Race* examines the processes by which members of the 6888th sought to obtain sociopolitical rights during a period in American history when these rights were systematically denied to racial minorities and women. These women identified with being American, had internalized the American ideal of "liberty and justice for all," and for the most part sought to work within the confines of the system, making appeals through letter writing and official organizational processes. A central factor motivating members of the 6888th to join the Women's Army (Auxiliary) Corps was a strong desire for social change. Their presence and their service in the military led to conflict, which facilitated such change.

2

★ ★ ★

A Changing Military Structure

Dominants can incorporate tokens and still preserve
their generalizations by inducting tokens into stereotypical roles that preserve familiar forms of interaction
between the kinds of people represented by the token
and the dominants.

—Rosabeth Kanter, *Men and Women of
the Corporation*

As society changes, so does the military, albeit often at a different
rate. Changes in social relations that began during World War II
resulted in part from an advanced industrial economy as well as
from the war itself. The transition from an agrarian to an industrial society was accelerated because of the need for more expedi-
ent war production. This war was more mechanized than previous
wars, and American factories were able to produce war goods at
unprecedented speed: automobile factories manufactured tanks;
typewriter factories manufactured machine guns.

With massive numbers of white men deployed abroad to fight,
millions of American women left their homes to work in the
factories. Members of racial and ethnic minorities who had been
previously passed over for jobs were able to find work in war
production. People migrated to cities en masse in search of jobs in
the burgeoning industrial centers. Much of the black migration to
cities was also spurred by new technology in southern agriculture:
the planting and harvesting of crops, formerly the work of black

sharecroppers, now were performed by such farm machines as tractors and cotton pickers.[1]

World War II marked the beginning of a complex era defined by wholesale changes in the social, political, and economic roles of the American populace. Entire new social classes composed of industrial workers and technicians emerged. Americans began to view the world and themselves in a new way, which led to unprecedented cultural and legal changes. As a whole, American society was gradually forced to become more tolerant of social change, as indicated by the gains made by women, African Americans, and other historically oppressed segments of the population. Social change, however, is always met with resistance, as demonstrated by the numerous race riots[2] of the time and (for the purposes of this book) by the slanderous rumors that women in the military were all prostitutes and lesbians. Many of these rumors originated with white male soldiers.

Technology exerted a strong influence on the military occupational structure. Because of the emphasis on technological innovation, this structure had shifted its emphasis from combat arms to greater administrative and technical support. Especially noticeable during the war was a growing similarity between the skills required in military units and those used in the civilian workplace.[3] As a result of modern technology, the military could employ large numbers of women and minorities to work in clerical and support jobs without changing its stratified structure; white men would remain at the top of the hierarchy. Neither women nor minorities were part of the elite group of leaders who made up the military establishment at that time. There were essentially two types of leaders during the war: The "heroic leaders," who embodied valor and glory, and the military "managers," who were more concerned with the rational conduct of war.[4] African American men and women were excluded from leadership positions in combat. The idea of assigning women to the battlefield was outside the realm of American imagination. African American men seldom received an opportunity to bear arms; when they did so, they almost never gained the recognition they deserved for their acts of courage.

The critical need for personnel during World War II was the major impetus for the process by which race and gender policies changed in the American armed services. Societal changes resulting from organized movements, coupled with the tremendous need for human power, affected how minorities and women eventually would be used by the War Department. African American men, for example, who were narrowly assigned to the supply services during World War I, now were given the opportunity to serve in other types of units and in more geographical areas (including overseas).[5] Women, who before World War II served almost exclusively as nurses, were now recruited into the newly organized Women's Army Auxiliary Corps (WAAC) to work as typists, switchboard operators, clerks, and technicians. Like Army nurses, Waacs (members of the Women's Army Auxiliary Corps) served under a separate command structure, without Army rank, officer status, or military benefits[6]—that is, until 1943, when the WAAC was converted to the Women's Army Corps and its members obtained full Army status and rank.[7] It is estimated that 909,000 African American men and women served in the Army during World War II, with a peak of 700,000 or 8.7 percent of the total Army strength in 1944.[8] Approximately 150,000 women served in the WAAC/WAC during the war, about 4 percent of whom were African American.[9] Yet even while the War Department expanded its boundaries to include African American men and women, these minorities remained in subservient positions to white males.

In this chapter I identify societal and organizational factors that led to these initial changes in race and gender policies in the U.S. military, and I discuss how these changes influenced the use of African American women in the war. Two separate campaigns had to be waged before African American women would even be considered for military service. First, campaigns to bring greater opportunities to black men were conducted by several civilian organizations and were linked to a wider campaign by African Americans for economic, political, and civil rights before, during, and after World War II. Second, a large-scale campaign for the mobilization of women was launched by the War Department after Japan bombed Pearl Harbor. The data presented in this chapter strongly support the "recruit/reject" hypothesis in military sociology: military organizations recruit minorities and women in times of great manpower shortage but reject their services at other times. This was clearly the case during World War II. The services of African American men were virtually rejected by the War Department until the great military buildup of 1940. Similarly, the idea of a women's Army corps was not entertained until the United States entered the war.

Expansion of Racial Boundaries

Limited access to economic institutions, vulnerability to social injustices, and political exclusion characterize the life of African Americans during World War II.[10] African Americans were virtually excluded from prestigious occupations; they held mainly undesirable jobs—those that offered neither financial stability nor opportunities for advancement. Black women were "still witnessing the lynching of their sons, brothers, fathers, husbands and lovers, and the raping of their daughters, sisters, mothers, and selves."[11] In many areas of the South, blacks had been disfranchised since the Reconstruction era.[12]

As early as 1938 African Americans campaigned for expanded opportunities to serve in the military. Black publications such as the *Pittsburgh Courier* and *The Crisis* urged their readers to send letters to political officials, requesting that African Americans be given greater opportunities to take part in national defense.[13] This effort was part of a more general struggle by African Americans nationwide to increase opportunities for blacks in employment and to improve their political representation in government.

Other causes were being pursued as well. The limited inclusion of African Americans in war production, for example, was an item in the black campaign in the 1940s. This particular issue led to the scheduling of a march in the District of Columbia; the march was canceled when President Roosevelt decided to sign an executive order abolishing discrimination in the defense industry.[14] This decision was a landmark in the struggle for black equality. In addition to the executive order, the President's Committee on Fair Employment Practices was established to investigate complaints of racial discrimination.

Many African Americans felt that through participation in the war effort significant political and economic gains could be achieved. Politically, African Americans viewed the war as an opportunity to prove their loyalty and thereby to be accepted as first-class citizens after the war. Economically, the demands of war would require labor, thereby creating job opportunities for African Americans. Furthermore, some African Americans perceived the military as an avenue of upward mobility, providing training in occupational skills that could be used in the civilian labor market once the war had ended. Political pressure was applied to various youth organizations to train African Americans so that they would be prepared for work in both defense industries and the active armed forces.[15]

Expanding black men's opportunities to serve in the military would benefit not only the African American community, but the War Department as well. Cognizant of the fact that black manpower was needed in developing an effective fighting force, the War Department made plans to open its doors. It grappled with the challenge of employing large numbers of black men to fill military needs while adhering to the social norms of racial segregation, and accordingly it formulated three plans before altering the existing policy on mobilizing African Americans. The 1937 plan, which stated that Blacks and Whites should be mobilized in proportion to their numbers in the general population, formed the basis for subsequent policies on race.[16]

Before the United States entered the war, the military was

opened to black men through the Selective Service Training Act of 1940 (the nation's first peace-time conscription). After France was occupied by Germany, the U.S. Congress supported a vast military buildup to aid England. The Selective Service Training Act expanded military opportunities for African Americans by prohibiting racial discrimination against volunteers and draftees.[17]

Shortly after this act went into effect, the War Department devised a seven-point policy outlining how African Americans were to be employed. The policy specifically stated that (1) the strength of black personnel would be proportionate to the black population of the country (10.6 percent), (2) black units would be established in each major branch of the Army, (3) black reserve officers who were eligible for active duty would be assigned to "Negro units officered by colored personnel," (4) African Americans would receive the opportunity to qualify for reserve commissions, (5) African Americans were to be given aviation training, (6) black civilians were to be accorded equal opportunity for employment at work, and (7) there would be no intermingling between "colored and white" enlisted personnel in the same regimental organization.[18] Items 1 and 7 were later applied directly to the Women's Army Auxiliary Corps.

The seventh point, prohibiting intermingling between the races, stirred tremendous resentment and anger in the African American community and continued to haunt the War Department throughout the war years. Such a policy conflicted with the fundamental value of the United States—democracy. On several occasions African American male soldiers openly protested racial segregation; in many instances people lost their lives or were wounded during these confrontations. Separating black from white personnel in the same regimental organization was both ideologically and logistically problematic. Simply stated, it was inconsistent for the War Department to mobilize masses of African American men (and later African American women) to go abroad explicitly to take part in a war for democracy, but to do so in racially segregated units. The policy was also logistically inefficient for the War

Department's goal of developing and maintaining an effective force.

Complications resulting from racial segregation were described expressively in the February 1942 edition of *The Crisis:*

The first implication of segregation is inferiority. . . . We believe this inescapable feeling of inferiority, and the shame and resentment of Negro soldiers and civilians that their government should force it upon them as a national policy in a war against racial bigotry and barbarity, are the underlying causes of all the headaches the War Department has had over Negro soldiers in training this past year . . . our draftees were not inducted for two or three months because Jim Crow "Negro" facilities at training camps were not ready. . . . Arrived in camps, our boys found themselves frequently in isolated stations, far from the other soldiers. They found separate busses "for colored," separate candy and cigarette counters, separate movie theaters (or Jim Crow "roosts" for them in regular theaters).[19]

Similar concerns were voiced later about segregation policies in the WAAC/WAC. In chapter 3 I recount several examples of protests against that segregation.

The War Department wasted a great deal of time and resources in trying to avoid black-white contact by implementing racial segregation policies. Ulysses Lee, the official historian on the employment of black troops during World War II, asserted that unused housing had to remain vacant if the personnel to be billeted were not of the race for which the housing was designated.[20] Camp locations where Blacks were to be sent were determined not by military need, but by (1) the availability of racially appropriate housing, (2) the proportion of white and black troops on the post, and (3) the proximity of the post to civilian centers of black communities.[21]

Finding enough cadre to train and lead African American male units presented another problem for the War Department. As a consequence of racial segregation, the supply of cadre was never sufficient.[22] Of the 228,715 black men in the Army in August

1942, only 817 (.35 percent) were officers.[23] African American men served in racially segregated units that were led almost exclusively by white officers. This trend among the men was the opposite of that among the African American women, who possessed trained leaders before they had enough recruits to instruct.[24]

The War Department resistance to employing black men in combat stemmed in part from the stereotypical belief that black men were inferior to white men. Relying heavily on testimony by World War I commanders of the 92nd Division (the only black combat division with the American Expeditionary Forces), military officials supported the notion that black men should be used "principally as labor organizations." The commander of the 367th Infantry is cited as stating, "As fighting troops, the Negro must be rated as second class material; this is due primarily to his inferior intelligence and lack of mental and moral qualities."[25] These testimonies always included reference to the 368th Infantry Regiment of the 92nd Division, which fled during combat because of inappropriate combat training. Omitted from the discussion was the valiant performance of the 369th Infantry, a black combat unit that served directly under the French during World War I and received high evaluations from its French commander.[26]

Regardless of how well trained black male soldiers were to be deployed overseas, the overseas commanders were reluctant because they feared racial conflict and, in some cases, objections by white foreign governments.[27] Black male troops were not deployed overseas in large numbers until 13 May 1942, when the War Department issued a policy on where they would be assigned and how they would be used. The Army's official study of black troops during World War II includes statistics revealing that on 12 May 1942 there were only 15,679 black men overseas (none of whom were stationed in the British Isles); seven and one-half months later this number had increased to 53,709 black men (7,315 of whom were stationed in the British Isles).[28] At one point American military officials in London stated that no black units should be sent to England. This recommendation was overruled, however, and it was decided that all African American men assigned to the British Isles would be restricted to service units.

Even though a great many African Americans during the 1940s identified the United States as their home, they were racially oppressed, denied full citizenship rights, and prohibited from bearing arms to defend the country. African Americans were divided over the issue of whether or not they should participate in the war abroad. Some felt that "the responsibility of the Negro is to fight fascism in Mississippi rather than Berlin";[29] others were highly motivated to serve in the military. For the most part black community leaders and the black press encouraged African American men (and later women) to participate in the war effort.

Employing African American men was more palatable to the War Department than using women. Before the United States entered the war, traditional gender norms decreed that military service was extremely inappropriate for women.[30] Once the United States entered the war, however, it was soon acknowledged that large numbers of women would be necessary to work in rear positions while men moved to the front lines.

Changes in the War Department's racial policies subsequently provided the Women's Army Auxiliary Corps with a reference point for employing African American women in subsequent months. Like their male counterparts, African American women were authorized to constitute 10.6 percent of the WAAC, equal to the proportion of their population in the country. They were also to be racially segregated and were to be assigned to camp locations on the basis of the same criteria as had been used to assign African American men.[31] Finally, racial restrictions were placed on the deployment of African American women overseas.

The Bombing of Pearl Harbor and the WAAC Bill

Social biases also prohibited white women from exercising their rights and responsibilities as citizens. War Department officials had been divided over the issue of developing a women's corps since World War I. Legislation to enlist women in the Army was introduced to Congress in 1917 but was disapproved.[32] Attempts to pass legislation authorizing a women's corps were also made (though in vain) before the United States entered World War II, and with sound reasoning. The military desperately needed office workers, and women were more numerous and more competent than men in occupations such as typing and switchboard operation. Furthermore, it was known that if the United States entered World War II, the employment of women would be indispensable. Many military officials, however, refused to take heed, and during the years following World War I they viewed women as inconsequential to their mission.

The passage of the Nineteenth Amendment, through which women gained suffrage, slightly altered the way some of these officials perceived women. Having recently gained the right to vote, many women supported a proposal to eliminate the military as a way of ensuring peace.[33] In response, military officials created a position titled Director of Women's Relations, United States Army, whose incumbent would serve as a liaison between the War Department and American women. The purpose of the position was to educate women on the necessity of a military and thereby to win their political support. Anita Phipps filled this position for ten years; during that time she developed a plan for a women's Army corps, which the General Staff rejected in August 1926.

Nearly two years later, bowing to pressure to develop a women's corps, the War Department appointed Maj. Everett Hughes as its chief planner. Major Hughes not only supported the notion that women should be allowed to serve in the military, but he also recommended strongly that they be integrated into the men's army with full benefits. Hughes's proposal was placed on hold for several months and finally thrown out in 1931.[34]

Eight years later the newly appointed chief of staff, Gen. George C. Marshall, resumed planning for a women's corps. In spring 1941 Congresswoman Edith Nourse Rogers consulted with him about introducing a bill to Congress. Subsequently, HR 4906 was prepared by officers of the G-1 Division.[35] The bombing of Pearl Harbor accelerated the War Department's plans for a women's corps. Secretary of War Henry L. Stimson sent his approval of the WAAC bill to Congress on 24 December; by the following week Representative Rogers had incorporated the War Department's proposed amendments into the bill and reintroduced it as HR 6293.[36]

Members of the 6888th remembered Pearl Harbor well, even though they had no idea at that time that they would later serve in the Army. Gladys Carter was moved deeply by the event:

If you lived during the bombing of Pearl Harbor, it [the event] was like a bolt of lightning. . . . everybody had to do something. . . . men volunteered and were later drafted, women worked in factories, everybody wanted to do their part. We knew how bad Negroes were treated in America, but there wasn't a question in my mind, nor anybody else's mind; this is our country too.

Elsie Oliver heard the news while she and friends were eating breakfast:

The morning of Pearl Harbor, I was eating breakfast. Seventh of December, 1941, in Boston. I was serving breakfast because I had guests from Camp Edwards, Massachusetts, and several girls were there to meet these fellas and we were all having breakfast together. They came up that morning, and while they were there it came over the radio of Pearl Harbor. And right away the notice came from Camp Edwards that everybody there had to report back to base for military orders. They would be on call to go to California, and the next stop would be Hawaii.

Myrtle Rhoden had gone to church that morning, but instead of returning directly home, she decided to go to a movie at the Lowe East Theater on West 125th Street in Harlem:

In the middle of the movie the lights came on and the screen went blank. . . . And they announced, "All military personnel report to your nearest base." Oh, it was very dramatic. And the theater was loaded with fellas in military uniform, Marines, Navy, Army. So all these guys got up and, I mean in an instant, they kissed their dates or whoever they were with, and they were taking the stairs two at a time. Just flying! I mean it was tremendous. . . . I got on the Seventh Avenue bus and went home. I lived on Fiftieth Street and Seventh Avenue. And when I went upstairs to my house, oh, my mother was upset. She said, "Oh, they bombed Pearl Harbor." I said, "Mama, what's going on? What's happening?" She said, "The Japanese bombed Pearl Harbor. That's American territory in Hawaii . . . and we're at war." The next morning President Roosevelt made that famous speech that "this date will live in infamy."

The bombing of Pearl Harbor resulted in the destruction of 8 U.S. battleships, 3 destroyers, 4 small ships, and 160 aircraft. More than 2,400 American personnel reportedly lost their lives.[37] Four days later Italy and Germany declared war on the United States.

Fighting a war on two fronts demanded the employment of women, despite the social norms. Women provided necessary support both in the military and in civilian war industries. There was little time for racial or gender bias. The fate of the country was in the hands of all Americans.

With great reluctance the House of Representatives passed the WAAC bill on 17 March 1942; the Senate passed it on 14 May. On 15 May it was signed into Public Law 554.[38] Oveta Culp Hobby was appointed as the WAAC director and later was given the rank of lieutenant colonel. The subsequent recruitment of large numbers of women for active participation in military service was unparalleled in the nation's history. Thirty thousand women applied for Officer Candidate School. Applicants from ages twenty-one to forty-five were given aptitude tests and were screened further by local interviewing boards.[39] Most of the selected candidates had been employed successfully in civilian life, had college training, and ranged in age from twenty-five to thirty-nine. One-fifth were married, mostly to men in the military. Some were mothers; a few had young children; many had sons in service.[40] On 20 July 1942 these women began Officer Candidate School at Fort Des Moines, Iowa, at the first WAAC Training Center.

Although the United States was engaged in a massive war, many women had been conditioned to be dependent and acquiescent. To put on a uniform and defend the country's constitution ran counter to the role for which most American women had been socialized. Although women surely continued to advocate change, the early women's movement all but disintegrated after the Nineteenth Amendment was passed.[41] Several women's organizations existed when the United States entered the war, but they were not unified and thus were not influential.

War Department officials realized that to mobilize large numbers of well-educated, middle-class women to serve in the military, they would have to organize a large-scale campaign. Portraying women in occupational roles that previously had been reserved for men was an essential element of the War Department's movement to change the image of the American woman.[42] In addition to advertising, the War Department employed an existing organization, the Women's Interests Section, to assist in this mobilization. Without such an organization the War Department probably would not have been able to recruit the approximately 150,000 women who served in the WAAC/WAC during the war. American women of so-called high caliber were encouraged to enlist in the military by the Women's Interests Section, which belonged to the Bureau of Public Relations. This organization was founded in 1941 by Oveta Culp Hobby, who also served as its first chief.[43] Its function was somewhat different from that of the director of women's relations, the position created by the War Department two decades earlier, in that the Women's Interests Section was directed toward soldiers' wives and mothers. The director of women's relations focused on educating American women about the importance of maintaining an army; the Women's Interests Section addressed specific concerns raised by relatives of men who were currently on active duty.

Recruitment and the Advisory Council to the Women's Interests Section

The Advisory Council to the Women's Interests Section (ACWIS) was a group composed of the presidents of thirty-three national women's organizations; later this number increased to thirty-six. The first meeting of ACWIS was called on 13 October 1941 in an effort to inform women all over the United States about how the Army cared for its soldiers. As a result of that meeting the group produced and circulated six pamphlets on what soldiers were fed, how their health was protected, and what their recreational and religious opportunities were. (These pamphlets were prepared before Pearl Harbor and pertained to a peace-time Army.)

Subsequent issues addressed by the group included what women could do to help the Army to victory and what could be done to help promote the image of the WAAC. On 15 June 1942 Emily Newell Blair, chief of the Women's Interests Section, urged the Advisory Council to publicly support the WAAC:

Mrs Hobby has told you about the WAAC. As the Corps will be recruited after regular Army methods and be under Army orders there is little needed from the women's organizations except and beyond what they do for the men in service. But I would point out that inasmuch as this is the first women's Army the attitude of the organized women toward the WAAC will go far in establishing the public's attitude towards it as a dignified, important branch of the service. I do not need to tell you how to do this, either.[44]

On the same day, as a follow-up, Oveta Culp Hobby, director of the Women's Army Auxiliary Corps, spoke confidentially to members of ACWIS about the plans for the WAAC.[45] By the end of the meeting, leaders of women's organizations throughout the country were supporting the idea.

The recruitment of massive numbers of women to fill positions that were traditionally considered inappropriate for women resembled a social movement in that it opposed the norms governing gender roles in society. Indeed, the War Department had no intention of changing the gender structure of military society or the reward distribution within its society; therefore, it was not deliberately launching a movement to redefine gender roles. Nonetheless, the change in gender relations that emerged during and after the war makes the WAAC/WAC recruitment effort comparable to those of social movements. The Women's Interests Section (WIS) was analogous to what some theorists in the study of social movements call a social movement organization. As defined by Zald and McCarthy, a social movement organization "is a complex, or formal, organization that identifies its goals with the preferences of a social movement . . . and attempts to implement those goals." [46] WIS identified the goals of ACWIS; the women's organizations belonging to ACWIS both adhered to those goals and provided resources for reaching them.

The first WAAC Officer Candidate Class was held from 20 July to 29 August 1942 and was followed weekly by a stream of graduating officers and "enrolled" (enlisted) women from the WAAC Training Center.[47] Lt. Gen. Dwight Eisenhower immediately requested two WAAC companies to serve overseas. Hobby was reluctant to allow women to be deployed overseas, however, because as members of an auxiliary corps they did not have military status and consequently were not entitled to hospitalization or life insurance. Nevertheless, 150 white Waacs volunteered for overseas duty in the winter of 1942 and were deployed to North Africa in December. White women were deployed in much greater numbers after the Women's Army Corps was established in 1943.

As the WAAC developed, ACWIS played an increasing role in influencing public opinion. The council would make sure that women had the opportunity to contribute fully "to the planning and establishment of world cooperation." To this end the War Department invited Marjory Fry of the British Information Service to a meeting with ACWIS on 28 October 1942, to suggest to council members how they might proceed with their plan for a women's corps based on the British experience. Fry spoke of the military background of British women, emphasizing that those women were equipped with specialized training to meet the problems of the day.[48]

ACWIS was perhaps the War Department's single most important vehicle for reaching the thousands of women who eventually would put on the uniform. In its 1943 annual report ACWIS listed a total of thirty-six organizations as members of the council, with a combined membership of twelve million to thirteen million women. Twenty of the participating organizations published magazines with "an aggregate circulation of approximately one million three hundred thousand."[49] Seventeen of the ACWIS organizations held annual, biennial, or triennial meetings.

The purpose of the council expanded from disseminating information to sponsoring projects, many of them devoted to recruiting women for the WAAC. Item 4 in the annual report, "Cooperation in the Recruiting Program of the WAAC," included the following information:

With great pleasure we undertook last fall to enlist the cooperation of the Advisory Council organizations in furthering the recruiting of the Women's Army Auxiliary Corps. The plan of cooperation involved four main points. All members of the Advisory Council were asked to send us or make available to us if possible their unit lists so that we could send them a WAAC direct mail piece and a copy of the plan of cooperation; to publicize the WAAC and call attention to its need of recruits by articles in their publications or items in their club letters and other communications; to urge their members to serve on local women's committees for WAAC recruiting in their own communities; and to invite WAAC recruiting officers to speak at their club meetings.[50]

According to Margaret S. Banister, organization director of the Women's Interests Section, twenty of the thirty-six organizations cooperated with this plan.

The War Department continued to solicit help from all thirty-six organizations to recruit women for the corps. At a meeting held on 25 June 1943 Colonel Hobby addressed ACWIS about the status of the WAACs after a year:

In the beginning there were four jobs open to these women. Their splendid record caused the Army to ask for additional jobs for them and to request over 400,000 women for the service. The enlisted men were not trained to do many of the jobs while the women were trained while civilians. Each woman replaced 1¾ man. At first the WAACS were additional personnel, now they release the equivalent number of men. The WAACS made a study of the 628 different jobs done by men—each has a specification serial number. 400 jobs were suitable for women. Yard stick applied—Is the work too heavy? Number of women needed. Were the hours such that women would be protected going back and forth, etc.? There was not enough personnel to train for 400 jobs, but 138 jobs are now being done by women.[51]

The WAAC had been in existence for a year. The new role of women was being severely challenged by the same military commanders who felt that there was no place for women in the military and by the American public, who had received a great deal of negative information about the WAAC. Hobby went on to report that the WAAC strength was 150,000, more than half the size of the standing peace-time Army. Among the problems faced by Waacs, she argued, were improper housing facilities, insufficient clothing, and slanderous stories, which appeared in the *New York Daily News* and the *Washington Times*. Hobby vehemently decried these stories as false:

Five hundred [Waacs] were said to have been returned from Africa to have babies. Three actually returned. One was legitimately pregnant before she left, one was ill with a gall bladder, the other was suffering with a concussion from a bomb. One hundred Waacs said to be in St. Elizabeth's. No truth in this statement. Nor was there any truth in the statements that a trainload of Waacs had been sent to Walter Reed to have babies, 86 discharged from Fort Devens with babies (3 were discharged), 172 lesbians in a hospital. Out of 65,000 women there [are] 7 illegitimate pregnancies, 9 cases of syphilis, and 41 cases of gonorrhea.[52]

Striving to persuade these civilian women on the Advisory Council to defend against the slanderous attacks on Waacs, Hobby further stated that the WAAC was the biggest professional opportunity American women had ever had and that members of ACWIS needed to educate American women about the WAAC's duties and to solicit their support. Improving the image of the WAAC was essential if the War Department was to meet its personnel goals.

The War Department employed several strategies to improve the image of women who had temporarily abandoned their roles as housewives, mothers, sisters, and daughters to put on the uniform. One such strategy was to circulate information about the importance of women to military goals. In July 1943 the Women's Army Auxiliary Corps was converted to the Women's Army Corps. The Women's Interests Section published "Facts about the Women's Army Corps," which contained information about eligibility requirements, the change from WAAC to WAC, why Wacs were needed, jobs that Wacs were doing in the Army, and how the Army praised Wacs. The document included the following information:

The WAC is filling and is prepared to fill the 155 jobs which fall into eight major types of work as follows: 1. *Technical and Professional,* including the following general classifications: medical, personnel, public relations, instruction and training, physical sciences and mathematics, photography, languages, drafting, and weather. 2. *Radio,* which provides jobs for radio mechanics, operators and repairmen, in 7 specialized capacities. 3. *Communications,* consisting of a dozen classifications, including many kinds of operators such as switchboard, telegraph, teletypewriter, and so forth. 4. *Mechanical Trade, and Manual,* which is broken down into jobs for mechanics, textile and fabric workers, motor vehicle mechanics and miscellaneous, with many sub-divisions in each classification. 5. *Administrative and Office,* having 32 classifications, among them accountant, auditor, bookbinder, cashier, cryptanalyst, fingerprinter, first sergeant, personnel noncommissioned officer, proofreader, and typist. 6. *Motor Vehicle Drivers,* fall into the following groups of work: chauffeur, motorboat operator, motor transportation noncommissioned officer, light truck driver, and truckmaster. 7. *Food,* consisting of jobs for bakers, cooks, dietitians, meats or daily inspectors, mess sergeants, and subsistence noncommissioned officers. 8. *Supply and Stock,* including 13 types, among them Army Air Forces technical supply noncommissioned officer, chief storekeeper, shipping clerk, shop clerk, and toolroom keeper.[53]

The document emphasized that the women in the Women's Army Auxiliary Corps had done, and were doing, an outstanding job. General Eisenhower reportedly praised the Wacs in Africa for distinguishing themselves in both neatness and efficiency. Col. George Teachout, commander of the post at Camp Crowder, Missouri, is cited as saying: "I want to say of every Wac at this installation I would be proud to have her for a daughter." Col. Floyd T. Gillespie, assistant chief signal officer in Allied Force Headquarters, endorsed the WAC in the following statement:

After the girls had a few weeks of experience in their jobs they were handling their assignments like veterans. They were fast and they were accurate. We could have used hundreds more. In fact, had we had enough of them, we could have used them to operate all our fixed communication installations—telephone and telegraph—throughout the rear areas. Every one of these girls released some man for signal corps duty up in the combat zones.[54]

By the end of the year the WAC recruiting drive had ended. In January 1944 Colonel Hobby reported to ACWIS that the drive had been a success: "American women enlisted at the rate of 903 per week. Hence the loss of WAC strength that had been antici-pated in the transition from the WAAC to the WAC was regained. The WAC strength increased from 20,943 in January 1943 to 62,859 in January 1944."[55]

In subsequent months a National Civilian Advisory Committee (NCAC) was formed under the Women's Army Corps; it imple-mented its recruitment efforts through the War Department's re-gional service commands (field sites in different geographical areas throughout the United States). Many of the members of ACWIS served on this new committee. Unlike the council, however, the committee was concerned exclusively with WAC affairs. The National Civilian Advisory Committee was charged with the task of employing innovative strategies to recruit women into the WAC. On 16 December 1944, for example, NCAC set up sites in the second service command (New York and Governors Island area) and submitted its quarterly recruiting activities report, covering the period from September to December. The strategies it employed included developing a list of schools, publishing a series of articles, running newspaper advertisements, and obtaining statements from leading industrial firms assuring women that they would be guaranteed their positions upon returning if they left to join the WAC. The Fifth Avenue Coach Company went so far as to paint a bus publicizing the WAC.[56]

NCAC continued to set up sites at different regional service commands during the early months of 1945. An NCAC site at the third service command, covering Maryland, Pennsylvania, and Virginia, was organized on 10 February 1945. In an effort to assist the WAC in its recruitment efforts, members of NCAC toured the Norfolk Army Air Base and visited Camp Patrick Henry so that they could see Wacs at work.[57] At the ninth service command (California, Washington, Oregon, Nevada, Utah, Idaho, and Montana) NCAC showed films such as *To the Ladies*, which portrayed women as responsible, mature adults, worthy of respect. Luncheons and teas were also sponsored in the ninth service command for the purpose of presenting the WAC program to newspaper representatives, radio commentators, and eligible women. The University of California was summoned to assist in the recruitment and complied by holding assembly programs preceded by tours of a hospital where Wac technicians were on duty. The state of Oregon employed sponsored advertisements and obtained support from 115 American Legion Auxiliary units throughout the state. The Arizona State Federation of Labor sponsored a medical WAC recruiting campaign. In Utah, approximately 500 persons, including 250 students at the University of Utah, attended a tea given at the home of Governor Herbert Maw of Utah in honor of women in uniform.[58] Apparently the National

Civilian Advisory Council succeeded in mobilizing a variety of organizations and institutions to support the WAC recruitment effort.

NCAC remained active in WAC recruitment until the end of the war; at that time the group focused on helping Wacs make a smooth transition back into civilian life. The image of the Wac was still unstable: Although ACWIS and (later) NCAC succeeded in recruiting women to serve in the Army, nasty rumors about Wacs being prostitutes and lesbians persisted. National NCAC chairman Mrs. Oswald B. Lord, concerned about employment opportunities for Wacs when they returned to civilian life, sent a form letter to various civilian organizations requesting that they provide written endorsements of Wacs.[59] The war was over, however, and the work of NCAC was coming to an end.

On 13 November 1945 a bulletin announced that the War Department was disbanding Regional Civilian Advisory Committees. The second service command was to be discontinued after 30 November. The NCAC was to be continued as an advisory board in all matters relating to members of the Women's Army Corps. The bulletin emphasized that civilian employers often did not credit Wacs with the intensive training and experiences they had received in the Army. Consequently, some women were finding that their service as Wacs worked against them rather than for them in their search for employment. In an effort to address this problem, the Veterans' Service Centers began exploring methods of giving women veterans credit for being medical technicians in the Army.[60]

In February 1946 several members of NCAC traveled overseas to visit WAC units that had not yet returned to the United States. Visiting Europe under the sponsorship of the War Department, these members observed twenty-two hundred Wacs assigned to the European Theater of Operations. Apparently the 6888th was not one of the units they visited, although the last of the battalion members did not return to the United States until March 1946. None of the members of the 6888th whom I interviewed remembers a visit by the Civilian Advisory Committee, and the 6888th is not mentioned in the report by Genevieve Forbes Herrick. Herrick, a member of the committee, circulated a report of her visit with more than a thousand Wacs, in which she stated that she got to know two hundred of them personally. She spoke with commanders of Wacs in Frankfurt, Munich, Vienna, Berlin, Paris, Bamberg, Salzburg, Nuremberg, and Berchtesgaden, all of whom were men, and reported that they all appreciated the work done by Wacs. In view of the negative image of Wacs, this was a meaningful disclosure.[61]

Some of Herrick's written observations support information about Wacs that had been revealed already and later was reported in the Army's official document on the Women's Army Corps. Among these observations was the fact that Wacs in Europe were on average older than male soldiers stationed overseas. The average male soldier stationed in the European Theater of Operations (ETO) was in his early twenties; the average Wac was in her thirties. The average Wac, in the United States as well as in Europe, was also better educated than her male counterpart.[62] Because of the relatively small proportion of women serving in the military and because women were assigned only to selected occupations that almost always required specialized skills, the War Department required higher aptitude scores on the entrance examination for women than for men.

Interestingly, Herrick reports that Wacs in Germany were heavily involved in community work, usually in youth activities programs. An American professor, Dr. Elizabeth Lam, worked for the Office of Military Government in Berlin and served as a senior specialist in youth activities for girls. A Wac officer or enlisted woman was authorized in each headquarters to supervise, organize, and conduct girls' activities. The Wacs met with girls from twelve to twenty years of age, made toys for orphaned German children, held discussion groups with high school and university students, and conducted classes in singing and folk dancing. While visiting Wacs in Germany, Herrick observed a Thanksgiving dinner that was held in an enlisted women's mess hall and a Christmas celebration in Frankfurt. She also reported that Wacs took donations and purchased three hundred pairs of shoes from Czechoslovakians to give to German children who had none.[63] Activities like these, which represent the humanitarian role performed by many Wacs during the war, are generally overlooked in the literature about the Women's Army Corps.

According to Herrick, Wacs in the ETO took advantage of courses in foreign language, music, art, and architecture. Their living conditions varied from rugged to the comforts of good hotels. At the Bamberg headquarters of the U.S. Constabulary, Wacs lived in austere conditions, with few light bulbs and poor lavatory facilities. In Vienna some of the enlisted women were billeted in a former orphanage for Jewish children (which housed German SS troops during the war). In Salzburg Wacs stayed at the Steinlechner Hotel, where the living conditions were pleasant. In Paris they lived in lavish, ornate hotels that had been taken over by the Army.[64] (These conditions were quite similar to those of the 6888th, which are described in chapter 5.)

Social clubs for Wacs also ranged from simple to luxurious; these clubs were exclusively for white Wacs. In Frankfurt the Underground was for enlisted women, while officers frequented the officers' club at the luxurious Kronberg Castle. The Cogen House was one of the more elegant clubs in Frankfurt, which a Wac officer could visit only if she was invited by a colonel or an officer of higher rank. Berlin had a "48" Club for both enlisted men and women. The most elaborate officers' club in Berlin was the Harnac House, operated by Wac captain Margot Reis—a graduate of Columbia University and Pratt Institute. Berchtesgaden was a recreational area in Germany, which some of the Wacs visited while they were on leave.[65]

Most Wacs in the ETO worked in such clerical positions as teletype and switchboard operators for the trans-Atlantic overseas operation in Vienna. Some Wacs, however, filled supervisory jobs, such as traffic chiefs for the military switchboard in Berlin. The supervisor of the finance department in Berlin and Bamberg was a Wac. Other occupations held by Wacs included serving as chief clerk of the public safety department, as court reporter, as photographer, as mess sergeant, as waitress, as German translator, as stenographer in the Judge Advocate General's office (JAG), and as exchange officer. Wacs also were attached to the social welfare department of the 98th General Hospital at Munich. A Wac officer served in the Education and Religious Affairs Branch of the Office of Military Government in Bavaria.

The activities of ACWIS and later of NCAC were directed toward women of European descent. Mary McLeod Bethune, as president of the National Council of Negro Women, was the link between African American women and the War Department's advisory councils. She was the only African American member of ACWIS. Consequently, African American women were influenced to some degree by the recruitment efforts of ACWIS and by the NCAC. Many of the white Wacs' experiences observed by Herrick were similar to those of black Wacs in Europe at that time. African American Wacs also took advantage of the educational opportunities available to them while they were in Europe, which were similar to those offered to Euro-American Wacs. The living conditions of the black Wacs in Europe also varied from poor to good, depending on where the unit was stationed. Many of the jobs performed by members of the 6888th were the same as those performed by white Wacs. The accomplishments of African American Wacs, however, were never highlighted in the reports of the Advisory Council of the Women's Interest Section or of the National Council Advisory Committee. It was almost as though African American women were invisible to these organizations.

Because of their double minority status, African American women would not have been employed by the military during World War II, were it not for preexisting racial policies that specified how black men were to be used and newly developing gender policies specifying where and how women were to be employed. Certainly, the expanding roles of black men and of white women created the context in which black women were employed in the U.S. Army during World War II. By the time the 6888th was formed, the War Department had already addressed the question of deploying African American men overseas, and several white WAC companies already had been deployed to the European and the China Theaters of Operations. Yet the African American Waac/Wac faced obstacles precisely because of her race and her gender, a situation that did not confront African American men or Euro-American women.

3

★ ★ ★

Fight Our Battles and Claim Our Victories

As a group, black women are in an unusual position in
this society, for not only are we collectively at the bot-
tom of the occupational ladder, but our overall social
status is lower than that of any group. . . . White
women and black men have it both ways. They can
act as oppressor or be oppressed. Black men may be
victimized by racism, but sexism allows them to act as
exploiters and oppressors of women. White women
may be victimized by sexism, but racism enables them
to act as exploiters of black people.
—bell hooks, *Feminist Theory:
From Margin to Center*

In their daily effort to negotiate the world, African American
women are forced to confront the indignities of either racism or
sexism, and often both simultaneously. This fact is conspicuous
in the experiences of African American Waacs/Wacs. As black
Americans they were forced to live, eat, and often work in separate facilities, in remote areas of military installations. As women
they were subjected to the harsh and slanderous rumors directed
toward all women in the military. African American Waacs/Wacs
struggled to influence policy changes within a hierarchically struc-
tured organization founded and operating on sexist and racist
principles.

The combination of racism and sexism confronting the African

49

American Waac/Wac put her into a category separate from those of African American men and Euro-American women. In addition to campaigns established to expand the use of African American men and to mobilize women, an additional effort was necessary before African American women were to receive a chance to participate fully in the Women's Army Corps, which included the opportunity to serve overseas. Unlike the campaign to develop a women's army corps, the pressure exerted on the military to deploy African American women overseas was external to the War Department. The campaign for racial equality in the WAAC/WAC was linked to organizations that dealt with racial injustices in general, namely the NAACP, the NCNW, and the black press.

Barricades and Bridges

Throughout the history of the United States African American women have fought to be recognized as citizens in civil, political, and social arenas. Actively seeking civil liberties such as freedom of speech and the right to human dignity, African American women played a leading role in the antislavery movements and the antilynching campaigns of the nineteenth century.[1] The Anti-Slavery Society, governed exclusively by men, focused solely on issues of abolishing slavery. Only four women were invited to attend the 1833 convention held by the American Anti-Slavery Society in Philadelphia, and their participation was restricted to that of passive observers.[2] At the World Anti-Slavery Convention in London, seven years later, Elizabeth Cady Stanton, a white American feminist who attended the meeting, was denied a seat because of her gender.[3] Many of the black women's early efforts to eradicate racism and sexism were made in alliance with white women in early movements such as the Female Anti-Slavery Society. Many of the black women leaders of this organization lived in Boston and Philadelphia.[4]

Although the early women's movement evolved from the abolitionist movement, racial biases had always been present to some degree. Racism, however, became even more prominent in the women's movement after the passage of the Fifteenth Amendment in 1869, because black men were granted suffrage and white women were not.[5] This situation exacerbated an already strained relationship between African American and Euro-American women; as a result many white women withdrew their support for the emancipation of African Americans and concentrated primarily on bourgeois, white feminist issues. In 1890 white feminists formed the National American Woman Suffrage Association (NAWSA). The typical member of NAWSA not only dissociated herself from African Americans but also supported the ideology of white supremacy in an effort to gain the support of the South.[6]

Black women, continuing to strive for social equality, developed political organizations such as the National Association of Colored Women. This group was founded by Mary Church Terrell in 1896, after black women's clubs were rejected for membership in the General Federation of Women's Clubs.[7] The Alpha Suffrage Club in Chicago was established in 1914 by Ida B. Wells for the purpose of mobilizing black women to struggle for local and universal suffrage.[8]

Indeed, African American women had a history of organizing for social and political change long before World War II. Issues associated with both race and gender discrimination were addressed by these early political organizations, as well as by groups that were formed in subsequent years. African American women were not always accepted as members of organizations dominated by black males or those governed by white women; thus, it was imperative for them to develop a separate political advocacy group. The years preceding World War II were inequitable toward women and especially detrimental to the welfare of African Americans. The National Council of Negro Women (NCNW), founded by Mary McLeod Bethune in 1935, was a prominent organization that addressed both race and gender issues.

During World War II Bethune, president of the NCNW, was an invited member of the Advisory Council for the Women's Interests

Section (ACWIS) and later of the National Civilian Advisory
Committee (NCAC) for the Women's Army Corps. This distinguished African American woman, who held a number of leadership positions in the country, was the link between these organizations and the African American community.[9] ACWIS and NCAC
officials constantly called on Bethune to influence African American women to support efforts that they, white middle-class
women, defined as important. One such effort was to encourage
educated women with "high moral character" to join the WAAC/
WAC. In 1943 Bethune received several communications concerning WAAC recruitment from Emily Newell Blair, chief of the
Women's Interests Section, and Margaret Banister, the organization's director. On 13 January Banister wrote Bethune informing
her of four regional conferences and confirming that invitations
would be extended to the list of NCNW representatives submitted
by Bethune five months earlier.[10] The NCNW consisted of several
black women's organizations that were particularly concerned
about employment issues, and working for the admission of black
women into the WAAC was consistent with the NCNW's broader
goals of racial equality. Bethune, in a show of complete support,
wrote back to Banister with the names of three additional representatives.

In the following month Blair wrote Bethune requesting that she
and the members of her organization actively assist the WAAC
recruitment drive by writing a personal column in the NCNW's
national publication, the *Aframerican Woman's Journal,* listing
the names of organization members' daughters who had joined
the WAC. Blair also asked Bethune to write an article urging
organization members to be hospitable to Wacs in their communities.[11] One of Bethune's philosophies was that African American
women should seize all opportunities to participate and to make
lasting contributions to American institutions.[12] Viewing the
Women's Army Auxiliary Corps as an opportunity for African
American women to advance themselves socially and politically,
Bethune encouraged them to enlist.

On 20 March 1943 Blair wrote Bethune asking her to disseminate information on a "code of wartime conversation." [13] War Department officials were concerned that classified information would be spread by women talking too openly about their spouses' and sons' military assignments. Women therefore were instructed not to reveal information about where or how their spouses or sons were deployed. Bethune replied to Blair that she would support the effort. Blair wrote Bethune again on 8 April, requesting that she encourage NCNW members to participate in the "Second War Loan Program for Women" by purchasing bonds for military equipment. Bethune was a liaison between African American and Euro-American women during the war.

Many such requests were made to solicit support from African American women in efforts defined by conservative white women. Bethune, however, realized how important it was for African American women to form a united front with white women against problems associated with sexism. Sexism affected the lives of black women as well as white, and these issues were rarely if ever addressed by organizations that focused primarily on race matters.

Bethune's efforts influenced many African American women to join the WAAC/WAC. She personally selected several of the African American women who attended and graduated from the WAAC's first Officer Candidate School, evidence of her plan to advance African American women's interests through black participation. Bethune took a leading role in instructing black candidates about the dual mission they were to perform. First, they were to carry out the duties of the Women's Army Auxiliary Corps, as they had sworn to do when taking the oath to join the WAAC. Second, they were to conduct themselves in such a way as to demonstrate that African Americans were capable soldiers and respectable persons, worthy of first-class citizenship.

While the first WAAC OCS was still in session, Bethune visited the black candidates. Noel Campbell Mitchell remembers that Bethune told the African American participants to set a good example: "She [Mary McLeod Bethune] came out there and talked to all of us and told us that they [the War Department] did not want us in this service in the first place, so we had to set an example. And we did. We did a beautiful job out there."

Bethune tried to sensitize members of ACWIS and NCAC to African American women's issues and concerns. She presented ACWIS with findings from her investigations of the WAC Training Center. In a written statement presented to the Advisory Council on 16 August 1943, Bethune stated:

As a member of the Women's Interests Section of the War Department, the National Council of Negro Women appreciates the opportunity extended to inspect the activities of the Women's Army Corps at Fort Des Moines, Iowa, and Camp Crowder, Missouri. The tour was informative and served to increase our interest in the program and anxiety for existing problems. We find it very difficult to make recommendations which will be effective for recruiting purposes in view of the existing policy of segregation. Full integration is the goal we seek. Working toward this goal we make the following recommendations.[14]

Among Bethune's nine recommendations was that more black officers be trained for recruiting duty, that black officers be given training in all specialized schools in the Army, that black Wacs be assigned in occupations that were presently closed to them, that no all-black regiment be established at Fort Des Moines (as was proposed by the War Department), and that the OCS not be moved to Fort Oglethorpe, Georgia (another proposal made by the War Department).[15]

Black WAC officers had been assigned to recruiting duty in 1942, but they were withdrawn from that duty in July 1943 and were returned to training centers to instruct black trainees. The War Department refused to reassign African American women as recruiters because of reports that the presence of black Wacs "in public places giving public speeches" created racial disturbances.[16] As for specialized schools, black Wacs were not trained or assigned in technical fields such as the Signal Corps, the Chemical Warfare Service, or the Corps of Engineers. These fields were open only to a limited number of white Wacs, most of whom (approximately five thousand) were assigned to the Signal Corps, in September 1944. No more than seven hundred Wacs were ever assigned to Chemical Warfare Services at any given time.[17]

As for the "all-Negro regiment," Bethune was referring to a reorganization proposed by the War Department in August 1943. According to the plan, African American Wacs at Fort Des Moines would be reorganized into an all-black regiment and thus would be segregated completely on post. This proposal met strong opposition by many black Wacs stationed at Fort Des Moines.[18] It is not surprising that Bethune, an integrationist, would oppose any plan for racial segregation. The reorganization plan was subsequently rescinded. Bethune's primary concern about opening an Officer Candidate School at Fort Oglethorpe was that black Wacs would not be well received in nearby Chattanooga. Her objections were in vain, however; Fort Oglethorpe opened its Officer's Candidate School in August 1943.[19] There were, however, relatively few African American Wacs trained at Fort Oglethorpe. Putney reports that the only black Wacs trained at Fort Oglethorpe were "those specifically recruited in late 1944 and early 1945 for assignment in army general hospitals and some of the black [Wac] officers who were commissioned between September 18, 1943, and February 17, 1945."[20]

Seeing to it that black women were among the first officer candidates of the WAAC was only one of the battles fought by Bethune. Once African Americans entered the Women's Army Auxiliary Corps, they were subjected to various acts of racism. To help keep their morale high, Bethune praised them effusively for their accomplishments. She also provided emotional, political, and economic support for African American Wacs who swam against the tides of institutional racism. For example, Bethune helped raise money to obtain legal representation for four African American Wacs who were court-martialed at Fort Devens in 1945. These women had disobeyed what they alleged was a racially discriminatory order (described more fully below). Bethune also defended the preservation of the Negro WAC Band when officials had decided to discontinue it. This situation was especially troublesome because black Wacs were prohibited from playing in the all-white WAC Band (see below).

Racial discrimination in the Women's Army Auxiliary Corps was obviously a major concern in the African American community. From the very beginning black organizations such as the Alpha Kappa Alpha (AKA) Sorority, the National Council of Negro Women (NCNW), the National Association for the Advancement of Colored People (NAACP), the National Urban League, and the Delta Sigma Theta Sorority lobbied for a clause that would prohibit the WAAC from discriminating against black women. Their effort was defeated by the Senate and the House of Representatives on the ground that such a clause was not necessary.[21] Although the Army offered African American women greater opportunities for active participation than did the other armed services, it was far from free of racial biases.

African American women were authorized to participate in the Women's Army Auxiliary Corps from its inception, but many faced a great deal of difficulty when they tried to apply. Although a few black women received personal invitations from the War Department to apply for the first Officer Candidate School at Fort Des Moines, many who attempted to join the WAAC were refused applications at their local recruiting stations,[22] because some recruiters, in acts of individual racism, took it upon themselves to deny applications to African Americans.

On a number of occasions African American women or their representatives, or both, wrote to WAAC Headquarters to expose local recruiters who had refused them applications.[23] On 18 May 1942 Earl Davis, president of the Winston-Salem Youth Council of the NAACP, sent Oveta Culp Hobby a telegram notifying her that the recruiting officer at Winston-Salem would not recruit blacks for the WAAC. In a reply to Davis by telegram on the following day, Hobby stated that the recruiter (a Sergeant Stephenson) had been contacted and would correct his mistake.

Complaints of racial discrimination at recruitment stations continued to be forwarded to WAAC Headquarters. On 29 May Mrs. E. P. Trezevant of Columbia, South Carolina, wrote a letter addressed to the U.S. Army Recruiting Corps, asserting that her local recruiting station had failed to give her an application. On 3 June she received a reply from the assistant adjutant general, Captain W. H. Nealing, stating that the Women's Army Auxiliary Corps's policy was not to discriminate on the basis of race, creed, or national origin. Not satisfied with that response, Mrs. Trezevant wrote the following week to Oveta Hobby and received a reply that the deadline for applying to the first OCS was 4 June. Refusing to give up, Mrs. Trezevant then wrote to Mary McLeod Bethune, who forwarded the complaint back to the WAAC director. Hobby wrote a letter to Bethune, which acknowledged that the complaint indeed was valid, but concluded her letter by saying, "I regret exceedingly that at this late date there is nothing which can be done." [24]

Another African American woman encountered an obstacle when she attempted to apply for the WAAC in North Carolina:

The most difficult part of it, but one that black women, a few of us, overcame, was to knock down the doors of the United States Post Office and get an application to apply. That was far harder than passing the mental alertness test. And I have heard other women who recount similarly. . . . That was really our first battle which became, across this country, a campaign. Why, if they could shut you out and you couldn't get in the door. . . . That's an easy way to eliminate you. [25]

The "mental alertness test" refers to the aptitude test that all applicants had to pass before gaining admission to the military. In this case the prospective applicant, at Bethune's advice, moved to Washington, D.C. There she was able to apply and subsequently enroll in the Women's Army Auxiliary Corps, to become one of the first 440 women to attend the WAAC Officer Candidate School.

While some of the other women had no difficulty in obtaining applications, almost all of those who attended the first WAAC OCS were stunned by the blatant racial segregation they encountered. Charity Adams Earley, for example, was shocked. She was inducted into the military at Columbus, Ohio, on 13 July 1942: "We were marched into a train and we came into Des Moines." When this group of inductees arrived at Fort Des Moines, they were taken to the training center by truck.

When we marched out of those trucks, and marched into a staging center—a reception center, I guess it was—we had to learn [military] terms. The first thing that took place literally shocked us. There had been twenty-five of us who had traveled together from Columbus, Ohio, and an officer came in and asked if the colored girls would move over to some seats he had way over in the corner. And then he proceeded to call the rest of them by name to send them to their quarters. . . . And of course we were sort of shocked that this kind of action would take place. . . . But we survived that and we went to our separate quarters, No. 54 at Fort Des Moines, Iowa.

Bernadine Flannagan was also surprised when she learned that the Women's Army Auxiliary Corps was racially segregated:

We [black Waacs] had our own barracks and white Waacs had their own barracks. We [black Waacs] had our own training facilities and they [white Waacs] had their own training facilities. I was surprised because in New London, Connecticut, where I grew up, everything was integrated. I left New London with white girls to travel to Fort Des Moines. We got on the train going south and we were separated when we got down to the Mason-Dixon line. I was told that I had to move to another section of the train. . . . The whole military service was a shock to me because I had no idea it was segregated. I don't know what I was thinking about. But being from an integrated town, I just didn't think that way.

Noel Campbell Mitchell reflects on the initial opposition from family and friends who wanted to shelter her from the cold military environment: "Having been born, reared, and educated at Tuskegee Institute, and because of my seemingly shy and dependent nature, my parents and friends were shocked when, after two years of teaching, I persisted, against everyone's advice and discouragement, except that of my father, in becoming a member of the first Officer's Candidate School of the Women's Army Auxiliary Corps."

On 23 June 1942 Mitchell and four other women from Tuskegee received military orders to report to Fort McPherson, Georgia.

By the time I had completed my physical examination I was thoroughly convinced that I didn't want to join the Army. We were told to wait in a room until we were called for an interview. When I was called I was scared to death. I walked into the room and there sat three Army colonels and two civilian women. One of the women broke the silence by saying, "I am disappointed in you." I stared at her because I had never seen her before and I knew she had never seen me. How could she say such a thing? It turned out that she happened to know my father, who was six feet, three inches tall and weighed 206 pounds. She had been certain that I would be about his height and weight. I could see why she was disappointed as I was only five feet, two inches tall and weighed 116 pounds. That broke the ice and I was more at ease.

Mitchell passed her physical as well as the interview and was informed that in a few days she would receive orders to travel to the induction center to be sworn in. At about noon on 16 July she took the oath and became officially a part of the Army.

As the train pulled out of the station I was never more homesick in my life. I resolved that since I was in it [the Army] now, I had to make good. The train was full of girls on their way to camp. I arrived in Des Moines on the night of 20 July 1942, about 7:30 PM. We were met at the station by enlisted men who were detailed to train the members of the Women's Army Auxiliary Corps. We were told to "fall in." I knew that Army life was tough but I hardly expected to have to ruin my traveling outfit falling into the dust. I never heard those words before in my life, so I looked around to see what the other girls were doing. I just followed the few who seemed to know that to fall in meant to form a straight line.[26]

Mitchell was the only African American in this group of women who traveled to Fort Des Moines. Upon her arrival at the training center Mitchell was met by an African American woman who had arrived earlier and who escorted her to the barracks reserved for "coloreds." Mitchell was the thirty-eighth black Waac to arrive; two more were expected. Surveying the area for a familiar face, she saw one woman who had attended college with her: "I hadn't known her well, but we greeted each other like long-lost friends. Anyone from home was welcomed at that moment." Mitchell vividly remembers racial segregation in the first Officer Candidate School: "There were 400 whites and 40 blacks at the time . . . and completely segregated. We had our own building, and we were the third platoon in a company." Racial segregation presented a serious logistic problem for the Army and a psychological problem for many African American Waacs/Wacs.

Initially the War Department was confused about what to do with black women in the WAAC. Much of the discomfiture stemmed from racial stereotypes. On 14 May 1942, for example, the executive director of the WAAC, Maj. Harold P. Tasker, sent a memorandum to Oveta Culp Hobby, informing her of a strategy to admit forty black women to the first OCS:

It was originally planned to admit twenty-three (23) colored women to the Officer Candidates' Course. Information from the engineer school at Fort Belvoir indicates a very high percentage of failures from the colored group in the Engineer Officer Candidate course. It is, therefore, believed that the number to attend our first officers' school should be increased to 40. . . . Based on that figure, and assuming for sake of argument that there will be no losses, the following plan is offered as a workable solution from all angles, including training and housing facilities.[27]

The overall plan was to train just enough black women to fill two companies consisting of 3 officers, 20 noncommissioned officers, and slightly more than 127 auxiliaries (low-ranking women of the rank and file). These companies subsequently were to be assigned to Fort Huachuca, Arizona, the largest black Army post at the time. At the end of the training period no black Waacs would be left at Fort Des Moines. This plan never materialized, however.

African American women participated in the first OCS graduation on 29 August and were commissioned as third officers. Because women did not actually belong to the U.S. Army but rather were a part of an auxiliary, the War Department created the rank of third officer, the equivalent to the Army's second officer.[28] The exact number of African American women who graduated in the first OCS class is unclear. In an article titled: "Announce Roster of Women in the Army Auxiliary Corps," the *Chicago Defender* listed forty names.[29] Several other documents state that thirty-nine African American women attended the first OCS class and successfully completed it.[30] In any case, the women were carefully selected from a pool of eligibles. All of them had at least some college experience before entering the military, and many were college graduates.

Two months before the graduation ceremony, in a news release dated 1 June 1942, Bethune announced that she had conferred with WAAC director Hobby and had been assured that black women would be welcomed with "a spirit of justice and fair play." The article read as follows:

Mrs. Bethune, speaking as president of the National Council of Negro Women, expressed the belief that this is an opportunity for the service of the best women of the race. She urged that the women who are fitted for this type of service by possessing strength of character, leadership, and cooperative attitude, register and become a part of this program. The National Council of Negro Women, declared Mrs. Bethune, reasserts its determination to stand shoulder to shoulder with all other women of the country in bearing our part of the responsibility for winning this war. The endorsement of the Women's Army Auxiliary Corps, asserted Mrs. Bethune, is wholeheartedly given, but is not to be interpreted as an endorsement of its policy of segregation. This, however, she declared, is the other half of our battle. It must not, in any way, lessen our support or participation in our country's victory effort.[31]

Several black organizations were skeptical, however, about black women's participating in an organization in which there was institutionalized racism and denied rights. These organizations voiced their concerns about racial segregation in the WAAC. E. J. Adams, acting secretary of the North Jersey Committee on Discrimination, wrote to Col. Don Faith, the commandant of the WAAC Training Center, requesting that the policy of racial discrimination be abolished. The letter was forwarded to WAAC Headquarters, and Adj. Gen. William Pearson replied formula-ically that the contents of Adams's letter had been duly noted.[32] On 25 August Harry McAlpin of the *Chicago Defender* sent Col. Harold Tasker, the executive director of the WAAC, a memo reporting alleged racial discrimination at the WAAC training cen-ter. Among the allegations was that the swimming pool was open to black Waacs only one hour a week; that signs were posted, designating which tables black Waacs were authorized to occupy in the mess hall; that black Waacs were required to sit in one section of the classroom; that black Waacs were banned from the officers' recreational facilities; and that racial slurs were used in the classroom. On 8 September McAlpin received a reply from Lt. Col. Noel Macy, assistant director of the War Department's Bu-reau of Public Relations, addressing each allegation separately.[33] Macy said that there was no discrimination with regard to the swimming pool; signs had been removed from tables in the mess hall; Blacks naturally would sit together in classrooms because the women were seated with their platoons, and that there were two service clubs: one for Whites and one for Blacks."[34]

In August, a few days after the first WAAC OCS held its graduation, Bethune asked Charles P. Howard, a black attorney in Iowa, to investigate conditions surrounding black Waacs at Fort Des Moines. In his report Howard wrote:

I reported to Captain Vann B. Kennedy, Public Relations Officer, advised him that I was making an investigation of the post at your request for the information of Mrs. Roosevelt, and asked for an interview with Colonel Don C. Faith. The Colonel was not immediately available, but upon his return I was granted an interview at once. I advised Colonel Faith that my mission was to investigate conditions at Fort Des Moines relative to the Negro girls and informed him that I had been requested to do so by you. Colonel Faith frankly informed me that as to housing, recreation, and eating, the Negro girls are segregated, and that segregation was done in conformity with "the policy of the Army;" that otherwise Negro girls are given absolute equality of opportunity. For the purpose of facilitating my investigation I prepared a series of questions, and the answers thereto are by me based upon questions propounded to Colonel Faith and Captain Kennedy, interviews made this date with individual Negro Waacs and groups of Negro Waacs, and my personal observations made daily since the first day of camp.[35]

Howard reported that the thirty-nine officer candidates were assigned to one platoon and were part of the First Company of the First Regiment WAAC with two other platoons made up of white officer candidates. There were a black and a white service club, one post canteen for both Blacks and Whites, and one swimming pool with a specified time for black women to swim. Black women were assigned special tables in the mess hall's southeast corner, marked "Reserved C." When black Waacs complained about the reservation cards on the table, Colonel Faith had them removed. Black Waacs attended classes along with Whites when training consisted of two or more platoons. Howard also reported that some black officer candidates visited white friends, and vice versa.[36]

This report makes clear that race discrimination was being practiced in the WAAC training center, even though the War Department wanted to give the impression that facilities were separate but equal. On 2 September Bethune forwarded Howard's report to Judge William Hastie, civilian aide to the secretary of war. Judge Hastie forwarded the report to Lieutenant Colonel Macy. In a memo to Lt. Col. David Page, Macy stated that the report appeared to be entirely accurate and recommended that it be cleared for release.[37]

Because African American women were accepted in the first WAAC Officer Candidate School, it sometimes appears, at least on the surface, that black female officers were more highly advantaged than black male officers. The number of black male officers was insufficient to lead black male troops; in contrast, there were initially more African American female officers than enrolled (enlisted) women. In December 1942 black women made up 3.8 percent of the WAAC officers as compared with 1.4 percent of the WAAC enlisted women. This ratio changed in the following months, however, as more black women were trained as enlisted personnel.[38] By March 1943, for example, Blacks made up 2.6 percent of the WAAC officers and 5.8 percent of the enlisted women.[39] For the first time in American history women in general, and African American women in particular, were being trained for leadership positions in an auxiliary of an exclusively male institution.

Even so, equal opportunity was far from reality in the Women's Army (Auxiliary) Corps. Racial restrictions influenced the assignments and activities of black Waacs/Wacs. Those who were assigned the position of company commander, for example, were restricted to commanding all-black female units. WAC director was the only position with an accompanying rank of colonel that was open to women, and all of the women who filled that position were of European descent. All of the few lieutenant colonel positions were filled by white women.

The highest rank assigned to African American women during World War II was that of major.[40] Two black women attained this rank: one was Harriet West, of WAC Headquarters in Washington, D.C.; the other was Charity Adams, the battalion commander of the 6888th Central Postal Directory Battalion.[41] Charity Adams Earley, then Charity Adams, was promoted to lieutenant colonel when she returned to the United States after the war. Thus, the highest position to which the average black Waac/Wac officer could realistically aspire was that of a company-level officer, for whom the highest attainable rank was captain. This fact dampened the spirits of some of the black Waac/Wac officers.[42] A more overt act of racism was reflected in the policy that forbade African American Waac/Wac officers from eating or socializing in officers' clubs.[43] Earley recalls being severely reprimanded by a white male officer superior for going to the officers' club while stationed at Fort Des Moines:

So you are the Major Adams, the negra officer who went into the officers club last night. I don't think any colored person has ever been a guest there before. What were you doing there? Who had the nerve to invite you there? I don't believe in race mixing, and I don't intend to be a part of it. I understand that you are from South Carolina. Well, I am too, and that makes it worse. . . . I can't stand having a negra from the same state that I come from socializing with the same people I do. Don't let being an officer go to your head; you are still colored and I want you to remember that. You people have to stay in your place.[44]

These peculiarly marginal black women occupied a paradoxical position of prominence and obscurity.

Many of the black graduates of the first WAAC OCS class remained at Fort Des Moines, were further trained as company officers, and served as officers for the black WAAC companies that were formed in the following months. These women were responsible for "the administration of black WAC companies, housing, feeding and getting troops to the right place at the right time."[45] They faced the same challenges as those encountered by their white counterparts, and they struggled with the additional burden of managing the problems resulting from racial segregation. Charity Adams Earley recalls that while white Waacs spent one week in the reception area, moved on to another area for basic training, and went to still another area for skill development, black Waacs remained in the same area for all three activities:

Because there were not many Negro WAACs, all of their routine schedules were done in Company 8 except for the specialist training. The result was that I commanded a receiving company, a basic training company, and a staging company. My officers and I learned in one company, in a short time, what other officers learned over long periods of time.[46]

Black company officers thus had to be more versatile than their white counterparts because of the racial inequality built into the institutional structure of the Women's Army (Auxiliary) Corps. As a result of such inequities, black Waacs' living, working, and social conditions were not only racially separate but also inferior to those of their white counterparts.

WAAC Detachment No. 2 (Colored)

The first all-black WAAC Basic Training Company began training at Fort Des Moines in September 1942.[47] All of these women had a basic training course that had been designed by the post commandant and patterned after the first four weeks of the men's basic course. The course consisted of military courtesy, Army organization, and drill. In lieu of combat courses (women were not trained in weaponry), Waacs had courses in current events, map reading, and property responsibility.[48] Some of these women received vocational training, becoming drivers, cooks, and bakers; others were sent to the field without such training. Some of the women interviewed for this study felt fortunate to have been selected among the few black Wacs to attend administration school. Mary Rozier recalls that a large number of black Wacs were sent to cooks' and bakers' school: "I was sent to administration school. They [the WAC] had administration school, and cooks' and bakers' schools; and there were a lot of girls who were teachers [in civilian life] who were sent to cooks' and bakers' school, but I was lucky enough to go to admin school."

In December 1942 the first two black WAAC companies, the Thirty-Second and the Thirty-Third WAAC Post Headquarters Companies, arrived at Fort Huachuca, Arizona.[49] African American Waacs were subsequently assigned to various Army and Army Air Corps installations throughout the United States. Most of them lived, worked, and socialized in racially segregated environments, but some worked in units in which they were the only African Americans, or in which they were among the very few black Waacs/Wacs assigned. Harriet West, for example, was the only black WAAC officer assigned for duty in the Personnel Division at WAAC Headquarters in the District of Columbia. Another Waac/Wac, Blanche Scott, was the only African American assigned to her recruiting station in Virginia: "There was a group of us in Richmond, in the headquarters, and I was the only Black, and there were about six or seven white WAC officers." Charity Adams Earley later became one of two black Wacs working in the WAC Training Center Headquarters.[50]

Largely because of racial discrimination in the larger society, as well as the military policy on racial segregation, the War Department was finding it difficult to recruit qualified African American women. The War Department defined eligibility by an applicant's score on the entrance examination. Because of poor educational facilities, however, the literacy rate was low in the black community. On 11 September 1942 1st Lt. D. F. Taylor sent a memorandum to the Military Branch Personnel Division stating that quotas for "colored WAAC auxiliaries [low ranking enlisted women]" had not been met because 85 percent of the black WAAC applicants had failed the mental alertness test. Taylor requested that the mental alertness test score be lowered for black WAAC applicants. Lieutenant Colonel Tasker rejected this request but stated that he would employ four "colored WAAC officers for temporary recruiting duty" in an effort to recruit more educated black women.

On the following day Col. Oscar Abbott, director of military personnel, circulated a memo titled "Policy Regarding Colored Personnel in the WAAC." The first two paragraphs of the memorandum read:

1. Colored units of the WAAC post headquarters type could be used on any post where there is a need for a WAAC Unit; provided the colored unit operates on the same basis of efficiency as the white unit. In this regard there should be no lowering of the standard test for applicants in order to fill the ratio requirements.

2. There is a definite reluctance on the part of the best qualified

colored women to volunteer in the WAAC. This is brought about by an impression on their part that they will not be well received or treated on posts where they may be stationed. This could be overcome by an intensive recruiting campaign with the idea in view of interesting the desired class of colored women in this project and arriving at a thorough understanding of their rights and privileges while in the service.[51]

The memo also listed the names and locations of colleges enrolling large numbers of African American women and stated that black WAAC companies should be assigned to locations where they would be well received.

The War Department was not aggressively addressing the concerns raised by African Americans. Aside from the question of low aptitude scores, much of the racial tension that existed in the Women's Army (Auxiliary) Corps resulted from the War Department's policy of racial segregation, which almost invariably led to unfair treatment of African American women. Even when black Waacs/Wacs scored high on the military entrance examination, they were not assigned to occupations commensurate with their abilities, nor were they promoted.

The issue of racial segregation became especially important to black leaders when several allegations were made about the racist practices of the WAAC. Edwin Embree, president of the Julius Rosenwald Fund in Chicago, was disturbed by these allegations and visited the WAAC Training Center on 23 September 1942. In a letter he wrote to Colonel Faith, thanking him for the hospitality they received, Embree assessed that facilities for "whites and coloreds" were equal and that qualified black women at Fort Des Moines had a positive effect on white Waacs, who claimed never to have associated on the basis of "equality, friendship, and common effort with Negroes of their own quality and education, in fact did not know such women existed." Taking a diplomatic tone, Embree wrote that the special table that had been assigned to colored girls in the officers' mess was a conspicuous form of segregation and was resented by black Waac officers. Embree ended his letter by urging that the "unnecessary [racial] segregation be corrected."[52]

Later that month a Mrs. Viola A. McAteea wrote to Eleanor Roosevelt requesting that Irma Moore, an African American Waac who held a master's degree in theology, be reassigned to a position more commensurate with her skills. "I'm hoping you could fly down to Des Moines and look over the training camp and see this Negro, (one would perhaps find her scrubbing floors)! You are so fine and so far above bigotry; I know you will do what you can for this dark skinned woman, Irma L. Moore, D.D. (5th Co.), (2nd. Reg.)."[53] Attorney S. Joe Brown of Iowa also lobbied on Moore's behalf. In a letter addressed to Colonel Faith he wrote, "Miss Moore enlisted for the express purpose of qualifying for a chaplaincy; but now that women are not being accepted as chaplains, she is willing to waive her clerical rank and enroll as a candidate for a third officer; and I am sure that you can make no mistake by giving her this opportunity."[54]

The problem of malassignment was rooted in structural inequality perpetrated by the War Department and not only discouraged qualified African American women from joining the Women's Army Corps, but also created unrest among black women who had joined. Several African American women openly protested being assigned to menial tasks; some were victorious in their protests, but other attempts were defeated. Before going overseas with the 6888th, Dorothy Dailey Jones was stationed at Fort Jackson, South Carolina. She arrived at Fort Jackson in the middle of an inflammatory situation: "The [black] women in the outfit, which was attached to the regional hospital, were doing the most menial work in the hospital. They were washing walls and carrying bed pans, and not much of anything else, regardless of training." When Jones arrived, three African American women already had been court-martialed for rebelling against the system, and one woman had slapped a white male officer. "Two of us stuck our necks out; we knew enough about military law to do it in a reasonably safe manner; we wrote a letter to the hospital commander through channels." Some of the women in Jones' company were already trained medical technicians. Others were unskilled: "We did have a meeting with the powers that be and some agreements were reached that there would be some training for those women who didn't have any skills." [55]

Many military hospitals at that time hired civilians to do the menial tasks that were assigned to black women at Fort Jackson who had been trained as medical technicians:

We convinced them [the powers that be] that it was a waste to use expensive Wacs for jobs that comparatively inexpensive civilians could do. Nobody had been promoted from the time the unit had been put together. We were WAC Detachment No. 2. In those days 2 always meant colored. I made PFC; our top sergeant finally got her sergeant stripes; she was a corporal. The company's rank went from PFC to corporal, and people were trained to be medical technicians and lab technicians. I didn't get beyond PFC until we went overseas. [56]

Jones was later assigned to special services in the Headquarters Company of the 6888th.

Grievances associated with racial segregation in the WAC reached many sympathetic ears. Emily Hickman, chairperson of the Public Affairs Committee of the Young Women's Christian Association, wrote a letter to WAAC director Hobby on 14 October 1942 and later to Secretary of War Henry L. Stimson, protesting racial segregation in the WAAC's Officer Candidate School:

We are particularly disturbed about this in view of the fact that we understand that there has been considerable modification of the customary Army plan of racial separation insofar as officers' training for Army men is concerned. We are tremendously hopeful that women may set ahead the cause of national unity and war morale, to which we believe the subject of our inquiry has direct relation. [57]

Emily Hickman was referring to the fact that although local and national legislation prohibited racial integration, in 1941 Army officials had integrated Officer Candidate Training in an effort to use manpower more efficiently.[58]

By this time Bethune's support for the corps was facing severe challenges. The black press and the National Association for the Advancement of Colored People were deeply concerned about the treatment of African American women in the WAAC. Bethune was criticized for approving an organization that had a racial segregation plan. On 4 November 1942 she wrote in her own defense to Walter White:

I have read with great alarm your findings on the status of segregation being practiced in the training of the Women's Army Auxiliary Corps at Fort Des Moines. Specifically, I am even more alarmed because of information coming to you and to Negro members of the WAAC indicating that I have given my approval to this segregated plan of operation. I think you and others who have known me during the years need no statement of my disapproval of segregation in any form. I have never at any time approved segregation at Fort Des Moines.[59]

Less than two weeks later, in an interview with the *Washington Tribune,* Bethune urged black Wacs to work for changing military racial policies through external organizations and not to take matters into their own hands: "It is unfortunate that the Negro Waacs must be segregated but it is much easier for them to remain in the camp and leave the fighting of the condition to those of us on the outside."[60] Later that month, partly as a result of political pressure and partly because there was only a small number of African American women training to be officers, the War Department desegregated the living and recreational facilities of the Officer Candidate School (OCS) at Fort Des Moines.[61]

Some of the officers of the 6888th attended OCS during this period of desegregation. Blanche Scott recalls: "The OCS wasn't bad. There were ten Blacks (they call them black now; then it was Negro). All of us [both black and white women] were in the same barracks; the ten Negro Wacs were in one little small room at the end. We [black and white Wacs] had classes together, ate together, socialized together, you know, and all that. We didn't have any problems at all as I recall." Similarly, Mildred Dupee Leonard remembers, "When we were in officer's training we lived in the same building as white trainees, but all of the Blacks were in one room because there were so few of us; there were nine of us in my class out of three hundred."

While the War Department received letters from African Americans protesting racial segregation, it also received correspondence from white Americans protesting alleged racial integration. On 17 April 1943 John C. McCormack, general manager of radio station KWKH.KTBS in Shreveport, Louisiana, wrote to John Ewing, apparently a prominent resident of Shreveport. When the letter was written, Ewing was in New York staying at the Waldorf Astoria Hotel. McCormack wrote to Ewing about recent rumors that the Women's Army Corps was racially integrated. In the letter he suggested that the WAAC be investigated for alleged racial integration:

Miss. Tucker's sister enlisted in the WAAC about six weeks ago. After completing her basic training, she applied for administrative school and was transferred over last weekend to the Chamberlain Hotel in Des Moines. A couple of days after moving into this hotel, she wrote Miss Tucker a letter commenting very strongly on the situation between the negroes and the whites in the WAAC. She said both negroes and whites were stationed in the Chamberlain Hotel, although they were on separate floors. They use the same dining room even though they have a section for the negroes and a section for the whites. She said she had seen them working side by side serving food, and it was her understanding that they did KP [kitchen police] duty together. She also stated she understood that in the cooks and bakers school they worked together, ate together, and lived in the same barracks. . . . I feel a little bit guilty in that we have . . . influenced so many girls to join this thing who no doubt find themselves in an unhappy situation after they arrive due to misrepresentation. . . . In writing this letter, I also have in mind having heard you mention that little Helen was thinking of joining the WAAC and felt you would want this thoroughly investigated before she did.[62]

Ewing forwarded the letter to Colonel Hobby, who replied to John McCormack as follows in a letter dated 7 May:

In the basic training section, Negroes are formed into their own companies, except in a few instances when the number of Negroes who arrive at a training center at any one time is insufficient to make up a company. In such a case, every effort is made to form at least a platoon of Negroes, so that the Negro women within the company may be housed in their own section of the barracks. . . . The number of Negroes who receive officer candidate training is so small that they cannot be formed into company units, and are consequently placed in regular officer candidate companies. . . . I am satisfied that such occurrences as you mention are infrequent, and when they do happen are temporary and practically unavoidable.[63]

The last sentence of this letter reveals that Hobby, the director of the WAC, sympathized with McCormack's complaint and supported the idea of racial segregation in the Women's Army Corps. Rather than defending integration, Hobby apologizes for it. Had the Women's Army Corps desegregated all of its facilities and assigned African American women to positions commensurate with their abilities, many of the racial problems that surfaced would have been alleviated. Instead, racism remained a problem in the Women's Army Corps because of its narrow-minded policy of racial segregation, which ran counter to the American ideology of democracy.

The African American community continued to press the issue of race relations in the WAAC. On 14 June 1943 a fact sheet was circulated among members of the Conference against Race Discrimination in the War Effort.[64] Some of the African American citizens wanted a more specific account of the situation in the WAC in order to make a better-informed assessment. Florence Murray, for example, of the Hotel Theresa in New York City, wrote to the War Department requesting a variety of statistics on Negro Waacs. First Officer Gretchen M. Thorp replied on 7 August 1943, stating that the WAC did not compile statistics by race. Thorp revealed, however, that thirty-nine Blacks had graduated

from the first Officer Candidate School and that some had received promotions; in addition, black officers served at WAC
Headquarters in Washington, D.C., at the WAC Training Centers
in Des Moines and at Fort Devens, and in ten Army installations
in the field.[65]

The atmosphere created by the WAC's policy of racial segregation spawned racial bigotry by creating an atmosphere in which
individual racists were inspired to act out their prejudices. Consider the case of Elsie Oliver, who while stationed at Fort Des
Moines was almost fatally injured by a military dentist who deliberately used soiled instruments to work in her mouth. Oliver
developed a serious infection and had to be hospitalized:

> I was notified to go to this dentist [one reputed as expressing disdain for
> African Americans] and his office was filled with Whites. When every-
> body else was out of his office but his assistant, they called me. I figured
> they would not see me that day at all. It was almost night when he called
> "Elsie Oliver." I went down to his chair, and when I sat down I noticed
> that all the instruments were soiled. . . . So I said: "Sir, you're not going
> to work on me with that!" He said: "I'm the dentist, you'll do as I tell
> you." So then he pushed me in the chair and started rubbing his hands
> up on my legs. I said, "I'm not here for anything but dental work. . . ."
> So that's when he pushed my head back and started pawing in my
> mouth. . . . The next morning infection had set in. . . . I was in the
> hospital for three or four weeks.

Oliver believes that the dentist was later court-martialed for his
deplorable act. Yet, although this individual act of discrimination
was not sanctioned by the institution, it was encouraged by the
War Department's policy of racial segregation.

On 4 February 1944 Lula Jones Garrett of the *Afro-American
Newspaper* in Baltimore forwarded a list of charges of racial
discrimination, compiled by black Wacs at Fort Des Moines, to
Maj. Harriet West, the African American Wac assigned as advisor
on Negro affairs, at WAC Headquarters in Washington, D.C. A
few days earlier a more extensive list of complaints from an
anonymous Wac had been sent to Major West at her home in the

District of Columbia. The grievances included allegations that black Wacs were forced to billet in crowded quarters separated from other billets, were subjected to racial slurs, and were not allowed to charge books out of Service Club "number 1" (a designation indicating that it was a facility for Whites). An investigation was requested. The list of grievances went up the chain of command at WAC Headquarters before it was sent back to Fort Des Moines for investigation. Maj. Charity Adams, serving at the time as the Training Center (quality) control officer, was assigned to investigate the complaints.[66]

Upon completing her investigation, Major Adams reported that there was no racial discrimination:

At no time have Negro officers been forced to live under the conditions stated. Housing facilities are equally adequate for both Negro and white officers. Reference books are located in the military science library and are available to all military personnel. They are not kept in either service club. Books kept in either service club may be available to personnel through the librarians of either Club.[67]

The final report was sent back to Headquarters and then forwarded to Lula Garrett. Racial slurs were not mentioned in that report, nor did the report address the specific allegation that black Wacs were denied access to library books at Service Club "number 1." In this instance, Major Adams replied as most WAC officials responded to complaints, by reciting military policy; she was not in a position powerful enough to permit anything else. Fulfilling a role with which she did not necessarily identify, Major Adams was merely a black Wac carrying out orders.

A number of allegations were made concerning the War Department's unequal and inferior treatment of black Wacs; although some may have been left unsubstantiated, others were supported by facts. In July 1944 Horace R. Cayton, manager of a hotel on the South Side of Chicago, wrote a letter to the armed forces induction station refusing to renew his contract to house newly inducted African American Wacs. One of his reasons for refusal was that the induction station neglected to reserve rooms for black Wacs before sending them to the hotel. Because of this lack of coordination, women were left without lodging. Black Wacs were sent to the South Side to look for housing late at night, while white Wacs were housed in the Loop (The downtown business area) in a protected environment. Cayton requested that the War Department revise its policy and house black inductees in the same way as white inductees.

During that month a number of letters were written to the War Department concerning discontinuing the only Negro WAC Band. One of these letters was addressed to Secretary of War Henry Stimson from Walter White, secretary of the NAACP. Several newspaper articles also protested the disbandment. The Negro Wac Band at Fort Des Moines initially consisted of thirty women, and later was reduced to twenty-eight (the standard size for an Army band). The band was established because black Wacs were excluded from the official band, which was composed exclusively of white Wacs. Pvt. Leonora Hull was the band director; and 2nd Lt. Thelma Brown was the officer in charge. Because the band was not officially authorized, the band members were carried as overhead. On 10 July 1944 they were given a band rating: some members were promoted to corporal, others to sergeant. They made numerous appearances, most notably at a conference for the NAACP in Chicago. A few days after that performance, however, the band members received notices that the band would be dissolved effective 18 July and its members would be reclassified and sent to different units.

As a result of widespread protest by black organizations, the black press, and private citizens, the War Department was compelled to rescind its decision. On 16 August Lt. Col. Jessie Pearl Rice wrote a letter to Bethune:

The order to disband this unit was issued as a part of an Army-wide program which called for the discontinuance of a large number of bands. After obtaining full information and receiving the recommendation of the commanding officer of the First WAC Training Center—a recommendation based on the importance of band to morale—the War Department decided to continue the band and its official activation has been directed.[68]

The War Department quickly found itself forced to modify its policy in an effort to be more racially inclusive. Yet, even though the War Department allowed the band to continue, it was not willing to include African American Waacs in its white band.

Racism and sexism continued to be defining characteristics of life for African American women in uniform. Even toward the end of the war African American women could be beaten unmercifully by police in the South for sitting in a "white only" section of a train station. The irony of such cases was that African American Wacs not only were terrorized by police in the very country they were willing to protect from foreign invasion, but they also were punished by the War Department for not adhering to racial segregation. One such case was described in New York City's *Amsterdam-Star News* on 28 July 1945:

Following an unmerciful beating by a civilian policeman in Elizabethtown, KY., because she dared sit in a waiting room reserved for white people, a WAC Private faces summary court martial this Saturday for breaking the Jim Crow Laws of the state. The woman, PFC. Helen Smith of Syracuse, who has served 26 months in the Corps and is now stationed at Fort Knox, lay ill in the hospital for a full week before she was able to write of her plight to relatives here and in Philadelphia.[69]

In other reported incidents as well, African American women were beaten while wearing the Army uniform. In one such report it was claimed that an African American woman was beaten for being a captain and "expecting white people to salute her."[70]

Two months before V-E (victory in Europe) Day, black Wacs continued to complain about racism in the corps. In a newspaper article titled "Disillusioned by Jim-Crow Washington Girl Quits WAC," Pvt. Ana Aiken testified:

I was sworn in the WAC on the 5th of February, 1943, and received basic training at Fort Des Moines. Conditions on the post were pretty fair. We only had segregated service clubs. After I completed my training I was sent to Fort Clark, Texas. . . . [There] when I went to the movies I met Jim Crow. . . . San Antonio was the nearest town and there we were barred from all recreation centers. . . . From there I went to Camp Gruber, Oklahoma, in June 1944. This camp was definitely not one for colored [Wacs] as provisions had been made for white Wacs only. . . . The morale of our group became very low. . . . We were finally sent to Fort Sam Houston, Texas . . . [where] civilians employed at the depot made it very unpleasant for us. . . . We were not allowed to work at the hospital (Brooks General). . . . Until we are able to live together as a people, colored units should be sheltered from the inconveniences of the south.[71]

In the same month four black Wacs in the North, rebelling against malassignments, were convicted for disobeying a direct order to work. These Wacs were protesting their assignment to perform only "dirty duties" (menial tasks) because of their race. On 20 March they were convicted by a nine-member court-martial on charges of disobeying a superior officer, received a dishonorable discharge, and were sentenced to one year at hard labor. Yet, unlike so many cases against black Wacs who refused to obey unfair and unjust orders, this case did not end in defeat. On 23 March 1945 three congressmen—Emanuel Celler, Vito Marcantonio, and Adam Clayton Powell—asked for an investigation of the court-martial. Again, several letters were written to the War Department by black organizations and the black press. On 3 April the court-martial sentences were voided on the grounds that the court was convened improperly (Gen. Sherman Miles, the accuser, also convened the court, which was both inappropriate and illegal). The Wacs were immediately restored to duty; this act represented a collective success by the African American community.[72]

At times racial discrimination against black Wacs reflected the fears of white ethnics living in neighborhoods adjacent to military installations. Residents rebelled against proposals made by the War Department to station black Wacs near their neighborhoods.

On 6 April 1945, for example, Col. John Nash, general staff corps to the Director of Personnel, wrote a memo claiming that a Jewish residential committee in Hyde Park (Chicago) protested the proposed placement of black Wacs at Gardiner Hospital.[73] Gardiner Hospital was located at 1660 East Hyde Park Boulevard, a predominantly Jewish neighborhood. One mile west of the hospital was Cottage Grove Avenue, the eastern boundary of Chicago's black neighborhood. Although Hyde Park had a restrictive covenants property owners' agreement, residents feared that African Americans would migrate into their community and cause a devaluation of their property. The residents also were concerned that if a black WAC detachment were assigned at Gardiner Hospital, the Wacs would be quartered in the immediate vicinity and would be tempted to use beaches reserved for Whites only. Furthermore, the committee argued, black men would pass through white segregated areas when calling on black Wacs for dates.

Black organizations, including the National Council of Negro Women and the Chicago Council against Racial and Religious Discrimination met with military officials to counteract the petition drawn up by Jewish protesters. These activists in Chicago sent letters urging the War Department to carry out its plan and to assign the black WAC unit to Gardiner. After long deliberation the War Department activated the unit—the Fifty-Fifth WAC Hospital Company—which began its tour of duty on 5 June. All official reports indicate that the unit performed well and encountered no racial antagonism during its time in Hyde Park.[74]

In some ways the military environment was merely a reflection of civilian society. Complying with the country's racial norms, the U.S. Army was racially segregated for the most part. Integration of the Officer Candidate School was an exception to the rule. Although the workplace was sometimes integrated, recreational and living facilities were separated almost entirely by race. By protesting race-biased policies in the Women's Army Auxiliary Corps and later the Women's Army Corps, African Americans actively sought change and sometimes achieved it.

Deploying Negro Waacs/Wacs Overseas

Among the issues concerning racial equality in the WAAC/WAC was the question of deploying African American Waac/Wacs overseas. Black political leaders addressed this issue in public speeches and wrote to the War Department. In a letter to Oveta Hobby dated 14 August 1944, Mary McLeod Bethune continued to raise issues that had not been satisfactorily addressed, including deployment of African American Wacs overseas:

In addition to seeing to it that Negro WACS are admitted to the 400th Army Band at Fort Des Moines, we also urge that colored WAC officials be assigned to duties comparable to their rank, that colored WACS be allowed to serve overseas, and finally that they be accorded all of the rights and privileges of a full fledged WAC, regardless of race, color, or creed.[75]

Several letters were written to the War Department requesting that black Wacs be deployed overseas. Secretary of War Henry L. Stimson's standard reply to these requests was simply that Negro Wacs were not being deployed overseas because they were not being requested by overseas commanders.[76]

The race barrier preventing the deployment of African Americans overseas was broken for black men in May 1942, when black soldiers were stationed in the British Isles for the first time. Three months later the War Department indecorously requested African American Wacs to serve as mates for black male soldiers. As early as August 1942 Gen. Dwight D. Eisenhower, commander of the American forces in the ETO, announced that the Army planned to send black Waacs to England "to perform duties such as car driving and secretarial work and also to provide companionship for thousands of Negro troops." An article in the *New York Times* stated:

Frankly recognizing the problem, the Army is attempting to deal with it on a sensible and practical basis, the General stressed. In the larger cities like London, where in the nature of things there is less home entertainment of soldiers, Negroes on leave wander disconsolately, one of them remarking: "There's no hot music and none of our girls."[77]

Newspapers heralded the announcement that black Waacs were going to the United Kingdom to serve as companions to black male troops. On 21 August the *St. Louis Arpug* carried the headline "Army Will Send Our WAACs to England to Help Troops." On the following day the *Philadelphia Tribune* wrote: "There is a possibility that Negro members of the Women's Army Auxiliary Corps will serve overseas. . . . The Waacs if they go will serve at such duties as secretaries, chauffeurs and at the same time bring a touch of home to the soldiers."[78]

This news hit WAAC officials particularly hard. They had struggled laboriously through ACWIS and the NCAC to avoid being tagged as an escort service. They battled constantly against depictions of Waacs as loose, highly sexed women with low morals and a predisposition toward "illegitimate" births. Rejecting the notion that black Waacs would be shipped abroad only to entertain soldiers, the WAAC director sent a statement abroad through Truman K. Gibson, Jr. (civilian aide to the secretary of war), outlining the duties expected of Waacs abroad:

The two companies of Negro women will be sent overseas some time during the fall for duty in various posts where American Negro Troops are stationed. This is in accordance with the procedure which is being carried out in this country where Negro units of the WAAC are being stationed on posts where the predominant population consists of Negro soldiers. Every member of the WAAC is enrolled and trained to perform a specific duty which will release a soldier for combat duty.[79]

Hobby, however, refused to allow black Waacs to be shipped to Europe under these circumstances, "to let women be scattered in uncontrolled small field units near male Negro troops." The requisition was canceled hastily, with the explanation that "colored Wacs will not be requisitioned until such time that the War Department announces that their shipment to [overseas] theaters of operation is a necessity."[80] Yet in the height of war the ETO was in dire need of skilled clerical workers to relieve male soldiers for combat. The combination of institutionalized racism and sexism prevented the use of educated, talented, and skilled black Wacs in overseas theaters in the early years of the war.

Meanwhile, Caucasian Waacs were preparing for overseas duty and were ready for shipment by September 1942. The greatest concern voiced by Hobby about their deployment was the fact that as members of an auxiliary they were not entitled to extra overseas pay, government life insurance, or veterans hospitalization. Nevertheless, General Eisenhower requested Caucasian Waac typists and telephone operators to serve in North Africa; 150 Waacs were selected from volunteers and departed for North Africa in November 1942. ETO officials continued to request white Wacs for deployment to Europe.

Black Wacs were not requested again until late in 1944. Gertrude LaVigne was working as a supply clerk at Fort Huachuca when she learned that she had been selected to go overseas: "By mid-1944 we were informed of the group to be selected for overseas duty. A commission of male officers came to the WAC area, interviewed enlisted women, and selected those of us who would comprise the first all-Negro WAC outfit to go overseas."

Many battles were won through the collective efforts of African American Waacs/Wacs, community organizations, political leaders, and the black press. Victory prevailed in the allocation of forty slots to African American women in the first Officer Candidate School, the desegregation of the WAC Officer Candidate School, the reassignment of black Wacs at Camp Breckenridge and at Fort Jackson, the reinstatement of the four African American Wacs who were court-martialed for protesting malassignments, the reinstatement of the Negro WAC Band when the official WAC band excluded black Wac musicians, the assignment of black Wacs to Gardiner Hospital, and the deployment of black Wacs to the European Theater of Operations. These events, milestones for black activists, influenced the lives of all African American Waacs/Wacs. Several of the members of the 6888th, including

Charity Adams Earley, Margaret Barnes Jones, and Dorothy Dailey Jones, actively confronted racial issues long before they were deployed overseas.

Although segregation was not new to most African American women who were reared in the South, several women who had grown up in northern cities stated that they did not experience racial discrimination until they entered the Army. In contrast to the segregation practiced in the southern region of the United States, the U.S. War Department sometimes made a conscious effort to provide separate but equal facilities for black and for white Waacs/Wacs. According to the findings of some inspections, in some cases the Women's Army Corps in fact provided separate but equal facilities.[81] Nonetheless, racial segregation was offensive and demeaning to African Americans and to white humanitarians throughout the United States.

Whether members of the 6888th had been stationed in the segregated South or in more integrated installations in the northern regions, by now they were keenly aware that they had the same political interests. They realized that in order to survive they had to work together, collectively, as a unit. They had developed a political consciousness.

4

★ ★ ★

Just American Soldiers Going to Do a Job

> No one knew when we were to leave. I must have had a premonition because after supper on the night of January 23rd I felt kind of homesick and I wanted to talk to Mom. I kind of felt the time was drawing near, so I called her long distance, and we talked for a long time. I told her that this would probably be the last time I would call; that I was not sure when we were leaving. . . . I said, I'll take care of myself and write often, and I told her not to worry about me.
> —A. Noel Campbell Mitchell, Unpublished Memoirs

Socioeconomic Status and Household Composition

Only a few occupations were available to African Americans before World War II. Although most black professionals in the 1940s were either schoolteachers or ministers, certainly African American doctors, scientists, and lawyers existed in black communities. In addition, only a small percentage of clerical workers in the labor force were African Americans. Most black businesses in the North were beauty parlors, barbershops, cleaners, and restaurants.[1] There were some black-owned insurance companies and manufacturing companies in the southern region of the country.[2] The largest proportion of black workers, however, was concentrated in domestic, service, semiskilled, and laborer positions.[3]

As indicated by the narratives in chapter 1, members of the

Table 1. Parent's Occupation and Interviewee's
Occupation before Military Service

Occupational Category	Parent's Occupation[a]		Interviewee's Occupation before Service	
	%	(N)	%	(N)
Professional	18	(9)	18	(9)
Clerical	2	(1)	19	(10)
Retail trade	0	(0)	2	(1)
Service[b]	17	(9)	11	(6)
Domestic[c]	6	(3)	8	(4)
Crafts	22	(11)	6	(3)
Operatives	4	(2)	0	(0)
Laborers	25	(13)	12	(6)
Farmers	4	(2)	0	(0)
Other[d]	2	(1)	24	(12)
Total	100	(51)	100	(51)

NOTES: [a]Father's occupation unless father was deceased or unemployed.
[b]Excluding private household workers.
[c]Domestic refers to private household service workers; Occupational categories taken from the Census of Population, Occupational Classification System.
[d]Includes unemployed and students.

6888th came from diverse socioeconomic backgrounds.[4] Most of the women interviewed for this study grew up in families where the heads of household were either skilled or unskilled laborers; the heads of household of the next largest group were craftsmen (table 1). Of the fifty-one women interviewed, nine were reared in households where at least one parent was a working professional, and in four cases both parents worked in professional occupations (table 2). Table 2 also reveals that in seven of these households parents were school teachers; there were two ministers' households; and one in which a parent was an agriculturist. In eleven households, parents worked in skilled crafts such as tailoring, dressmaking, auto mechanics, and construction, and in two of those households parents were entertainers—musician and playwright. Parents in nine households worked in such service occupations as catering, hairdressing, and barbering; parents in three households were domestic workers. In three households the parents were operative workers, in two households they were farmers, and in one household both parents were unemployed.

Although most of the women interviewed for this study grew

Table 2. Interviewee's Age, Education, Rank, Civilian Occupation, and
Father's and Mother's Occupations

Age[a]	Education[a]	Rank with 6888th	Civilian Occupation[a]	Father's Occupation	Mother's Occupation
22	12	E-5	typist	bank clerk	housewife
23	12	E-3	**secretary**	laborer	domestic
23	13	E-3	clerical	farmer	housewife
20	15	E-3	**teacher**	caterer	caterer
33	12	E-5	factory worker	elevator operator	housewife
23	12	E-3	factory worker	factory worker	domestic
20	15	E-8	clerical	contractor	seamstress
27	14	E-5	student	laborer	domestic
21	14	E-3	student	contractor	housewife
19	13	E-3	factory worker	factory worker	domestic
25	14	E-3	student	restaurant owner	housewife
23	15	E-6	student	farmer	housewife
21	16	E-2	unemployed	**teacher**	**teacher**
21	12	E-3	waitress	contractor	housewife
24	17	0-4	teacher	**minister**	housewife
36	12	E-3	clerical	laborer	housewife
23	12	E-3	unemployed	janitor	housewife
22	12	E-3	clerical	presser	cook
20	12	E-3	clerical	factory worker	housewife
21	14	E-4	artist	tailor	housewife
24	16	E-4	factory worker	pullman porter	housewife
25	16	E-4	teacher	laborer	housewife
27	16	E-3	**librarian**	principal	**teacher**
22	12	E-4	factory worker	disabled vet	seamstress
25	16	E-3	unemployed	laborer	deceased
20	12	E-3	sales clerk	pullman porter	housewife
32	14	0-2	clerical	**chef**	**teacher/politics**
22	11	E-6	caterer	deceased	caterer
21	16	0-2	unemployed	deceased	beautician
19	12	E-4	domestic	factory worker	farm worker
21	13	E-2	dancer	producer/playwright	singer
25	16	E-3	engraver	**teacher**	**teacher**
23	16	0-3	**teacher**	**agriculturist**	housewife
28	12	E-3	beautician	farm worker	farm worker
21	12	E-4	clerical	laborer	housewife
20	12	E-3	unemployed	unknown	WPA/public aid
18	13	E-2	clerical	contractor	**teacher**
23	14	E-5	beautician	**chef**	**music teacher**
26	13	E-3	**secretary**	**minister**	housewife
27	15	0-2	clerical	**teacher**	**teacher**
23	13	E-3	domestic	deceased	domestic
28	12	E-3	unemployed	construction	housewife
18	12	E-3	domestic	laborer	housewife
36	12	E-5	factory worker	musician	domestic
21	12	E-3	dressmaker	mechanic	laundry worker
31	12	E-6	beautician	barber	**teacher**
25	16	E-4	**teacher**	laborer	domestic
18	13	E-3	student	refrig repairman	seamstress
22	9	E-4	domestic	mechanic	domestic
25	12	E-6	**teacher**	domestic	domestic
20	14	E-4	student	domestic	domestic

NOTE: [a] On entering service.

up in traditional nuclear families consisting of two parents and siblings, some lived in what today might be called alternative households. Some lived with relatives other than their biological parents. Mary Ragland's parents were killed in a car accident, and she was reared by adoptive parents: "I was born in Atlanta, Georgia, but I was raised in Wilmington, Delaware. My father, from what I gather, was from Atlanta, and my mother was East Indian; I don't know how they got together. She and my father died at a very young age in the early thirties and I was raised by some friends of theirs in Wilmington, Delaware." Ragland describes her adoptive parents as entrepreneurs, "They had two Safeway markets, so they raised me very well."

One interviewee, Boston native Enid Clark, was reared by a foster parent: "My parents weren't interested in me but another lady was very interested. . . . I was in a one-parent household. My foster mother had never married. She always wanted a child, so she got one." Clark suffered physical defects at birth and required special care:

I was in bad shape when I left the hospital after I was born because I had rickets and a few other things. And she took care of me up until about age eight or nine, and then my real mother somehow or other thought she wanted me back. And all she did was to shove me into different homes. The court sent me back to my foster mother when I was eleven; they wanted me to be with someone who loved me. We lived in a section of Boston called Roxbury. It's a terrible mess now, but it was kind of nice then. It was multiracial, mostly Jewish and Irish. We had good times there.

Clark's foster mother did domestic work for some of the wealthy residents of Boston. A pediatrician for whom she did laundry provided Clark gratis with much of the medical care she required. Clark completed high school and a few months of clerical school before entering the military. Being an only child, she felt that she had to represent her family in the war effort. Clark served as a postal clerk in the 6888th.

In another uncommon situation, a woman who had grown up in a white nuclear family did not learn that she was black until she applied to enter the Army. Anna Tarryk was born in Brooklyn, New York, and lived with her mother, her adoptive father (a construction engineer), and five half brothers, "My mother is Austrian and my background is a little different than most. When I applied to go into the service I was told that I would have to be segregated; but up to that point I didn't have to be." Because she appeared to be of European descent, Tarryk was never questioned about her race when she was growing up. She lived in an all-white neighborhood, attended all-white schools, and had graduated from an all-white high school before entering the service.

Tarryk never knew her biological father, and her mother never discussed her African heritage: "She just said one thing, that he was a dark-skinned man, and when he learned that my mother was pregnant he left." Of her mother, Tarryk says, "She married my father while she was pregnant, and he adopted me." Tarryk joined the Army even though the recruiter tried to dissuade her: "She felt very compassionate toward me. I think she felt that she tried to save me from going into the military. But being young, I had my own set of ideas." Tarryk entered the Army with a waiver: "The waiver was that if I wasn't able to adjust I could get an honorable discharge."

Like Tarryk, there were other women of mixed heritage in the unit. Dorothy Jones recalls a good friend from Minneapolis named Toni Smith:

If the recruiting sergeant hadn't known her and her family, there probably would have been no questions asked, and she would have been listed as white, and that would have been that; and I probably never would have met her. . . . But the woman who was recruiting at the time knew her background, knew that her family was sort of mixed, and asked her, "Are you white or colored?" And Toni said that she never stopped to consider it before. She decided she was colored. And she said, "Probably a mistake but I did it."

In some cases the fathers were either dead or physically disabled, and the mothers were generally the primary breadwinners.

Gertrude LaVigne, for example, lived in a household headed by her mother; her father had died when she was still an infant. As mentioned in chapter 1, LaVigne's mother moved her family to Ohio and started a family catering business.

Age Distribution

The age limit for enlistment in the Women's Army Corps was 20 to 50 (it was 21 to 45 for the Women's Army Auxiliary Corps before 1 July 1943).[5] Members of the 6888th represented all of the age groups that existed in the WAC during the 1940s. According to an article in *Stars and Stripes,* 20-year-old Pvt. Hilda E. Wood of Philadelphia was the youngest member, and 52-year-old Erma L. Fifer of Chicago, a grandmother of three, was the oldest. These members were part of the first contingent, which arrived in England in February 1945.

In some cases women younger than age 20 joined the military with parental consent. Such young women were in the second contingent of the 6888th, which arrived in Europe in April 1945. Mary Ragland and Willie Whiting claim that they were "not quite 18" when they entered in 1944. Both had to have written permission from a parent or a legal guardian before joining the WAC. A year later they were assigned to the 6888th. Most of the women interviewed for this study were in their early to middle twenties when they entered the military. As highlighted in table 2, the interviewees ranged in age from 18 to 36.

Education

As a group the members of the 6888th, not surprisingly, were less well educated than white Wacs stationed in Europe at the time. Forty percent of the unit was reported by the War Department to be unskilled, as compared with 1 percent of white Wacs in this theater; and 40 percent scored in the two lowest AGCT (Army General Classification Test) grades, as compared with 10 percent for white Wacs.[6] These discrepancies in occupational skills and aptitude scores obviously reflect racial inequities in educational opportunities during that period. In the 1930s fewer than 10 percent of African Americans age twenty-five or older had completed high school. Only 1.3 percent had completed college.[7]

Well-educated African American Waacs/Wacs, on the other hand, tended to do well on the military entrance examination. This was demonstrated not only by the black women who entered and completed OCS, but also by those who entered as enlisted women. Dorothy Dailey Jones, a private first class with the 6888th, scored exceptionally high. Jones, born in Richmond, Virginia, was the oldest of eleven children. Her father was a Pullman porter, her mother a homemaker. When Jones was three years old her family moved to Cambridge, Massachusetts, in an effort to escape, "good old Jim Crow" (legalized racial segregation in the South). Jones's mother taught her how to read when she was only three:

Mom was a remarkable woman. In another time and another place, she would have had a couple of degrees and be doing all kinds of things. As it was, until the youngest was in school, she wasn't able to work or anything. Mom was always interested in what was happening in the world. As long as I can remember, I could read the newspaper and we would discuss things. She never discouraged me from having a lot of friends of different types of people. In fact, I am constantly quoting her. She used to say that people who restricted themselves to one group were cheating themselves of the opportunity to grow.

Jones had gone to predominantly white public schools in Cambridge. Although she had completed only high school and a few hours toward a college degree when she entered the military, she scored in the highest bracket of the AGCT:

It's not that I am brighter than other people. A lot of people I think would have scored higher if those tests really tested intelligence, but they don't. They test knowledge. What they test is how well you can handle middle-class communication. So I don't feel particularly proud that I scored high. I just happen to be a good test taker because, for one thing, I had been a reader all of my life. Secondly, and related to that, is my ability to deal with the English language. I had excellent teachers . . . and they encouraged my use of English, my exploration of English. I did a lot of reading outside of class, linguistics and stuff like that, just because I was interested in communication. I also had knowledge in depth of French and a little bit of Spanish, and a little bit of German. All those things helped. I'm a rapid reader, which is another thing that helped. The more questions you can get to, the better off you are. So those are the things that contributed to my being a good test taker, and some basic intelligence. But I know people who are as smart and smarter than I am who don't test well.

Members of the 6888th in general appear to have been better educated than the average African American woman in civilian society. Few members of the 6888th had not completed high school, and several had at least some college. All of the officers and a considerable proportion of the enlisted women were university graduates.[8] A newspaper clipping distributed by the War Department stated that 85 percent of the unit were ex-school-teachers and held college degrees.[9] The battalion commander, Charity Adams Earley, had graduated from Wilberforce University and completed one year of graduate study at Ohio State University before entering the military. Her successor, who served most of her time with the 6888th as a company commander, had received her master's degree from Ohio State University in 1937.[10] The executive officer, Noel Campbell Mitchell, had completed four years of college at Tuskegee Institute before joining the military, and the special service officer had graduated from Sargent College in Boston before entering.[11] Of the fifty-one women interviewed for this book, more than half had had at least some college, and more than one-fourth were college graduates. All but two had graduated from high school. Table 2 shows the years of school completed by each interviewee before she entered the military; the numbers range from 9 to 17.

Civilian Occupational Skills

Before the war African American women were concentrated in three occupational categories: domestic workers, farm laborers, and service workers (beauticians, lodging house keepers, janitors, waitresses, and midwives). In 1940 fewer than 5 percent of African American women in the labor force were professionals such as teachers, physicians, or lawyers.[12]

The previous occupational experiences of members of the 6888th were not typical of the average African American women of that period. Many members of the unit had worked at professional and skilled occupations before entering the military. Although 40 percent were reported to have been unskilled workers, the remaining 60 percent were either unemployed, semiskilled, skilled, or professional workers. Betty Smith of Kansas City, for example, had been a student nurse before going into the military. Jacqueline and Winona Fuller, sisters from Chicago, had been clerical workers. Jacqueline was also a graduate of the Art Institute of Chicago.[13] Jennie Moton was an accomplished pianist.[14]

Most of the interviewees were either unemployed or students before they entered the military. Ten of them were clerical workers, and nine were professionals (see table 1). Table 2 highlights the nine professional occupations of interviewees. Tessie Barr, Charity Adams Earley, Margaret Jackson, Noel Campbell Mitchell, Johnnie Walton, and Essie Woods were schoolteachers. Dorothy Johnson was an assistant librarian. Gladys Anderson and Mary Rozier were secretaries. Unlike women of their parents' generation, many members of the 6888th had worked in clerical positions; this fact suggests that these positions were becoming more available to African Americans than they had been in previous years. Four of the women were domestic workers, three worked in a skilled craft, and six were either skilled or unskilled laborers in factories (see table 2).

Some of the interviewees had graduated from college with degrees in teaching and were unemployed. Several women emphasized how limited the occupational opportunities were for them before they joined the WAAC/WAC. Mildred Leonard's comments characterize the unemployed African American woman professional of that time:

I entered the service in October and actually there were no jobs available. I was in teaching and of course we were segregated at the time; and the teachers who taught had tenure and you had to wait for somebody to die before there was a vacancy. And so there just weren't any jobs that were available for a college trained person. . . . Teaching was closed out.

Lavinia Johnson also reports that she had completed college and was seeking employment before joining the Women's Army Corps, "I had a teacher's degree but I didn't have any place to teach, so I decided since I had no job in the teaching field that I would go into the military."

Geographical Origin and Neighborhood Characteristics

According to my roster of 742 names, ranks, and serial numbers of members of the 6888th, most of the women entered the military from the eastern region of the United States (see Appendix C).[15] The first digit of the serial number represents the geographical area (service command) from which the member entered. As shown in the first column of table 3, most of the women entered the military from the third service command (Maryland, Pennsylvania, and parts of Virginia), and fewest of them entered from the ninth service command (western states). When the states of Maryland, Virginia, and Washington, D.C., are classified as belonging to the northern region of the United States, almost half (44 percent) of the women entered the military from the northeastern region of the United States (first, second, third, and tenth service commands in table 3). Approximately 16 percent of the women entered the military from the fourth service command, or south Atlantic states, 27 percent from the midwestern region

Table 3. Service Command from Which Members of the 6888th
Entered the Military

N	Service Command	States
22	First	Connecticut, Maine, Massachusetts, New Hampshire, Rhode Island, and Vermont
117	Second	Delaware, New York, and New Jersey
130	Third	Maryland, Pennsylvania, and Virginia (Except Alexandria and Arlington)
116	Fourth	Alabama, Georgia, Mississippi, North Carolina, South Carolina, and Tennessee
87	Fifth	Indiana, Kentucky, Ohio, and West Virginia
75	Sixth	Illinois, Michigan, and Wisconsin
31	Seventh	Colorado, Iowa, Kansas, Minnesota, Missouri, Nebraska, North Dakota, South Dakota, and Wyoming
91	Eighth	Arkansas, Louisiana, New Mexico, Oklahoma, and Texas
17	Ninth	Arizona, California, Nevada, Oregon, Utah, and Washington
56	Tenth	Alexandria, Virginia; Arlington, Virginia; and Washington, D.C.
742	Total	

SOURCE: AR 170-10, August 1942, *Service Commands and Departments,* U.S. Army Center of Military History, Washington, D.C.

(fifth, sixth, and seventh service commands), 12 percent from the west south central region (eighth service command), and 2 percent from the western region (ninth service command).[16]

Some of the women had lived in racially segregated communities; others grew up in ethnically diverse neighborhoods. Noel Campbell Mitchell's was all black: "I had never been around white people before in my life. [In Officer Candidate School] there were 39 of us and 400 Whites. . . . Three of us were from Tuskegee, and all three of us graduated [from college] too. . . . I didn't know too much about segregation because I'd only been around blacks all of my life." Although Mitchell lived and grew up in the "Jim Crow" South, her family was able to shelter her from the dehumanizing aspects of racism. All of her activities were confined to an African American community, and thus she had no contact with the white world.

Other women who grew up in the southern region of the nation knew all too well the impediments of racism. Sadie Belcher found life difficult as a young African American woman living in Atlanta: "Life wasn't easy for Negroes. It was a time when the South was segregated, and that's all we knew because we were brought up in it." Several women interviewed for this study spoke about growing up in the segregated South, being made to attend segregated schools, and riding in the back of segregated buses after paying the same fare as white passengers.

But not all of the women lived in segregated neighborhoods. Myrtle Rhoden, for example, describes her neighborhood as racially diverse. Her residential community of New York contained not only African Americans but also Jewish, Spanish, and Hindu children:

To this day I am still friends with those children. They're grown, but we're still in contact with each other. We lost Inez Enriques [who was Spanish] last December. She passed away. But I'm still in touch with the Hindu family. Quentin and I just chatted not too long ago. He moved to Atlanta, but we're still friends even to this day.

Bernadine Flannagan also lived in an interracial neighborhood, "There were all types of people living in my neighborhood. We had Syrians, Poles, Portuguese, French, as well as Afro-Americans." Virginia Frazier speaks similarly of her integrated neighborhood in Minneapolis: "We never had segregation—well, when my parents and them came on the underground railroad, they had it, but I never experienced it." She goes on to say that she never experienced racial segregation until she attended basic training at Fort Des Moines.

Some of the former members of the 6888th reveal that their parents were very active in civic affairs. As a result of their parents' political activities, these women were exposed to political issues at an early age. Charity Adams Earley, for instance, speaks of her father's confrontations with the Ku Klux Klan when he was president of the South Carolina branch of the NAACP.[17] Gladys Carter recalls that her father was very active in civic affairs in Harlem:

My father was an activist; I remember going with him to forums. And 125th Street was a business street for Harlem; that's where the five and dimes were, and there was a department store and a lot of shops, and of course the Apollo Theater was there. And there were no colored sales clerks in any of the stores; they were all white. And Adam Clayton Powell led a rally. I was eight or nine years of age when I marched in the parade with my dad; and I thought that was great. I had a little sign. I learned later that we were demanding that the stores on 125th Street hire black clerks and managers.

Growing up on 127th Street and then moving to 145th Street, Gladys Carter has fond memories of Harlem. Most of all she remembers it as a very safe place to live: "Harlem was a wonderful place. Not at all like you hear about today; I felt very safe." Carter, who was active in sports, used to practice at the YMCA on 135th Street. "When we left basketball practice, sometimes eleven, ten-thirty at night, some girls went uptown and some girls went downtown. I lived the farthest, 145th Street, so the last couple of blocks I usually walked by myself; and sometimes I had to walk over across to St. Nicholas Avenue; and I went through those streets feeling very, very safe."

Military Occupational Statuses before the 6888th

Members of the 6888th had been assigned to military installations throughout the United States. They had performed in a variety of military roles, including administrative and clerical assignments. Six of the battalion's thirty-one officers, Charity Adams, Noel Campbell, Vera Harrison, Mary Kearney, Mildred Carter, and Corrie Sherard had attended the first Officer Candidate School together two and a half years earlier. Most of the officers of the unit had been either company or executive officers in field units just before being deployed for overseas duty and therefore had plenty of experience in leading troops. Vera Harrison, for example, was the executive officer for the 33rd Post Headquarters

Company at Fort Huachuca, Arizona, when she received her orders for overseas. Violet Hill and Colonia Powell were executive officers of WAC detachments at Fort Lewis, Washington, and Fort Bragg, North Carolina, respectively. Noel Campbell Mitchell, Margaret Barnes Jones, Blanche Scott, and Mercedes Jordan were all company officers of WAC detachments. Mitchell, who had been trained to be a supply officer, was commanding a WAC detachment at Fort Oglethorpe when she received her orders for overseas duty. Blanche Scott, who previously had been assigned to the Recruiting Command in Virginia, was at Walla Walla Army Air Base in the state of Washington when she received the news. Margaret Jones was assigned to the Staten Island terminal in New York; Jordan was at Douglas Army Air Base.

Some of the 6888th officers, however, had not been commanding units in the field, but had held administrative positions before "coming down on orders to go overseas." Lillian Duncan was the plans and training officer for the WAC section at Fort Knox, Kentucky. At Fort Des Moines, Corrie Sherard was a mess officer, Charity Adams Earley was the Training Center control officer, and Mildred Dupee Leonard was a librarian. These officers' wide and varied experiences were assets to the battalion once they were overseas.

Most of the enlisted women I interviewed reported that they had worked in either clerical or administrative positions before being assigned to the 6888th. Some of the battalion members had held highly responsible positions. Lucia Pitts, a postal clerk with the unit, reveals in her published memoirs that she was assigned to the provost marshal's office at Fort Huachuca, where she replaced a male sergeant major and became the acting sergeant major. Her duties included administering and supervising all of the office work and supervising 150 military police.[18] Mary Rozier was trained in administration at Fort Des Moines and later worked as a medical secretary in the psychiatric ward of a hospital at Camp Atterbury, Indiana. Some of the women worked in service occupations: Kitty Smith, for example, was assigned as a chaplain's assistant and then as a dental assistant at Camp Sibert in Gadsen, Alabama.

Other interviewees were cooks before they were assigned to the 6888th. Gertrude LaVigne attended the Army's Cook and Baker School at Fort Huachuca, where she was assigned as a cook after completing the course. She continued to take classes in clerical work; later she was assigned as a supply clerk, and then as a mail clerk, before learning that she had been selected for overseas duty. Elsie Oliver, Mary Williams, and Edith Tyrell worked as cooks before their assignment to the 6888th.

Preparing for Overseas Duty

Members of the 6888th assembled at the Extended Field Service Battalion, Third WAC Training Center, Fort Oglethorpe, Georgia, to receive training and to be outfitted for overseas duty. Many former members think of the event as a homecoming. Most of the women I interviewed greeted old friends whom they had not seen in years. Some of the women had been friends before they joined the military; others had met during previous military assignments. Former commanding officers and former enlisted trainees were reunited for the first time since basic training. "There were girls who took their basic training under me," remembers Noel Mitchell, "and whom, after their four weeks with me, I hadn't seen until they arrived at Fort Oglethorpe. Charity Adams Earley recalls, "Other officers and enlisted women who were to belong to our outfit arrived and, with the arrival of each group, we had another reunion. We told stories about what happened to us during the time we had been away from each other on our various field assignments." [19]

All of the women knew and thought highly of their battalion commander, Maj. Charity Adams. Even if they had not trained under her, they knew of her because she was one of two highest-ranking African American women in uniform at that time. Major

Adams was discussed on the radio and written up in all of the black newspapers; she was truly a celebrity. In her orientation speech Adams welcomed the women in the unit. She emphasized that they were the first black Wacs to go overseas and that "the eyes of the world" were upon them. Noel Mitchell recalls Charity Adams saying that as the first black Wacs to serve overseas, "we could either do a good job and receive praise, or do a bad job and receive ridicule."

Mitchell, who already had been stationed at Fort Oglethorpe, was responsible for familiarizing the group with the military installation.

I pointed out that Fort Oglethorpe was not a segregated post, and that I was just as surprised as they were when I found this to be true. . . . I did stress one point that the commanding officer of the post made clear to me: that although the post would not be segregated, he had no jurisdiction over civil authorities off the reservation, so the girls would have to conduct themselves accordingly.

None of the women were told what their assignments would be, where they were going, or when they were going to leave. After ten days of orientation, still completely in the dark about their destination, the unit was issued equipment and winter clothing. Although they had not been informed about where they would be stationed, everybody speculated. Noel Mitchell took part in these deliberations:

We assumed that our destination was Europe since the prescribed uniform for the ETO was winter. It seems we were being issued enough clothing to wear the rest of our lives. We were given wool shirts, ski suits with liners [which were to be the women's work clothes], knitted caps, twill fatigue trousers and shirts, and field shoes, which were hightop brown shoes to be worn with trousers.

During training the women were taught how to recognize enemy aircraft, ships, and weapons of all types. They also learned what to say and how to react if captured by the enemy, how to board a ship via cargo net, and how to climb ropes. Dorothy

Bartlett remembers, "We had a mock ship, and we had to learn how to get up and come down. Some of the girls froze, and some of the sergeants had to go up and get them." Gladys Carter says:

We had to climb ropes . . . and come down the side of a ship as you would if it were sinking. We had to do some crawling under wire. . . . We had to put on gas masks and we had to learn to put them on properly. And then they took us into a room while there was gas in there, and told us to lift up. . . . It seems to me, if I remember correctly, we were to lift up just to get a whiff [of gas], and then they ushered us out. So that was part of it. A lot of marching and just getting ready, getting outfitted, that kind of thing.

Enid Clark describes the training at Fort Oglethorpe as an "infiltration course" consisting of "all the stuff the men went through except we didn't have live bullets shot at us." Sammye Davis recalls, "We had all of the technical training that the men had . . . climbing that wall, making long trips with packs on our backs for endurance, and that kind of thing." Mildred Dupee Leonard recalls, "The training at Oglethorpe was just training us to go overseas and for what we might expect. We went through Army training and did boarding and evacuating the ships. They weren't training women to use weapons, but we were trained on the obstacle course and hiking, and things like that." Mary McBride remembers that the activities at Fort Oglethorpe consisted of

falling and crawling and stuff. Climbing ropes and mess. Coming down and stuff. It was havoc. You know when you're crawling under barb wire and they're shooting, do-do-do, and you're crawling. They say if you raise up, they'll kill you. They scare you half to death. I don't know whether it was live ammunition or what, but you had to learn how to do that stuff to save your life.

Myrtle Rhoden will never forget receiving immunization shots, new uniforms, and overseas equipment at Fort Oglethorpe: "We were trained how to detect gas bombs and gas attacks. We were trained how to disperse over to the side of the road to go down in the ditch . . . that type of warfare training. Then one night they packed us up around two in the morning. Fog was up to your keister [buttocks], and we finally got in trucks and ended up on a railroad train. The next thing I knew, we were going to New York City."

Three Separate Journeys Abroad

Members of the 6888th actually traveled overseas in three waves. First the battalion commander and her executive officer (Charity Adams and Noel Campbell, later Mitchell) flew to Europe at the end of January 1945. Shortly afterward the first contingent of the battalion sailed to Europe on the *Ile de France*. Finally, the second contingent sailed to Europe on the *Queen Elizabeth*. Each journey was different from the others.

On 24 January 1945 Adams and Campbell received orders to report to Washington, D.C. They arrived at the airport in Chattanooga and had to wait a few hours before their plane departed. Noel Campbell Mitchell began to have second thoughts about flying:

I began to wonder if I would like flying to Europe. I had flown before with my brother and enjoyed it, but pleasure flying is one thing and flying the Atlantic Ocean was another thing. I couldn't say I was scared. Later, Edna admitted to me that she felt the same way, but she didn't tell me for the same reason I didn't tell her.

They flew from Chattanooga to Washington, D. C. on a commercial plane and arrived in Washington at 9:30 that night, "tired, cold, hungry, and with no place to stay." It had not occurred to them that all of the business offices would be closed by the time they reached their destination. The War Department had not made boarding arrangements for them. After looking through her personal phone book, Adams called a friend and was able to secure a place for them to stay that night. Mitchell says:

Edna called her friend and greeted her as if she had seen her only a few days ago. The friend, after listening to our problem, said, "Wait a minute while I ask my mother if it will be all right." We waited with our fingers crossed. She came back to the phone after what seemed like hours and said it would be all right to come out. We took a taxi, went out, and found Josephine and her mother to be very nice. After serving supper and preparing their own bedroom for us, they slept on the couch. They wanted to know our mission and how long we would be in Washington. Although we had missed security class at Fort Oglethorpe, we knew that movement of troops or personnel was a top secret, so we told them we didn't know; we would find out in the morning.

The following day the officers reported to Gravely Point, Virginia (just outside Washington, D.C.) to be processed for overseas travel. They went to the finance office, a clothing supply room, and a medical section. Both Adams and Campbell remember the strange looks they received at the reception center. Not only were they the only Negro Wacs in the building, but they were officers — one a major, the other a captain. Most of the people in the processing area were white male soldiers; the two women did not see any African Americans until they went to the cafeteria for lunch. Mitchell recalls:

As I was going through the line someone called, "Noel!" I couldn't imagine who it was. I knew it must have been someone from home since I was known as Abbie in the Army. I turned, and there to my surprise was Mrs. Edith Washington (the widow of Booker T. Washington's son, from Tuskegee) and her daughter, Edith. I had known them all of my life. I asked what she was doing there. She said she had been working there since shortly after the war started. I was so glad to see her, or anyone else I knew at this time. She asked me the usual thing that I had been asked since I had arrived in Washington. I told her the usual thing.

Earley and Mitchell were given orders in a sealed envelope and were instructed not to open them until they were in flight. The next day they boarded a C-54 cargo plane (equipped with a rubber lifeboat) along with sixteen men and one civilian woman. Among the men were "one major, several captains, first and second lieutenants, mostly with thick southern accents, and three civilian men in Army uniforms without insignia."[20] One of the civilian men, Mitchell recalls, was a war correspondent and editor of the *Christian Science Monitor*. After the plane had been in flight for an hour, Earley and Mitchell read their orders and discovered that they were en route to London.

When I interviewed Noel Campbell Mitchell and Charity Adams Earley, they both described the other passengers on the plane as sociable and friendly. Neither racism nor sexism surfaced during their journey abroad. The passengers spent many hours together, experiencing a journey that was novel and sometimes anxiety provoking. Under these circumstances race and gender were inconsequential.

The plane stopped in Bermuda, where the passengers disembarked and ate dinner at the officers' mess hall. Adams and Campbell dined with two of the white men they had met on the plane. The next stop was the Azores Islands, where they ate breakfast. By this time the passengers had been traveling together for several hours and, as Mitchell said, "were one big family, calling each other by our first names. There was no restraint in our talking, for we were just American soldiers going to do a job."

The travelers arrived in Prestwick, Scotland, at 2:00 A.M. and were taken to an American Red Cross hotel, where they spent the night. The group separated in Prestwick, where Earley and Mitchell boarded a DC-3 for London. Landing approximately three miles outside the city, they were taken the rest of the way to London by an Air Transport Command bus.

Although London had been bombed quite heavily in the months preceding their arrival, Adams and Campbell did not find the ravages of war as they had expected. Noel Campbell Mitchell remembers, "I was quite surprised to see houses standing. From all of the reports I heard at home, London was in shambles. I learned later that the English had cleared all the debris as soon as possible after air raids."

Adams and Campbell were the very first black WAC officers to arrive in Europe; as they might have expected, they were met with astonished looks:

While we were observing what was strange to us, we were being observed. We had forgotten how strange we seemed to military as well as
civilian personnel. Again, we were among U.S. military personnel who
could not believe Negro Wac officers were real. Salutes were slow in
coming and frequently [were] returned with great reluctance. The old
familiar problem was beginning all over again.[21]

Adams and Campbell reported to Maj. Margaret Philpot, WAC
staff director in the United Kingdom, who saw to it that they were
processed and briefed about their new assignment. Noel Campbell
Mitchell liked Major Philpot from the moment she met her: "During my stay in England we became fast friends." Mitchell recalls
how cordial Philpot was upon their first meeting:

Major Philpot was sitting behind her desk when we walked in. She
smiled and said, "Hello. I am glad you are here. I have a copy of your
orders but I did not know just when you were going to arrive. Your
troops have not left the States yet, but there is plenty to be done before
they arrive. They are tentatively due to arrive on February 12th; that
will give you two weeks."

That evening at dinner, according to Mitchell, Philpot briefed
Adams and Campbell about their assignment in Europe:

I am sure you know you will be working with mail. Up until now, the
mail has been serviced by white Wacs at the First Base Post Office at
Sutton Coal Field. . . . These Wacs have been servicing the mail for
almost two years. Most of them are being sent home, so there is a real
need for you."

A few days after that conversation Adams and Campbell met Maj.
Dudley C. Jernigan, commanding officer of the First Base Post
Office, to which the 6888th would be temporarily attached. They
learned that they would be stationed in Birmingham and quartered at an old boarding school, which they were responsible for
preparing for their battalion's arrival.

After Earley and Mitchell's departure, members of the 6888th
traveled overseas in two waves. At the end of January 1945 nearly
seven hundred black Wacs boarded a train and went to Camp

Shanks, New York, for final processing. Gertrude LaVigne remembers being delayed in New York:

Our unit was at the dock ready to board our ship for overseas. The Red Cross was there with coffee and doughnuts. It was terribly cold and I, and others, thought of pouring the coffee on our feet to warm them up. There was a delay on our boarding and we learned that there were enemy ships and submarines in the north Atlantic, so we were sent back to the quarters area for an indefinite delay. There were [male] soldiers there also waiting to board our ship, and other transport ships in the dock. . . . Our stay was extended several times before we finally boarded our ship and set sail for England.

Colonel Hobby, director of the WAC, traveled to New York to see the first contingent off. The unit went by ferry to the dock of the *Ile de France,* which they boarded on 3 February. This exquisite ship, which had been used for transporting wealthy and famous people to Europe, had been modified to transport troops to Europe during the war. Myrtle Rhoden remembers that the ship

was loaded with troops and equipment and bombs and ammunition and whatever else they needed for war. It was loaded to the brim. We [members of the 6888th] were on the top deck in the staterooms. There weren't any other women; all of the other people on board the ship were men. . . . I looked out on the deck before we went into our quarters and saw ships everywhere. We pulled away from the harbor and we were out in the sea, not in the middle, but we were way out in the water, and we could see other ships; many, many ships were out there.

All of the women I interviewed remember the ship as large and impressive. Ruth Jefferson Wright states, "You know, it was a nice ship; and all I remember is that I was sick the whole time. They had so many of us in one room." Some of the former members describe the trip overseas as being "exciting, fascinating, and beautiful"; others complained, as did Wright, about being seasick all the way. During the voyage the women were put through boat drills and exercise sessions.

Mildred Dupee Leonard, a first lieutenant with the 6888th, found the journey overseas to be wonderful:

In the Army, the conditions under which officers live and the conditions under which enlisted personnel live are not the same, and so we [officers] were living in the best quarters. It had the best of everything. It may not have been quite that good for enlisted personnel because some of them were down in the hole. It would be just like traveling on an ocean liner: the further down on the ship you go, the less pleasant the trip.

Gladys Thomas Anderson, a young and fun-loving private first class, found the voyage most enjoyable in spite of the conditions:

Believe it or not, I was enjoying it. We had a hectic trip because we had heavy waves; and then one night they told us that there was a sub behind us, and I woke up and heard it. But I didn't believe what they told me and just turned over and went back to sleep; I found out later it was true. During the day, oftentimes when we ate our meals, we had to go down to the dining room, and the ship would be listing from right to left. I remember enjoying it because I couldn't put my foot down like I wanted to. The ship would come up to meet my foot, and I laughed about that. But you had to do something to while away the time, and I couldn't see being sad and not enjoying myself. So I just enjoyed being with my friends, and talking, and laughing at the ones who got seasick. I was one of the fortunate ones; I didn't get seasick.

The "sub" that Anderson mentions was indeed a German submarine. Before the *Ile de France* reached Glasgow Harbor, it was engaged by German U-boats.

Not all of the women experienced the trip as cheerfully as did Anderson. Rhoden, for example, was frantic: "Our ship was engaged, and we went into what was considered a zigzag type of formation to avoid the attack. That lasted, they tell me, forty-five minutes; but honestly I thought it was much longer than forty-five minutes." There were twelve women to a room, six in double-deck bunks on each side. Rhoden remembers being tossed and turned:

You had to hang on with all your strength because the veering was so severe—the pulling and turning. I could hear the noise outside; the sirens, the banging, the horns, and the whistles; the galvanized garbage cans were banging and clanging; everything we had on our shelves went flying through the air like marbles; perfume and cosmetics went everywhere; lots of screaming. Everything was going at one time.

Rhoden, like many of the other women, prayed: "I thought, this is the end. I really did. I said my prayers. One or two girls were crying in my squadron. I didn't do any outburst; I don't know what was wrong with me; I just didn't scream out loud. And finally it ended. It just stopped."

LaVigne also mentioned this event as most memorable, and especially that they reached their destination without casualty: "About one day out of the Glasgow Harbor our convoy encountered enemy submarines. The ship zig-zagged, rolled, and pitched as our convoy, escorted by fighter ships, planes, and submarines engaged the enemy. . . . Fortunately we docked in safety." [22]

Accompanied by an armed convoy of ships, the first contingent of the 6888th arrived in Glasgow on 11 February 1945. The unit was met by bagpipe music, their battalion commander, Charity Adams, and Brig. Gen. Benjamin O. Davis, Sr., the highest-ranking African American officer. In a letter to his wife, Davis wrote:

Charity Adams a Wilberforce girl is the Major commanding the battalion. I visited them aboard ship and rode with the first section from Glasgow to Birmingham where I am now. I am being nicely handled and the girls are being beautifully taken care of. They are in good spirits. [23]

Fifty days later the second contingent of the 6888th arrived in England. Their ship also traveled in a convoy, but the journey was less eventful than the first contingent's. Nobody reported any attack by enemy submarines, or anything of that sort. The few women I interviewed who were with the second contingent, such as Dorothy Johnson, remember the journey as pleasant:

We went over in a very high style because we went over on the *Queen Elizabeth*. So we had quite a commodious ship, and we were not the only ones that were being transferred at the time. . . . The whole ship was peopled with troops going overseas, and we were, of course, in a convoy. . . . And it was a rather luxurious journey over.

The second contingent was also met by the battalion commander. Unlike the members of the first contingent, who were met with bagpipes and a big celebration in Scotland, the second contingent did not receive its welcome until it arrived in Birmingham. Charity Adams Earley states that the group was greeted by the earlier arrivals as well as by military dignitaries.[24] The welcome given to the second contingent, however, was not nearly as jubilant as that which the first contingent received.

5

★ ★ ★

Serving in the European Theater of Operations, January 1945–March 1946

Welcome! Welcome! Welcome!

During the first few days in Europe, Adams and Campbell flew to Paris to report to Lt. Gen. John C. H. Lee, the commanding general of the Communication Zone, ETO. Upon arrival in Paris they were met by Maj. Mary Weems, assistant WAC director for Headquarter Communication Zone, ETO. Later they met with Brig. Gen. Benjamin O. Davis, Sr., Headquarters Staff, Communication Zone, ETO. Noel Campbell Mitchell told me that General Davis's aide and nephew, Lt. John Overton, was once a high school classmate of hers. Mitchell also said that she had known General Davis for many years at Tuskegee Institute: Davis had taught military science and tactics at Tuskegee when Mitchell was a student there. Adams and Campbell spent a few days attending various receptions, some of which were given in their honor. One such event was held in Paris in General Lee's suite at the Hôtel George Cinq, with several other officers.[1]

Much of their time, however, was spent in preparing for their unit's arrival. They selected rooms for offices, separated the battalion into companies, made a list of the equipment they would need, and performed numerous other logistic and administrative tasks. They were responsible for making sure that beds were available for the unit and that their mess hall was sufficiently stocked with food and utensils. They saw to it that plumbing and electrical work was done and that telephone lines were connected. Soldiers from a nearby male unit were assigned to assist in preparing the living and work quarters for the battalion's arrival.

The kitchen was cleaned, food was prepared, and the dining hall had been decorated with welcoming signs only hours before the 6888th arrived in England. As an added feature, a dance band was engaged to greet members of the incoming unit as soon as they arrived. On 10 February Adams departed Birmingham to meet the troops in Scotland. Mitchell recalls that she stayed in Birmingham, overseeing the work that had yet to be done.

A special inspection of the 6888th was made by General Davis when the first contingent arrived in Europe. On 11 February 1945 Davis, accompanied by an inspection team, inspected the unit aboard the *Ile de France*.[2] On the following day Davis accompanied the battalion's first section from Glasgow to Birmingham.

War correspondent Edward B. Toles, a spectator, wrote the following about the unit's arrival in England:

As trainloads of the smartly uniformed women, equipped with full field packs, poured onto the station platform, a 30-piece white army band blared out "Beer Barrel Polka." Past the lusty cheers of townspeople and down the blackout streets, the first overseas group of Negro Wacs marched to its home, a swanky steam-heated frame structure that formerly housed a first class boys' school. In two huge dining rooms, roast lamb awaited the new arrivals. The huge building provides living quarters, workrooms, headquarters, and even a regulation-size basketball court in the modern gymnasium was ready for the women's recreation.[3]

The group was met by Colonel Herr, company officer of the western district; Colonel Darnell, district engineer; and Major Jernigan, company officer of the First Base Post Office. General Davis, along with Colonels Herr and Darnell, inspected the King Edward School, where the 6888th was to be quartered, and reported that the building was in excellent condition. As stated in General Davis's report, the King Edward School "was clean and comfortably heated. Beds were made and nicely arranged, and sufficient for accommodation of the personnel." General Davis also reported that the unit's morale was high.[4]

Upon arriving in Scotland, Mildred Dupee Leonard remembers hurrying from the ship to board a train:

We arrived in Scotland and transferred from the ship to the train to go into England. Traveling in a large group like that in a troop train, so to speak, the conditions were just like those of anyone traveling on a crowded train. But of course we had been issued C rations and things like that. We had our own duffel bags in which we carried our own personal items, and the C rations, which sufficed as our meals until we got to where we were going.

Several women commented on the beauty of the countryside on their way to Birmingham. In her memoirs, Lucia Pitts describes the scene as living up to its celebrated reputation:

[It] was a first impression never to be forgotten. The farmlands looked lush and green, but at intervals there was snow. Everything was laid out so neatly and precisely, with trim hedgerows separating the plots, and little splashing falls here and there; and the land looked so clean it seemed it had been swept by a broom.[5]

The women arrived at the King Edward School at night and received the welcoming that Edward Toles described in his news release. Margaret Barbour, remembers that, tired from the long, arduous journey, they found that they had makeshift bunks. "The guys [male soldiers] had made double deckers for us and beds were all made when we got there."

On 13 February a special assembly was held at the school. The male officers mentioned above were accompanied by Maj. Virginia Hurley and Captains Mary Miller and Ellen Hays, all of whom were Transportation Corps WAC officers. The program consisted of speeches by General Davis, Major Jernigan, Major Weems, Major Adams, Captain Mildred E. Carter (the 6888th special service officer), and Chaplain Beverly M. Ward.

According to General Davis's report, the detachment consisted of 26 officers and 687 enlisted women. He stated, "The commander, Major Charity E. Adams appears to be competent, and displayed excellent leadership and control."[6] He also said that the detachment was organized into a provisional battalion, assigned to the First Base Post Office, APO 640, for duty under Major Jernigan. In actuality, the unit was attached to the First Post Office until 8 March 1945; it then received its official designation as the 6888th Central Postal Directory and became a self-sustaining battalion and the largest U.S. Army unit in Birmingham at that time.

The battalion's living facilities varied with the location. In Birmingham and Rouen the women were housed in much smaller quarters than in Paris. Contrary to some of the information in General Davis's report, many of the interviewees described the King Edward School in England as being in shambles when they arrived. The building showed signs of bombing and other ravages of the war. There were holes in the roof, which some members remember patching themselves. The living quarters had very limited heat, and hot water was scarce. Mitchell says: "I had never been in a more depressing place in my life. The corridors were narrow and dark. The rooms were small, ill-lighted, and poorly ventilated."

Members complained about having to go outside to take showers in the cold. Myrtle Rhoden recalls,

The first night I took a shower with about four or five other females. I was so tired that the fact that we had no shower curtains or anything

Figure 1. 6888th Living Facilities in England

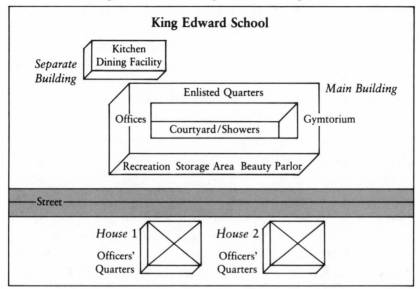

still hadn't registered with me until much later. It was cold and we took our showers as quickly as we could and went to bed. I remember that in the following days I bathed by my bed out of my helmet most of the time.

Figure 1 shows the layout of the work and living facilities. Most of the unit's activities took place in the main building, where enlisted quarters, administrative offices, recreation and storage areas, a beauty parlor, and gymtorium (gymnasium) were located. In the center of the quadrangle was a courtyard, where outdoor showers were located. In a separate building on the grounds was a kitchen and dining facility. Officers lived in two houses across the street from the main building. During their stay in Birmingham, members of the 6888th transformed the King Edward school into very livable quarters.

The primary mission of the battalion was to sort and redirect mail. All of the women interviewed for this study describe the work objectives similar to those recounted here:

The 6888th Central Postal Directory Battalion was responsible for the redirection of mail to U.S. personnel in the European Theater of Operations. The total number of U.S. personnel involved was estimated to be about seven million. . . . This number included people in the Army, Navy, Marine Corps, Air Corps, and Seabees, uniformed civilian specialists and technicians, nonuniformed specialists, congressmen and their aides on inspection trips, Red Cross workers, and every person involved in and with military and paramilitary activity in the ETO.[7]

Because so many of the Army units were moving from one combat area to another, and because there was a civilian and military manpower shortage, mail had been accumulating in British warehouses over several months. Mattie Allen remembers that loads of mail were continuously transported to their facility: "We were a postal battalion and we had train loads of packages and mail that came to us as a unit." Dorothy Bartlett recalls: "The gym was stacked practically to the ceiling with delayed mail, like boxes and letters and things that people had sent for soldiers that had moved to another post or something." According to Virginia Frazier, "We were just stymied by the mail stacked all over."

The mail was handled rather intricately. Locator clerks had boxes of locator cards, which contained the unit numbers for all of the American personnel stationed in Europe. When a unit moved, the postal directory was notified, and new locator cards were made for all of the people in that unit. Common surnames often required several boxes: Mail for people named Smith, for instance, may have filled three boxes. When a postal clerk received letters for somebody named John A. Smith, for example, she found John A. Smith's locator card, which contained his unit number, and forwarded the mail to his unit. Often mail was forwarded to soldiers after the unit had moved and before the postal directory received a new unit locator card. In those cases the mail was returned to the postal directory and held until a new locator card was received from the soldier's unit. If the mail was marked "deceased," it went to a special area and was handled separately. The 6888th, organized into five companies, was a self-sufficient unit. The Headquarters Company handled all administrative and service support duties. Companies A, B, C, and D were made up of postal directory personnel.

All of the interviewees described the working conditions as poor. Some of the strains in performing their job were associated directly with war. Lighting, for example, was poor in England because windows were painted black for war-related blackouts. Many of the women suffered eyestrain as a result of the badly lit work areas. Work space was also a problem: the limitation on space required that mail clerks be assigned to rotating eight-hour shifts. Another source of stress was the lack of adequate heat in the workplace; work areas were so cold that the women worked in their ski pants and field jackets. Ventilation was especially poor at the King Edward School. Mitchell describes the gymnasium, where the mail was stored, as smelling like a distillery.

All Aboard!

In May 1945 the 6888th was assigned to Rouen, France, where Joan of Arc was burned at the stake in 1431. The unit members traveled from Birmingham by train to the port at Southhampton and boarded a small boat in which they crossed the English Channel. Lucia Pitts recorded that the women traveled in very tight quarters: "On this boat we slept sailor fashion—in our clothes, on pieces of canvas that let down from the wall shelf-fashion. Nothing was on these shelves but us, our lifebelts, and our overcoats for covering. Since we slept in tiers of four to six, if you lifted your head from your bunk without thinking, you popped it against the bunk above you."[8] When the boat docked at Le Havre, the first thing most of the interviewees recall is the mass of rubble they saw. Lavinia Johnson's first impression was that the French did not clean up as the British did: "The British, as soon as the bombing occurred, would clean up. The French, they just let the rubble stay there."

The unit boarded a train that had holes in the roof and no

windows, a somewhat uncomfortable situation during the periods of rain. When they arrived in Rouen, they received an enormous welcome from African American male soldiers stationed in the area. "The whole place was jammed full of black soldiers," recalls Gladys Carter:

They came in every vehicle imaginable. They were in trucks and jeeps and wagons; and they were up on the roof and every place waving. "My name is Joe." "Where's Susie?" And some of them, of course, knew some of the women and were asking for them. They were just surrounding us, yelling, "Let me carry your bag. What's your name?" . . . And so you had to laugh. . . . The next thing I remember is going through some big gates and I heard my name being called, "Schuster, Schuster" (my maiden name is Schuster). And I looked up and it was a fella named Joe Judkins. Joe Judkins had been at Virginia State with me. . . . He greeted me with a kiss, you know, kind of a smack on the cheek as I walked along.

Not everyone found the welcome as flattering as did Carter. Women of the unit varied as to age, personality, and responsibilities. The executive officer, Mitchell, for example, found the excitement disruptive: "We were besieged with soldiers and civilians. We asked for male MPs [military police] to guard our gates until we could get organized and use WAC MPs." This response is not surprising in view of the officers' responsibility for ensuring a flawless transition from Birmingham to Rouen.

In Rouen the battalion was housed in the Caserne Tallandier, an old French barracks that had once been occupied by Napoleon's troops. Several brick buildings were surrounded by an eight-foot wall with a high iron gate. This facility was much larger than the King Edward School. The battalion's headquarters and medical facility occupied one building. A large two-story building provided space for supplies, storage, and the motor pool. The mess hall, kitchen, and recreational space occupied another building. There were separate small buildings for laundry and additional storage. The largest building was a four-story brick structure in which the work area was located on the ground floor; the enlisted personnel were quartered on the other three floors. Two houses on the post were used for officers' quarters. The officers' club occupied the first floor of one of these houses.

In Rouen, as in Birmingham, the facilities included a post exchange, a special services office, a library, a beauty parlor, and a recreation hall. Although beds were not available, and the women slept on canvas cots that were stacked in twos, several battalion members told correspondent Edward Toles that they were pleased with their new quarters because of the "breathing space."[9] Everyone agreed that the living facilities were much larger in Rouen than in Birmingham, but not everyone thought they were comfortable. Bernice Thomas, for example, remembers the quarters in Rouen as less than favorable: "We lived in an old place. . . . I believe someone told me that Napoleon had been there, horrible old place, with no windows, and we had to take our mattress covers to the barn and fill them up with straw for a mattress."

Lucia Pitts described the enlisted women's living quarters in Rouen as follows:

All of the enlisted women were assigned to the largest building, about thirty-two to a room. We still had double bunks, made of frames into which Army cots had been fitted. For mattresses we were handed covers as we entered, which we had to stuff with fresh straw from a pile outside. We found that when one lay down on it, it had a tendency to knot up, sticking one in the wrong places and sometimes biting. We had no sheets, no pillows, just blankets. . . . But little stumps a Wac. Those who felt they had to have pillows made them out of extra blankets or coats or robes. Those who couldn't bear the rough blanket scratching their necks . . . found a piece of rag and folded it over the blanket edges.[10]

Despite the poor facilities, the close quarters in Birmingham and later in Rouen promoted social bonding. The physical structure of the King Edward School and of the Caserne Tallandier forced the unit's members to have daily close face-to-face contact and to develop primary group ties and a strong sense of sisterhood.

Unlike the work environment in Birmingham, the workrooms

in Rouen were large, well ventilated, and well lighted. There was enough space to allow all of the postal clerks to work during the day, thereby alleviating the problems associated with rotating shifts. The battalion commander was authorized to hire French civilian workers. Two French interpreters were employed, and a French woman to clean the officers' quarters. Approximately three hundred German prisoners of war worked to prepare the post for the unit's arrival and continued to maintain the post throughout the unit's stay in Rouen. Capt. Thomas Campbell (the executive officer's brother) was assigned to the unit in Rouen as the medical doctor.

Although some of the strains of the workplace were alleviated in Rouen, they were not eliminated. Some women recall that the heating was never really adequate. In addition the workload was extremely heavy. Myrtle Rhoden recalls, "We found the same conditions in France that we found in England; the mail had been held up for months. There was mail that was two or three years old. So we had to rewrap packages and reroute mail. They gave us six months to get the mail out in France, and we were determined to get it out in three."

Seventy Miles Southeast to Paris

In October 1945 the battalion was moved by motor convoy to Paris, seventy miles southeast of Rouen. According to Earley, the convoy consisted of thirty-five vehicles (jeeps and 6 x 6 trucks). All of the interviewees who had not returned to the United States remember being delayed by an accident that had occurred in a convoy ahead of them, but they weren't sure what had happened. Earley explained that a piano had fallen on a male soldier, holding up the convoy for hours.[11] The unit did not arrive in Paris until the wee hours of the morning. This was the unit's final destination in Europe; in contrast to the warm welcome that the 6888th had received in Birmingham and Rouen, no soldiers or dignitaries greeted them in Paris.

Living facilities in Paris far surpassed those in Birmingham and Rouen. Members of the 6888th describe these quarters as lavish. The battalion was housed in two hotels; enlisted members were housed at the Bohy Lafayette, and officers at the Hôtel États-Unis. All of the unit's members enjoyed maid service, and their meals were prepared by hotel cooks. The hotels had self-service elevators, and the rooms were ornate with thick carpeting, large beds, walk-in closets, mirrors, and easy chairs. Some rooms were furnished with desks and lamps. The living conditions in Paris, although more plush, were not conducive to the cohesiveness that was present in Birmingham and Rouen (see chapter 7 for further discussion.)

The working area in Paris was located in a large garage about a half-hour's drive from the living quarters. The major grievance that surfaced in Paris was the shortage of workers. Large quantities of mail continued to be delivered to the unit for processing. As before, American soldiers brought mail to the work area from the railway station, and French civilians assisted in handling heavy mailbags. The unit had decreased drastically in size, however, while the workload remained the same.

Several members had rotated back to the United States before the unit was deployed to Paris; others returned home shortly afterward. Both the battalion commander and the executive officer were among those who returned to the United States in December 1945. By March 1946, when the war had been over for a few months, all of the remaining members had returned to the States.[12] Many of the members soon returned to civilian society, but some remained in the military and retired several years later.

In both England and France work conditions ranged from poor to barely adequate. Although the strains of limited space, poor ventilation, and poor lighting were alleviated somewhat in Rouen, the heating was still less than desirable. In Paris, on the other hand, work-related stress was less attributable to the physical environment than to the reduction in unit size and to the fact that many of the members wanted to return home. Although well over half of the unit had rotated back to the United States, the remaining members were expected to process the mail at the same level of productivity. Yet, in spite of the voluminous workload and reduced size of the unit, many of the women were able to adjust and were still motivated to do an outstanding job. Myrtle Rhoden says, "The 6888th was knitted together into one group and were determined to get the job done in France as we had in England."

Different from the Coloured Women Portrayed on the Films

Members of the 6888th were the first black women ever seen by most of the British residents of Birmingham. "They stared at us," Frances Johnson recalls. "It seemed like they had never seen black women before in their lives." "Curious," "friendly," "warm," and "hospitable" are the words used by members of the 6888th to describe the British people they met.

In general, residents of Birmingham were very hospitable to members of the 6888th. Several former members of the unit recall that British families invited them into their homes. Dorothy Bartlett received many invitations: "The majority of the people in Birmingham were very pleasant. There were times when I was downtown and everything shut down; and they would invite me to their homes to have tea with them."

The British people had been given erroneous information about African Americans by white American soldiers who had been stationed in England. Many of the African American Wacs were approached by British people, as was Sadie Belcher: "Some of the British said that the Americans had said that Blacks were like animals and they had tails; and one woman even told me that they said Blacks barked at midnight like a dog." In spite of these rumors, African American Wacs found the British quite cordial, and many lasting friendships developed.

Dorothy Carter made friends with a family who considered themselves relatively high class:

The English are very class-conscious and you didn't meet people in a certain class unless you happen to be one of them. But I happened to meet this family who, if I had been a citizen, I would not have [met]. And I met people of a higher class through them. They used to show me places where black men would go to party, and described the type of women that black men dealt with as being low class.

Carter spent some of her weekends with this family: "They called every weekend a holiday. I learned to love the outdoors, the museums, and things of that sort because that's where we went most of the time." She discovered that her high-class friends lived rather modestly: "I was not impressed with the standard of living there. They lived in narrow houses with little gardens. Even the family I met had an outdoor bathroom and toilet."

British people treated African American Wacs with a respect that they seldom received in the United States from white Americans. Moreover, the British refused to allow white American servicemen to show disrespect to black Wacs in their presence. Myrtle Rhoden recalls the following incident:

As we [a few members of the 6888th] walked into the pub they [white American servicemen] were already there. They started verbally abusing [us] and declaring how dark the room had gotten as a result of us walking in. British men came to our side and rescued us, and sat down. They [British men] told the [white] American servicemen that they were out of place at which point the American soldiers got belligerent and were thrown out. We [members of the 6888th] stayed at the pub and had a wonderful time, and the British men escorted us to our barracks afterwards.

Virginia Frazier remembers a similar act of cordiality on the part of a British family who provided her with shelter when the Red Cross refused to. When the 6888th was stationed in France, Frazier, and two white Wacs were selected from a pool of applicants to attend Portsman College of Art in England. She received special orders to report to the American Red Cross in Bath:

It was about ten at night when I arrived at Bath, England, and I reported to the American Red Cross. Much to my surprise, they [Red Cross officials] didn't really know what to do with me because I was black.

The other two guys coming from different companies in Europe were white. They didn't count on a black person, and at that time the Red Crosses were [racially] separate. They called this English guy from the school—I guess he was the head guy at the school—and he said he had a place I could stay with an English family. This wonderful English family took me in. Their names were Deetan. It was just the boy, Timmy Deetan, and his mother took me in, gave me a room, and it was beautiful.

The British community thought highly of the members of the 6888th. Many of the stereotypes and myths about African American women that they had acquired were apparently dispelled by the presence of a Negro WAC battalion in their country. This fact is reflected in a British newspaper article: "These WACs are very different from the coloured women portrayed on the films, where they are usually either domestics or the outspoken old-retainer type or sloe-eyed sirens given to gaudiness of costume and eccentricity in dress. The WACs have dignity and proper reserve." [13]

All of the women in the study claimed that racial segregation was not practiced in England while they were stationed in Europe. There is well-documented evidence that British people tended to gravitate toward African Americans as early as 1942, when the first black soldiers arrived in England. Many British people approved of interracial marriages between black and white people, and many British women married African American men. [14] According to a report on the relations between American troops and British citizens provided by the U.S. embassy in London, the British people condemned the American practice of racial segregation in 1945. [15] Thus, the warm reception that members of the 6888th received from citizens of Britain and France reflects a cultural difference between the United States and those countries during World War II.

Although none of the women I studied married British men, some, including the battalion commander, dated them:

During the course of attending ceremonial and civic functions, I met a young man, a civil engineer, whose job had kept him working for the city rather than off in the service. He took quite a fancy to me and, after struggling to overcome his English prejudice against "blacks," he asked me to accompany him to the theater. Before I could accept his invitation I, too, had a few personal and cultural adjustments to make. . . . One day he took me for tea at the home of friends of his.[16]

Most respondents spoke of the British men they met as "friends" and reported that social activities with their new friends were held in groups. Myrtle Rhoden reports:

We [three members of the 6888th] made friends with a gentleman, Mr. Hicks, in a public park. He invited us to his home. He was living in a lady's house, Mrs. Granger, Audrey Granger. Twenty-one Reservoir Lane. I'll always remember that address. I know exactly where it is. We would go there to visit Mr. Hicks and he introduced us to Audrey Granger. . . . Her two sons were prisoners of war somewhere and she was very concerned about them. . . . She was a little lady about five feet three, big blue eyes, and pure white, pretty silver hair. Clarice Blackett, Ruth Bean, and myself went to her house, and when she opened the door she just devoured us. The little teeny woman embraced all three of us in her arms at one time.

Several of the interviewees stated that the unit was not given as large a reception in France as in England. Some perceived the French as indifferent toward them. Lavinia Johnson observed that the atmosphere in France was different from that in England: "They didn't care anything about you. They didn't go out of their way to serve anybody." In her published memoirs, Earley wrote about the people the unit encountered in France, "We sensed the French resented the 'you owe us; we saved your country' attitude expressed by many American personnel. As long as we spent our money to shop and to enjoy the culture and atmosphere of the city, the [French] people did not care whether we were Negro or white."[17] Similarly, Gladys Carter observed, "France was different from England; I don't think the [French] people were as friendly or as outgoing. I don't remember socializing as much in France as we had in England." Myrtle Rhoden did not befriend as many people in France as in England:

There was one family in France that was very nice to me. They had a cafe not far from the Caserne Tallandier, the building we lived in. Whenever I went to the cafe the woman would invite me upstairs, and her little boy, Keith, would play the violin for me. I just enjoyed visiting them but I didn't go there often.

Other women, however, describe more involved relationships with French residents. Ruth Wright, for example, found that the French people she encountered were very friendly. She met a family in Rouen by the name of Lamont and visited them quite often. Later Wright named her son after the Lamonts. Bernice Thomas recalls,

I made quite a few friends [in France] with whom I corresponded when I returned to the United States. I was treated fine; I stayed overnight with some of the French people. One woman in particular couldn't speak English, and I couldn't speak French, but we managed to get along. I would go to her home and we would have dinner, and I even spent the night with her in the same bed.

Diverse Skills and Talents

Members of the 6888th brought diverse skills and talents to their military service; this fact helps to explain why they were successful as a group. Unlike other WAC units deployed to the ETO, the 6888th was not attached to a male unit, but was self-contained. In England, members of the 6888th managed and operated their mess halls, motor pools, and supply rooms. They had their own military police to patrol their barracks. They also had a chapel, with their own organist and their own choir. During most of the unit's tour in Europe, all of the support services, such as cooks, security, communication, recreation, and supply were performed by African American women.[18]

Most of the members of the 6888th were assigned as postal clerks, processing mail, but others held service and support positions. Edith Tyrell, for example, served as a cook. Virginia Frazier worked in the personnel office as a payroll clerk. Gertrude

LaVigne was a supply sergeant: "I was quite busy. At first I was a company supply sergeant and then I was the battalion supply sergeant, and I remained battalion supply sergeant all the while we were in England and when we moved to France."

Margaret Jones, the public relations officer, was in charge of interviewing members and sending newspaper stories about the unit's activities back to the United States, "My job was to publicize what the girls were doing, and I wrote releases to their home newspapers. I had a photographer at my disposal, and I would take photographs of the girls on the job sites, and those were all forwarded through a public relations office and sent to the United States." Jones was also in charge of organizing fund-raising activities for charitable organizations such as the United Negro College Fund. The battalion waged a very successful United Negro College Fund drive in June 1945, raising $4,503.70.[19] The public relations officer also published a mimeographed weekly battalion newspaper, *Special Delivery,* which reported current events and contained articles written by battalion members.

One of the greatest advantages of a unit as diverse as the 6888th was the wealth of civilian work experience that the various members had had. Many of the skills the women had acquired in civilian society were great assets, enabling the unit to provide its own support services (as mentioned above) as well as the services of beauticians, actresses, and dancers. Mildred Carter had been a professional dancer in civilian life and had appeared in several Broadway musicals. She was born in Boston, graduated from Sargent College, and had founded the Davenport School of Dance before entering the military. Because of her theatrical talents, Carter was appointed special service officer of the 6888th and organized a highly acclaimed entertainment troupe.

Mary McBride, Willie Whiting, and Leatrice Lowe were among the dancers assigned to special services; they were part of a dance group that performed shows all over Europe. Whiting recalls, "I traveled with a small group . . . we were a dancing trio. Mary McBride, a professional dancer before she became a Wac, was in charge of the trio." Later I interviewed McBride; she informed me that Mildred Carter had encouraged her to form a dance group:

She [Carter] said, "I know you teach dancing Mary, that's good." So I said, "Well, I have two friends, Willie Whiting (who didn't know her right from her left) and Leatrice Lowe, and we'll be a trio from Chicago." And you talk about working with them. All we did was straighten up and fly right. A very corny thing, when I go back in my mind, but anyway we got to travel. See, they would take us to various hospital bases.

McBride added that there were about twenty-five women in their performing arts group. One member was a singer named Phyllis Branch, who had performed in New York City. McBride recalls that Branch had appeared with world renowned entertainers: "She sang with Frank Sinatra and Sammy Davis, Jr., and believe it or not, when she first came into the military, she was an MP."

Other members of the battalion were quite competitive in such sports as softball, table tennis, volleyball, and basketball. Gertrude LaVigne played on the basketball team and later became the noncommissioned officer in charge. The athletic teams traveled throughout Europe, participating in tournaments. LaVigne says, "The Ping-Pong tournament was played in Wiesbaden [Germany]." The city had been partially destroyed during combat, but "people were clearing away debris and getting on with their lives. The children were happy, mostly playing children games; but still their eyes were like baby rabbits, frighteningly searching for a way out."

While members of the 6888th played table tennis, children begged for chocolate, chewing gum, and cigarettes. LaVigne recalls that her team placed in one of the table tennis tournaments: "There were many good players at this tournament. We visited the places of interest in and around the city and returned to our home base to prepare for other scheduled tournaments." Gladys Anderson also had entered the table tennis tournament in Wiesbaden: "I didn't win because I was knocked out of the first round. But when we had the basketball team, I got into basketball, and we were fortunate to win the tournament in Europe . . . and we got a ten days' R and R [rest and recuperation] leave."

The basketball team was issued men's swimsuits and T-shirts: "We used colored materials," explains LaVigne, "and put stripes down the sides, numbers on the back, and trimming on the neckline and sleeves. We were also issued gym shoes; we were ready!" Team members refused to allow any racial opposition to dampen their spirits. LaVigne remembers a potentially demoralizing event that occurred on the way to the championship tournament:

Well, the time came to go to Stuttgart, Germany, for the ETO championship basketball tournament. The team reported to the train station's departure point. A number of the fourteen teams who would be participating in this tournament were all gathered here. As we were ready to board the train, we were stopped and told that we would not be permitted to board that train.

The team was not permitted to board, according to LaVigne, because the members were African American. She reported the incident to General Lee, the commanding general of communications zone:

Upon stressing the urgency of our mission, we were permitted to see the general. I told him the situation about not being permitted to board the train for the tournament. He asked: "Do you think you have a good team and can win?" Our reply was enthusiastically, "Yes sir!" The general ordered a delay on the departure of that train and had his special car attached, and the 6888 CPD [Central Postal Directory] team rode to Stuttgart in style all the way.

Some of the unit's athletes were selected to take a two-week recreational specialists' course. Among those selected was LaVigne: "This was a training trip that was a dream vacation and training all rolled into one. We were quartered in the beautiful Alhambra Hotel, one of the elite hotels in Nice, with all the amenities." All of those who attended were able to do a little sightseeing: "We visited Marseille, France, went into northern Italy across Spain's southeastern border, and many places within driving distance."

The 6888th also had a softball team that played several games and reached the tournaments in Europe. In August 1945 the team traveled to Namur, Belgium to participate in the regional tournament. One officer, 1st Lt. Violet Hill, was among the players. Novella Auls was the team's coach. The battalion commander, along with 1st Lts. Blanche Scott and Margaret Barnes, traveled to Namur to cheer the team on.[20] The 6888th's softball team did not win the tournament because, according to LaVigne, key players' strategies were revealed during their warmup. Nonetheless, team members enjoyed watching the remainder of the game. "While we were spectators in the bleachers for the remainder of the tournament, the two teams playing the championship started fighting on the field. A soldier stood up and shouted: 'Ladies, ladies, let's be gentlemen, please.' This seemed to settle and quiet the teams, and they went on to finish the game."

For the women who played sports, living in Europe was most enjoyable. Not only did they benefit by improving their cardiovascular endurance, conditioning, and overall fitness; they also developed teamwork. Moreover, active involvement in sports helped them to deal with the stress they faced in their day-to-day lives. Anderson found that "being in sports, you learn how to roll with the punches."

Members of the 6888th could participate in several organized activities in the little free time they had. Mary Daniels Williams remembers touring England: "Anyone who wanted to sign up could go on tours. We went to London and we visited the countryside to look around old castles. We went through Windsor Castle, which is the place where the king and queen live when they're not in Buckingham Palace."

Leadership Style and a Hierarchical Rank Structure

You cannot promote yourself; the people under you are
the ones who move you up.   —Charity Adams Earley

The 6888th, segregated by race and gender, was given full responsibility for governing itself and carrying out its assigned mission without male or white female control. Leaders of the 6888th filled roles that African American women had never occupied before, and they were viewed by their subordinates as pioneers and role models rather than as controllers. These women led by example rather than by an impersonal management style. Unit members were able to perform effectively largely because their leaders were competent. Margaret Jackson recalls, "We had some very strong black officers who were interested in our maintaining our sense of self and pride and race." Cleopatra Cohn, when asked how well she thought the 6888th performed its mission, replied, "I think we did real well because we had some officers who were really concerned about our welfare." Elsie Oliver stated, "We could go to any officer with any problem, and they would give us friendly advice."

Members of the 6888th had what the organizational literature calls "vertical cohesion" (bonding between leaders and subordinates) and were not inhibited by the hierarchical rank structure. Virginia Frazier explains that Blanche Scott, the officer in charge of her work, also had been her company officer at Walla Walla Air Base, just before they were assigned to overseas duty. Scott also had been her company officer during basic training at Fort Des Moines. Frazier states, "Our unit, that left the administrative school, stayed together all the way through [the military]. That's why Lt. Blanche Scott and I are such good friends [today]— because she was always an officer with our company." When I asked whom she would have sought out first if she had had a personal problem while stationed overseas, Frazier replied, "I would go to Lieutenant Scott, who was head of my company."

The highest-ranking officer in the battalion, her executive officer, and all of the company's commissioned and noncommissioned officers were African American women. These leaders were sensitive and responsive to the needs of the women under their jurisdiction. Figure 2 illustrates the chain of command of the 6888th. At the top was the commander in chief (the president of the United States); directly under him, for Wacs, was Colonel Hobby, followed by the commander of the ETO, General Eisenhower, and then by the commanding general of the Communication Zone of the ETO. Next was the commander of the Communication Zone of England (later of Normandy), and then the ETO WAC Director, who was not actually part of the formal chain of command but was involved in all WAC affairs in Europe. Directly under her was the battalion commander of the 6888th. Within the battalion an executive officer ranked directly beneath the battalion commander. Thirteen officers were assigned to headquarters company in charge of offices such as special service, personnel, public relations, post exchange, transportation, dining facilities, and supply. The five companies were headed by company commanders, executive officers, and, except for the headquarters company, two postal officers. In addition there were the noncommissioned officers, the enlisted women, and the administrative staff or the support personnel assigned to the unit (not shown in figure 2).

Major Adams represented the nexus between legal and charismatic authority.[21] On the one hand, she was appointed by higher military officials, on the basis of her technical qualifications, to serve as the battalion commander of the 6888th. Her appointment carried the impersonal, official obligation of ensuring that the mission of redirecting mail was accomplished effectively, while her subordinates' physical and emotional needs were met. Adams achieved these goals well, and her superiors decided to promote her to lieutenant colonel before her term of service had ended. According to Frazier, "Charity Adams was very thorough and businesslike. She did things strictly military. When we were at work it was strictly business."

Figure 2. Chain of Command of 6888th Members

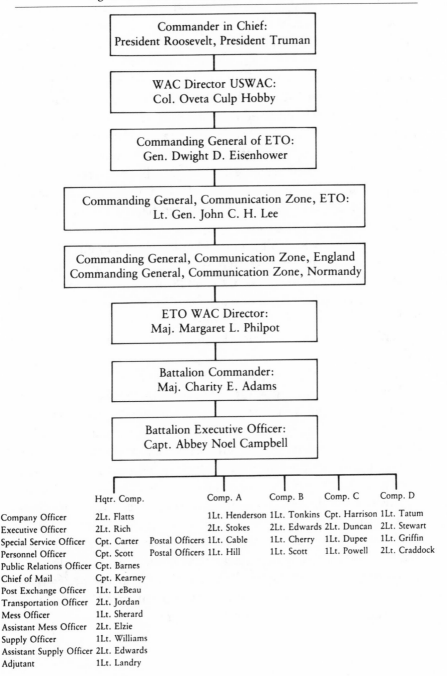

Commander in Chief:
President Roosevelt, President Truman

WAC Director USWAC:
Col. Oveta Culp Hobby

Commanding General of ETO:
Gen. Dwight D. Eisenhower

Commanding General, Communication Zone, ETO:
Lt. Gen. John C. H. Lee

Commanding General, Communication Zone, England
Commanding General, Communication Zone, Normandy

ETO WAC Director:
Maj. Margaret L. Philpot

Battalion Commander:
Maj. Charity E. Adams

Battalion Executive Officer:
Capt. Abbey Noel Campbell

	Hqtr. Comp.		Comp. A	Comp. B	Comp. C	Comp. D
Company Officer	2Lt. Flatts		1Lt. Henderson	1Lt. Tonkins	Cpt. Harrison	1Lt. Tatum
Executive Officer	2Lt. Rich		2Lt. Stokes	2Lt. Edwards	2Lt. Duncan	2Lt. Stewart
Special Service Officer	Cpt. Carter	Postal Officers 1Lt. Cable		1Lt. Cherry	1Lt. Dupee	1Lt. Griffin
Personnel Officer	Cpt. Scott	Postal Officers 1Lt. Hill		1Lt. Scott	1Lt. Powell	2Lt. Craddock
Public Relations Officer	Cpt. Barnes					
Chief of Mail	Cpt. Kearney					
Post Exchange Officer	1Lt. LeBeau					
Transportation Officer	2Lt. Jordan					
Mess Officer	1Lt. Sherard					
Assistant Mess Officer	2Lt. Elzie					
Supply Officer	1Lt. Williams					
Assistant Supply Officer	2Lt. Edwards					
Adjutant	1Lt. Landry					

On the other hand, Major Adams was a charismatic leader who possessed certain qualities that set her apart from the average American woman of the 1940s. She had obtained a college degree with majors in mathematics, physics, and Latin and a minor in history, and she was physically beautiful. Adams also held the highest rank awarded to a black Wac at that time. Her subordinates greatly admired her educational and military achievements; Willie Whiting recalls that "she had brains and beauty. She had it all." Frazier remembers that the battalion commander was well respected by her subordinates: "She was liked. Everybody admired her for who she was because she had a rare rank." Gladys Carter also speaks highly of her former battalion commander: "We were in support of her. And to this day I don't know any 6888th member who isn't proud of her. She was a tough lady; she made us toe the line, but we were so proud to be in her outfit." In 1988, at a reunion, members of the 6888th paid tribute to Charity Adams Earley. Gladys Carter recalls that Earley asked to be called by her first name: "I had the greatest difficulty when I saw her at a reunion to call her Charity. I said, You will always be Major Adams to me."

Battalion members were willing to accept Charity Adams's authority because she possessed both military skills and human character. Her subordinates saw her almost daily. Her office was close to the central work area, and she is said to have attended chapel every Sunday. Major Adams was a role model to the women in her unit, a powerful yet benevolent leader. She looked after their needs and was considerate of their well-being. Major Adams's subordinates testify that she never senselessly insulted the women under her command.

Charity Adams Earley herself acknowledges that she did not find it necessary to use coercive tactics to obtain her subordinates' cooperation. Also, her subordinates realized that the better they performed, the more strongly they would enhance the image of their leaders and of black women in general.

Race and Gender Discrimination Revisited

Discrimination stemming from the racial and gender attitudes that prevailed then in the United States periodically surfaced in Europe. In many such instances members of the 6888th put up an ardent struggle to fight racism and sexism. There were a few accounts of resistance to outright racial discrimination, on the part of members of the 6888th in Europe. The American Red Cross in England, for example, allegedly attempted to provide segregated recreational facilities for black and white Wacs by opening a hotel for blacks only. The battalion commander asked all of the members of the 6888th to support her in resisting racial segregation by refusing to patronize the segregated club. "I am very proud of my service as CO of the 6888th, but one of the proudest times was when the women of that unit supported me in this action. I have never deluded myself that this support came out of love for me. What we had was a large group of adult Negro women who had been victimized, in one way or another, by racial bias." [22]

Another incident occurred when the 6888th basketball team was on its way to London. Just before the unit departed for Rouen, the former supply NCO recalls that several members of the team were selected to go to London to try out for the all-star team, which consisted of members from all the WAC teams in England. They were a very disgruntled group of women when they learned that because they belonged to the only black WAC unit overseas, and because of the U.S. policy forbidding racially mixed teams, they were not permitted to compete. This act of discrimination just made the 6888th basketball team more determined to win the games they were permitted to play. "When the time came to go to Stuttgart, Germany, to the ETO Championship Basketball Tournament . . . we were victorious. The 6888th Central Postal Directory won the ETO Basketball Championship." [23]

Most of the women I interviewed stated that they generally got along well with African American male soldiers in Europe. Mattie

Allen states, "They loved having people of their own color overseas, and we [members of the 6888th] were treated with the utmost courtesy." Similarly, Virginia Frazier says, "Boy, were they glad to see us. When we arrived in Rouen there was a mob of them waiting outside the gate for us to arrive. . . . Each black [male] outfit stationed near us would have dances and trucks sent for us to go." Frances Johnson remembers that many of the black male soldiers were "cousins, uncles, and other kinds of relatives to members of the 6888th." Mary McBride says, "Oh, they just loved [having members of the 6888th stationed in Europe]." She added, "You had to put them in their place. They would make [sexual] suggestions, but I wasn't for that. So there was a certain respect that some of us received. . . . I know I received some respect."

Several members married African American men who were also stationed in Europe. In many cases the couples met in Europe, as did Geraldine and Paul Beaumont.[24] In other cases the men and women had known each other before entering the military. Ruth Sloan's marriage to Emmett Williams in Paris, for example, was a result of a romance that had begun when they were in college.[25]

Many of the interviewees had mixed feelings about the African American men they met in Europe. Allie Davis states that "some were nice; others resented the presence of black women." Ruth Hammond says that her experiences with black men in Europe were "sometimes good and sometimes bad. . . . It wasn't anything ever physical, but sometimes little snide remarks. I didn't let that stuff bother me." Odessa Marshall recalls, "They kind of resented us in the first place because we thought they thought that we were sending them to the front line. But mostly, in my experiences, they were pretty nice." Similarly, Mary Rozier states, "Some were happy to see us; others treated us as though we were there for them. Some would be offended if they asked for a date and were turned down. And of course they would say that you were a lesbian and that was why [you turned them down]. But then, there were others who were just nice."

Other women, however, spoke of negative experiences with African American military men in Europe. Some alleged that African American male soldiers behaved as though members of the 6888th were assigned to Europe specifically to provide companionship for them. The former personnel officer of the unit, Blanche Scott, stated, "So many of the black fellows seemed to have the idea that we were in the Army for the soldiers and johns, and they treated us that way. . . . We resented that." Ardella Pitts says, "I didn't find anything wrong, but some of the girls said that when they tried to carry themselves like real ladies, guys said they were stuck-up or something and called them all kinds of names. I don't know. I sort of stayed by myself. I didn't like running around and partying and stuff like that so I had no problem." Elaine Bennett recalls:

Charity Adams found out that a rumor had left the United States that the black women in our battalion were being used to accommodate the black males and she had a fit. She just had a fit . . . because it wasn't that [we were there to accommodate men]. We were there to serve our country. We were there with a responsibility. After working with that mail all day, you were so doggoned tired you were really glad to pile in your bunk and wait until six o'clock the next morning to get up and do the same thing all over again.

Other accounts suggest that the African American male soldiers in Europe were not interested in dating African American women. Elsie Oliver states quite emphatically, "They [African American men] were busy with white [European] women overseas. That is why there were so many war babies. They would say such things to black women as 'We want something we can see at night.' " Johnnie Walton recalls, "The African American men didn't have time to fool with you [members of the 6888th]; they were more interested in the mademoiselles." Yet African American men allegedly were enraged whenever they saw black women dating British or French men. As Ruth Wright says, "There's one thing about the black male soldiers in England and France, they were very protective of their women. Now, they could go out with British girls and whatnot, but if they caught a black girl walking with a white fellow, they sometimes would go nuts! That was a no-no."

Surely, when the women of the 6888th behaved in ways which were consistent with the roles that American culture prescribed for women, they were less likely to meet with disapproval from the black male soldiers. Several traits, however mythical, are stereotypically ascribed to women of all races in the United States. Women, by American standards, are supposed to be unaggressive physically, sexually passive, nurturant, friendly, attentive to their appearance, dependent, and possessed by one man. Men, on the other hand, are supposed to be aggressive physically, sexually assertive, emotionally tough, and independent. This list of gender stereotypes is by no means intended to be exhaustive; many more are not included here. The point is that members of the 6888th found themselves in conflict with the expectations of African American male soldiers when they did not adhere to the typical gender roles. Some of the men felt their masculinity threatened when they were turned down for a date, and they retaliated by calling the women names. Because it was commonly believed that women belonged to men of their own race, black men were upset when they saw black women socializing with British and French men. The women, on the other hand, could not make the same claim on the men because of the differences in social standards and because of the traditional belief that what was good for the gander was not good for the goose.

Earley described the tension that sometimes existed between black male soldiers and Wacs in terms of competition. She wrote: "Negro males had been systematically degraded and mistreated in the civilian world, and the presence of successfully performing Negro women on the scene increased their resentment. The efforts of the women to be supportive of men was mistaken for competition and patronage."[26] This thought is developed further in the following statement by Elaine Bennett: "Some of the male soldiers were very unhappy with the amount of rank black females had in comparison to the rank they had."

The gender discrimination encountered by members of the 6888th was more pervasive than the personal confrontations that surfaced between them and black male soldiers. It stemmed from norms governing gender roles in the American society. Mattie E. Treadwell discussed the slanderous attacks against women in the WAAC, which were widespread as early as May 1943. These attacks included an "onslaught of gossip, jokes, slander, and obscenity about the WAAC which swept along the eastern seaboard." [27] In fact, gender discrimination was rooted in the infrastructure of the military institution and continued to surface throughout the war years; it remains a problem in military organizations today. [28]

The Silent Minority

Homosexuality was also a fact of life in the 6888th, as in other organizations both inside and outside the military institution. Many of the interviewees acknowledged that there were lesbians in the unit. "Things weren't as open then as they are now. At that time it [the homosexual lifestyle] was not open at all, most of it was kept hush-hush." A few interviewees made unsolicited comments about homosexual activity in the unit, stating that they would have preferred that such activity had never existed. But homosexual activity did occur, and regardless of how hush-hush it was, nonparticipants generally were aware of it. One interviewee says that she had not been aware of a homosexual lifestyle until she was assigned to Fort Oglethorpe, Georgia, in preparation for overseas duty: "It was like going to a circus to see women so masculine. . . . They tried to stay in clusters; all of their friends in a little unit in and of itself. . . . One buddy got in touch with the other buddies and they formed their own little clique."

The fact that lesbians were in the unit did not pose a problem for everyone. Dorothy Jones says:

I had known lesbians from the time I was a kid. Long before I knew what it was, or even the word, there were a couple of women, friends of my aunt, who became friends of mine. When I wanted to study the violin, Miss Chili was the one who gave me the violin she had learned on. . . . I began to realize what her lifestyle was, but she was a really wonderful human being, so how could I be upset by it? As I grew through pre-adolescence, she began to pull away; she would no longer take me places, and so forth. And I asked Mom if I had done something to offend her. Mom replied, "Oh no, she just doesn't want you tagged with her reputation. You're getting to be a young woman now."

People as tolerant as Jones were sometimes questioned by straight members of the 6888th. Jones, for example, recalled being ridiculed sometimes for not supporting derogatory statements about lesbians in the unit:

I felt flak from people [members of the 6888th] who didn't understand my approach to the whole concept of sexual preference: "What you do in your time in your bedroom is your business. It doesn't concern me. And the fact that I am civil and even friendly to you doesn't mean that I'm joining you in your bedroom." Some of the straight people really could not understand how I could be friendly with lesbians. But I believe that when you're doing what you consider to be right, don't worry about what other people think about it. So I didn't.

Although the interviewees had mixed feelings about the presence of lesbians in the unit, all agreed that their presence did not in any way impair the unit's performance. Referring to homosexual activity, the battalion commander wrote, "I cannot swear to the kind of social activity that took place with all members of the 6888th, but I will swear that the efficient performance of the unit was not impaired." [29] Jones sums the situation up in the following statement: "There were always homosexuals throughout the military. Some of them were extremely competent military personnel who either were known or were not known to be so. In the cases of some that I knew or knew of, they were so competent that their commanding officers closed their eyes to the fact that they were gay."

Morale and Job Performance

For the present analysis I define morale in terms of the unit's ability and determination to perform its mission. According to Louis Wirth, morale is the pursuit of collective goals. It is a group's capacity to maintain its integrity and steadfastness of purpose until its objective is attained.[30] Although most of the people I interviewed stated that morale was high in the 6888th, a few people recall that it was somewhat low at times. Willie Whiting, for example, remembered that the work was dull and that there was little chance for advancement because of the limited number of slots for promotion. She added that she felt she was competent to perform at a higher rank if given the chance.

One event that dampened the battalion members' spirits while they were stationed in England was the news of President Roosevelt's death. The president was greatly respected by African Americans, largely for his government intervention programs and his employment of black officials. Members of the 6888th were moved deeply by his death. Lucia Pitts wrote in her memoirs that the news was revealed to the women while they were in formation, "We continued to stand there stunned. I remember finally stamping my foot and saying out loud, 'Oh, no!' Some girls openly wept. The sergeant announced a memorial retreat for the next day and dismissed us. We wandered blindly away, the usual high spirits and chit-chat missing." [31]

Several women I interviewed remembered that three members were killed in an automobile accident while the battalion was stationed in Rouen. That event temporarily lowered the spirits of the unit. Blanche Scott recalls, "We did have a few people who got killed over there in an automobile accident and people got down in the dumps. But [other than that] I thought morale was A-1. If it wasn't 100 percent, it was at least 96 percent." Similarly, Sammye Davis states:

Morale was high because for all of us it was a totally new experience, and especially the traveling. We weren't like a lot of the Wacs in that we didn't stay in one place very long. We went from Birmingham—we were only there about four months—and then we went to Rouen for three or four months, and then we went to Paris. So you see, it was like a vacation, so morale was high. There was one incident in Rouen where three Wacs [members of the 6888th] were killed because they were riding in a jeep, and the driver was going too fast. . . . That was something sad that happened, but it wasn't a long-lasting low-morale thing.

The remains of the women killed in the car accident—Delores Browne and Mary Barlow of Connecticut and Mary Bankston of New York—are buried at the Normandy American Cemetery in Bayeux.[32] This event saddened the women in the unit, but it did not demoralize them; in fact it brought them closer together. The War Department did not make provisions for funerals, so members of the 6888th donated their services and their money to see to it that two funeral services were held: one for the two deceased women who were Protestant, and one for the woman who was Catholic. Noel Campbell Mitchell reflects upon this event:

It occurred to us that something had to be done to the bodies before burial. We wondered how we would have them fixed up. It dawned upon Lieutenant Scott, our personnel officer, that with as many girls as we had in the unit, surely there was someone who had done embalming or had been a mortician in civilian life. She went to the personnel office and checked their service records. . . . She found the names of three of the girls who had once done that kind of work. . . . I called them into the office and told them what we wanted done and asked them if they would do it, and they said they would.

Battalion members donated money that was used to purchase caskets. Mildred Carter, the special service officer, arranged the funeral programs and memorial services. The women in the battalion who had worked as morticians in civilian life prepared the bodies for burial. The executive officer, the public relations officer, and an interpreter went out into the French community and purchased caskets. Through a unified effort by members of the battalion, the deceased were buried with honors.

Virtually all of the women I interviewed stated that overall morale in the unit was high. Margaret Jackson recalls that, "for the most part, people whom I knew were in very good spirits. We worked; we accepted the bad along with the good. There were a few complaints, but we knew what the circumstances were and that they were not permanent. In Birmingham, England, where we first stayed, we had difficulties with plumbing. But it was not unbearable."

Frances Johnson says, "We tried to keep up our morale. We staged shows ourselves. We put on variety shows." Margaret Jones stated that the morale of the unit was "quite high. . . . We had our own beauticians; that was part of our special services setup. And of course, with 850 women in the organization who needed to have their hair done, they were in demand. We [also] had about twenty or twenty-five women in the organization who were musicians." Ruth Wright comments, "I don't think the morale was ever low. We had so much fun among ourselves that I don't think that it was a problem." Johnnie Walton remembers that "morale was very high because everybody was looking forward to seeing as much of Europe as they could. [Members of the 6888th] had a chance to go to different sections of the European continent and had a chance to visit historical sites and to do all of the things that typical tourists do." Janyce Taylor recalls, "I don't think there was ever a morale problem. I really don't. I think we had pretty good officers; most of the NCOs were pretty good."

A central factor contributing to the favorable morale in the battalion was the cordial welcome that the group received from the English and the French. If nothing else, the congeniality expressed by the host countries provided a safety valve for the stress of the working and living conditions. Although at times members of the 6888th were reminded of the dehumanizing effects of racial discrimination, the citizens of England and France treated them with dignity and respect. Each of the members I interviewed has fond memories of the friendliness they encountered. Not only were members of the 6888th entertained by Europeans at public establishments such as ski resorts and pubs; they were also welcomed and entertained in private homes.

How well the unit performed overseas has sometimes been a subject of debate. All of the women whom I interviewed stated unequivocally that the unit fulfilled its mission outstandingly well. Both the battalion commander and her executive officer praised the members of the 6888th for working day and night to prepare thousands of pieces of mail for delivery under less-than-desirable conditions.

The women worked diligently and broke previous records for redirecting mail; they carried out their mission with a great deal of pride. The battalion commander and the executive officer recall that there were no notable disciplinary problems among the members. These statements were confirmed by the following passage, taken from the official account of women in the Army Corps during World War II:

No particular difficulties were reported in discipline and administration. The unit [6888th] was congratulated by the theater on its "exceptionally fine" special services program. Its observance of military courtesies was pronounced exemplary, as were grooming and appearance of members and the maintenance of quarters.[33]

Hence, there was no problem with members of the 6888th going AWOL (absent without leave). Similarly, pregnancy was not a major problem in the unit. The former first sergeant of Company D, Bennett, said, "I don't think I had a half dozen women out of 250 who were discharged because of pregnancy."

There is some evidence that the morale of the unit's members declined somewhat after they moved to Paris. Four months before the entire unit was returned to the United States, members were beginning to look forward to going home. Many of the women had gone, leaving the unit at about half its original size. Probably the most important reason for the members' lowered spirits was the fact the war was over, and they were ready to go home.

There was an official report that the unit's performance, although high in England, had fallen while they were in France. The document suggests that the unit may have performed well while at full strength, but that the performance level dropped when the unit's size was reduced. In November 1945 Maj. Frances A. Clements and Capt. Velma Griffith inspected WAC units in the ETO. The 6888th was inspected on 15 November. According to Major Clements's evaluation report, the strength of the battalion had fallen from 850 to 558 Wacs, 210 of whom were eligible for discharge by 1 January 1946.

Major Clements stated further that morale of the battalion was low for the following reasons: (1) The battalion commander was confronted with many problems and had failed to counsel her women wisely, as she had done in the past, to help them through the difficult period they faced. (2) The workload had fluctuated from heavy to light and then to heavy again without adequate time for the Wacs to adjust. This problem was compounded by the deep reduction in unit strength just when a large influx of holiday mail was received. (3) Heating was extremely poor, creating poor working conditions.

Major Clements recommended that the 6888th be returned to the States. She spoke with Mary Halleren, the ETO WAC staff director in Frankfurt, and later with the G-1 adjutant general about the problems she saw in the 6888th. ETO officials, however, decided to retain the unit, contrary to Major Clements's recommendation.

This efficiency evaluation reflects the unit's work performance for only a small segment of their overseas tour. The report also implies that when the unit was functioning at full strength, its overall performance was quite high. Mary Rozier recalls that the members of the 6888th were told by high-ranking officials in the European Theater of Operations that they had done an exceptionally good job: "We were surprised that we didn't get a citation."

6

★ ★ ★

Life after Military Service

In chapters 1 and 2 I examined what civilian life was like for members of the 6888th before they entered the military. In this chapter I discuss how military service affected their lives after the unit was disbanded. Although some members of the unit remained in the active armed services after they returned to the United States, most of them immediately reentered civilian society to reap some of the benefits of service. When these women joined the military, they expected the United States to win the war; they looked forward to expanded opportunities when they returned home. Not only did they expect to receive a good education, full employment, and adequate health care; they were willing to work for them by fulfilling the obligations that accompany citizenship, including defending the U.S. constitution.

As illustrated in chapter 1, many of the interviewees stated that before they joined the Women's Army (Auxiliary) Corps they had believed they would have greater occupational and educational opportunities after the war. This positive attitude parallels earlier findings on African American men who served in the Army during the same period.[1] Modell, Goulden, and Magnusson found similar results when they reexamined survey data collected during the war by Samuel Stouffer and his associates.[2] Evaluating responses to two variables (generalized optimism and residential plans), Modell and his colleagues found that African American men, to a greater extent than men of European descent, assumed they would be better off as a result of their military service. In addition they discovered that African American men from the South were more optimistic about returns for military service than were those from the North.

Both the members of the 6888th and the men in Modell's study emphasized their expectation for a better quality of life. Unlike the question in the current study, however, the question used in Modell's study is worded vaguely and is closed-ended: "Do you think things will be better or worse for you personally after the war than before the war?"[3] The African American men answered that things would be better for them personally, but they did not specify how. In the present study, by contrast, members of the 6888th stated specifically that they expected to attain a better quality of life after military service through educational and occupational advancement. The open-ended question for the present study was worded as follows: "What were some of the reasons that you joined the military?" (See question 2 in Appendix B.) Most of the interviewees maintained that advanced education and occupational advancement were among their reasons.

Another difference between the present study and Modell's is the effect of geographical region on the interviewees' responses. Whereas Modell found that southern black men were more optimistic about the effects of their military service than northern black men, I found no such regional variation among the women in my study. Members of the 6888th were generally optimistic about advancing educationally and occupationally after the war, regardless of their geographical background.

Another distinction between the two studies is that of interregional migration. Modell, Goulden, and Magnusson showed that African American men expected to relocate after the war was over. Many of them had entered the military from southern states and expected to live outside the South when the war ended.[4] In contrast, although several members of the 6888th in fact changed their domicile at the end of World War II (thereby contributing to the massive interregional migration that took place in the United States during that period), the women interviewed for this study did not emphasize geographic relocation as one of their expectations before joining the military.[5] A few of the women who were born and reared in southern states entered the military from northern states; hence they had migrated before enrolling. Blanche Scott, for example, was born in Boydton, Virginia, and was inducted into the military in the Washington, D. C., area, where she still lives today. Other interviewees, such as Charity Earley, Elsie Oliver, Mary Rozier, Elizabeth Eastman, and Gertrude La-Vigne, also had moved to northern cities before entering the military.

Some women mentioned that Wacs were stigmatized when they returned to the civilian society. When I asked interviewees whether they suffered any disadvantages for having served in the military, most of the replies were similar to Odessa Marshall's: "Disadvantages? No, I can't see any at all." A few women, however, reported that military women were stigmatized as being "whores" or "lesbians." Lavinia Johnson, for example, answered, "I don't know of any disadvantage other than that people have misconceptions of military personnel; that you [women veterans] are like a hardnose combat soldier. Once in a while I would run into someone who said that military women did not have feminine qualities." Mary Rozier remembered that when she returned to the civilian world, "people still said the same thing as the soldiers felt; that you just went in [the military] to run around, to be with the men or to be with the women, one or the other. Not many people really accepted the fact that I was going in because I wanted to be a part of the war effort too."

Some women simply did not mention that they had served in the Women's Army Corps. Willie Whiting, for example, stated,

I think we would be kidding ourselves if we did not accept the fact that being a woman veteran gives a little stigma. How often it works to your advantage, I don't know. When you come home from the service you're faced with all of these things. And as my occupations have developed, I have never done any bragging in reference to my veteran status because I recognize that there is a stigma attached to it. I think that I lived long enough to outlive that [stigma], but everyone did not have that luxury.

A few former members of the 6888th complained that they could not cash in on their military benefits because the Veterans Administration (VA) was insensitive to women's needs. The following account by Dorothy Jones is a case in point:

When I moved back to Boston, after my oldest child was born, I decided that it was time to go back to school. And I did go, and Ellen [Jones's daughter] went to nursery school. By the time the second year was coming around, I was pregnant again. And it was also the year the Veterans Administration had announced that World War II vets had to either be in school on October 1 or lose their benefits. You could apply for an extension based on circumstances beyond your control. Well, I applied for an extension based on my pregnancy. (I was due the beginning of October and therefore wasn't going to register for the fall semester. I went to summer school. Everybody was teasing me; they'd give me two seats instead of one, you know that whole bit.) And the VA turned me down. They told me that being pregnant was not, in their opinion, something beyond my control. I asked, "In Massachusetts?" Birth control was highly illegal in Massachusetts in those days; the use, the prescription, or the advice. All that was illegal. Doctors were being arrested. . . . When I asked, "What is beyond one's control?" they [the VA representatives] replied, "Well, if you were called to service in Korea, that's the only thing that you can get an extension for. . . . So I filed for an appeal, and Alice [the baby] took her good time coming into this world. My appeal was scheduled for 10:00 A.M., the morning of October 21st; Alice came into this world the night of the 20th. . . . [Jones called the VA on the afternoon of the 21st.] They said, "Sorry, you didn't show, so by default you've lost." I probably could have started writing my congressman and all but I had a three-year-old and a newborn to take care of. I let that one drop.

Complaints like these did not surface often in the accounts given by members of the 6888th; yet all of the women were aware of negative stereotypes of the female military veteran and of women veterans' difficulty in reaping benefits. Most of the women did not feel they could do anything to change negative sentiments toward the female veteran and chose to ignore them and to concentrate their energies on the bread-and-butter issues of improving their economic lives.

★

How does the effect of military service on the lives of former members of the 6888th compare with that on former military personnel in previous studies? Research conducted during World War II did not concentrate on the effect of military service on the subsequent lives of military personnel, but rather on how well soldiers adjusted to military life. In the 1940s, for example, studies in social psychology conducted at the Research Branch, Information and Education Division of the Army examined American soldiers' problems of adaptation and morale.[6] During the same period Edward Shils and Morris Janowitz published a study on cohesion and disintegration of German soldiers during the war, accentuating adaptation.[7]

The effect of military service on postservice life did not emerge as a central theme in the social science literature until the 1960s, when controversy arose about the military draft. A few of the resulting studies are highlighted in this section. Most of them differ from the present work in that they focus on the military in a different period. Several were conducted during the Vietnam War era, when the military was scrutinized closely and the morality of military service was questioned seriously. All of the studies referenced in this section, with the exception of Fredland and Little's works, examine the effects of a racially integrated military, in contrast to the racially segregated Army of World War II.

The present study also differs from those referenced below in that it is based on qualitative information (individual case studies and historical documents) rather than quantitative data (from large samples of the population). Another significant difference is that none of the earlier studies focus on women's military experiences. Yet, although these previous studies are not always directly comparable to the present inquiry, they are instructive in providing a general framework by which to analyze the effects of military service.

These studies, based on a human capital approach, examine the effect of military service on civilian income; they attempt to explain observed inequalities in the distribution of labor income in terms of differences in investment in training. Human capital theory assumes that human services can be augmented through training, education, and experience. A further assumption of these studies is that wages are positively related to productivity and that people's wages increase as they become more productive. Jobs that require a great deal of training or formal education pay higher wages than those requiring less. Some of these propositions are generally applicable and, as illustrated below, are supported by the findings of the present study.[8]

Military service has various possible effects on the subsequent lives of those who served. Some studies found that military service created a discontinuity in service members' lives by removing them from life in the civilian world and subjecting them to an environment in which their past was insignificant.[9] Several investigations conducted by economists in the 1960s illustrated that participation in the armed services negatively influenced male soldiers' postservice income, primarily for two reasons. First, the military pay scale was appreciably lower than that of civilian organizations. Second, interruption of service members' lives disrupted higher education, on-the-job training, and job seniority, forcing them to sacrifice educational or employment opportunities, or both, as well as career advancement. Thomas Willett's article "Another Cost of Conscription" and Walter Oi's published study "The Economic Cost of Conscription" fall into this category.[10]

Members of the 6888th, by contrast, did not view military service as a disruption in their lives. Unlike the men in the studies cited above, the women in general, and the members of the 6888th in particular were not conscripts (draftees) but volunteers. This fact would largely explain the differences found here. Many of the women I interviewed regarded the hiatus in their lives caused by the war as a moratorium, allowing them time to reflect on their pasts and to think about their futures. As mentioned earlier, most of the women who had been working before they joined the military were guaranteed their positions when they returned to the civilian world, and therefore they did not fear losing their jobs when they chose to enter the military. Interviewees who had been employed in a professional career complained that regardless of their capabilities, they were limited to teaching. The lower pay offered by the military for their services did not discourage them from joining; on the contrary, these women were looking forward to a change. Most of the interviewees who had been attending college before they entered the military were eager to become military veterans to help finance their education.

In successive studies published in the late 1960s and early 1970s, social scientists criticized economists for focusing narrowly on the consequences of military service for white males and overlooking possible variations due to demographic characteristics such as socioeconomic status, race, and gender. They expanded the human capital model to examine variation resulting from former servicemen's class and race differences. Many of these subsequent studies showed results dramatically different from those produced by economists. Sociological research, for example, discovered many benefits of military service. Several sociologists illustrated that service offered opportunities for self-improvement through facilities such as technical training, continuing academic studies in off-duty programs, and educational attainment in subsequent years.[11] A case in point is a study conducted by Kattenbrink in 1969. Controlling for socioeconomic status, Kattenbrink found that military men of relatively low socioeconomic status made more occupational gains when they returned to the civilian world than military men of higher status. The reason for this difference, according to Kattenbrink, was that military men of lower socioeconomic status, while on active duty, made more progress academically and socially than did the men of higher status.[12]

Later studies raised questions about Kattenbrink's claim that military service influenced the occupational gains of men of low socioeconomic status. A study conducted in 1970 by Mason found no relationship between military service and subsequent earnings, regardless of socioeconomic status. Mason further compared the earnings of black and of white men and found that service did not affect black males' civilian earnings any differently than those of white males. He concluded that neither racial group derived any earning advantage from military status or experience.[13] When examining veterans' educational attainment, however, Mason found a strong relationship between military service and education: education contributed more to an officer's civilian status than to that of an enlisted man. This difference, argued Mason, existed because officers generally have more schooling than enlisted personnel initially.

As in Kattenbrink's findings, some of the members of the 6888th made occupational gains when they returned to the civilian world. Unlike the subjects of Kattenbrink's study, however, the members of the 6888th displayed no real difference based on class; most of the women interviewed, regardless of class, stated that they matured through their military experience. Similarly, the present study gives no indication that socioeconomic status influenced the propensity of former 6888th members to continue their education; many of them pursued academic studies in subsequent years regardless of their economic background. Unlike Mason's findings, statements by former members of the 6888th suggest, that although some did not obtain real occupational advantages for their military service, others did. Some members of the 6888th increased their earnings by acquiring civil service points for being veterans and thus receiving higher job ratings.

The strong relationship that Mason found between education and military service seems to be supported by the experiences of members of the 6888th. In the present study education was mentioned most often as the most important variable leading to upward mobility, whether the interviewees were officers or enlisted members. This finding is not surprising when we consider that many of the women interviewed for this study entered the military for the express purpose of completing their education.

Browning, Lopreato, and Poston's research, unlike the studies mentioned above, discovered that military service resulted in an income advantage for racial minorities. They further observed that the military institution created a "bridging environment" for members of minorities, which provided the conditions they needed to advance occupationally. This bridging environment had subsequently boosted the earning power of African Americans and Mexican Americans when they returned to the civilian world.[14] Lopreato and Poston produced additional evidence in support of the bridging environment theory in a subsequent study, which revealed that minority veterans converted education into earnings at a greater rate than did minority nonveterans.[15] Poston found later that minority veterans were paid more than nonveterans for their age, education, and class of work.[16]

The data for the present study are insufficient to prove or disprove this research, because we lack comparative information on African American women of the World War II era who did not serve in the military. Many of the interviewees, however, describe the military structure as providing a bridging environment. As reflected in some of the accounts to follow, several former members of the 6888th, such as Mary Daniels Williams and Bernice Thomas, speak of the military environment as having created a break from their past and having prepared them for the civilian labor market that they confronted later.

As illustrated in the narratives below, the preparation to which members of the 6888th refer did not take the form of vocational training, but consisted of intangible benefits such as discipline and the tangible benefits of the GI Bill. This finding is consistent with that of an earlier study by Fredland and Little examining long-term contributions of vocational training on the subsequent earnings of World War II veterans. Those authors discovered that military training, on the whole, was less significant in influencing earnings than was civilian vocational training. After separating military training into three categories (professional/managerial, skilled manual, and all others), they found that the only military training that yielded high premiums in civilian life was that in the professional and managerial area.[17] Similarly, almost all of the women interviewed for my study stated that the vocational training they received while on active duty was not relevant to their subsequent work in the civilian world.

Like many of the military occupational tasks required during World War II, those performed by members of the 6888th did not demand much skill. Very few African American women received professional or managerial training while in the military, although some had entered the military with civilian professional training. Nonetheless, some of the women in this study, like other veterans of World War II, were able to translate their military experience into material rewards through the GI Bill or civil service points, as discussed further below. The gains in human capital achieved by members of the 6888th were largely a function of the historical period. These women joined the military during a period when the GI Bill was signed into law. They returned to a civilian world that offered women many more occupational opportunities than the one they had left; thus, they could cash in on the human capital gains they had made in the military. For the present inquiry I have separated the influences of military service on interviewees' lives into four categories: intangible rewards, educational and occupational benefits, marriage, and military service as a turning point.

Intangible Rewards

Among the intangible rewards, military service has been found to broaden one's perspectives, social knowledge, and self-awareness.[18] Elder and his colleagues assert, "Mobilization increases the scope of awareness of oneself and others through an expanded range of interactional experiences, including new people and places, which promote greater acceptance of social diversity."[19] This intangible effect of military service is supported strongly by data of the present study.

A few interviewees found that their military service did not translate into material rewards. They did not acquire any usable occupational skills in the military for the civilian labor market, nor did they make use of the GI Bill after they were discharged from the Army. Although they did not gain materially, these women almost invariably said that they benefited spiritually for having served. Military service provided them with rare and valuable experiences. Ruth Hammond, for example, stated that the military did not help her to advance educationally or occupationally. She had completed college before entering the military; she did not use the GI Bill for additional education when she returned home from overseas because she wanted to work. When the war was over, Hammond's services were forgotten. She was never able to find the job for which she felt she was qualified because of what she perceived as racial discrimination:

I applied for an opening at the Veterans Administration to help with discharges and whatnot. The first thing that I was told [by a woman who was screening applicants] was "You have to have a degree for that." I said, "Well; you haven't looked at my resume so you don't know what I have." . . . She read it. She didn't say anything, but I didn't get the job.

Even though Hammond believes that the military did not provide her with an avenue of upward mobility, she stated that she met and interacted with wonderful people while serving overseas. That experience in itself was invaluable: "I wanted to travel and I did. I met some very nice people, I saw some wonderful things, and I enjoyed a lot of things, so I don't regret serving in the military."

Gladys Anderson also stated that she did not obtain material rewards for serving in the WAC. Her situation was somewhat different from that of Hammond's in that she started working as soon as she returned home from service, and she attended college part time. Anderson says that the military did not help her to advance educationally or occupationally, "because I went in as a stenographer clerk and came out as a stenographer clerk." Anderson went to school part time until she discovered that she was not progressing as fast as she had wished: "My instructor told me that I would be forty years old by the time I finished and got the degree that I wanted; I wanted to be a domestic science teacher. . . . After thinking about it I realized that I could not quit my job just to continue college on a full-time basis, so I decided to quit [college]." Although she did not advance occupationally or educationally, Anderson's military experience made it easier for her to get along with people: "I learned how to accept people and not to fret too much when things don't come out as they should."

Former members of the 6888th who claim to have benefited materially by military service almost invariably benefited psychologically as well. Most of these women also recognize that the military provided them with enlightening experiences. Tessie Barr, for example, remarks, "The service gave me an insight on the world. . . . I can accept things more." Other women stated that they reached a higher level of maturity as a result of their military service by learning to live and work with others. Odessa Marshall claims, "The military changed my life in a number of ways." Among the many effects of service on her life, she declares, "It gave me a little more independence, and it made me more aggressive." Largely through the influence of her military experience, Marshall is currently an advocate of women's rights. Vernelle Davis also credits military service for teaching her how to live with people: "I can respect anyone. I don't care what you're doing; I have respect for you. I don't say I want to associate with you, but I can live with you."

The military institution is famous (or infamous, depending upon one's point of view) for its regimented way of life. Consequently, personnel on active duty give up much of their personal right to life, liberty, and the pursuit of happiness upon entering the military. Sammye Davis remembers the military as strict, but she feels that the austere lifestyle had a positive effect on her life: "Of course the lifestyle was very rigid, which was very good because as a result I'm now organized, more so than many people I see. It [the Army] was good for organization, self-discipline, self-control, getting along with people. There were many good things that I got out of being in service."

Willie Whiting also acknowledges military service for the discipline she acquired:

To the extent that discipline plays a major role in my life I say I have benefited by being in the military. . . . There I learned the necessity of discipline and exactly what it means; and of course the results if you fail to discipline. I'm very glad for the experience in service. If it taught more discipline, I needed it. I had resigned myself to the fact, when I went in, that there probably would be many times when something would be suggested that I would rather not do, but the military was not designed for me personally, so I did it.

Allie Davis also appreciates the military for its discipline. She says that service made her "tough, disciplined, and self-controlled," attributes that helped her later in both her personal and her professional civilian life.

Some interviewees, such as Gladys Carter, said that military service helped them to develop self-confidence:

The military had a great impact on my life and the type of person I turned out to be. I always was assertive, and a person interested, concerned, and . . . not . . . afraid to get involved. But I think the military gave me more direction. It gave me even more of a willingness to take on a job and to take on a challenge. I just think that I can do anything damn well if I put my mind to it. The military had a lot to do with that [feeling of confidence].

Some women claimed they had been sheltered all their lives until they entered the Women's Army (Auxiliary) Corps. Military service altered their view of life by expanding their horizons. Lavinia Johnson, for example, credits the service for the insight she acquired about people in general: "I learned so much about other people. I came from a small town and had led a sheltered life. [In the military] I learned to accept different people." In retrospect, Mildred Dupee Leonard also credits the service for exposing her to diversity: "I just think that the training and the assignments I had and the maturity that I developed during this period of time certainly prepared me to handle the situation in the civilian world. I was young and had never worked or been away from home, or experienced any of the real life outside of home." Leonard explains that during the time she spent in the military, "I had an opportunity to have four more years of maturity, with responsibilities. So when I came out of the military I really felt prepared [for adult life]." Sadie Belcher also became more independent as a result of her military service: "I think maybe it helped me to grow. . . . It gave me independence, because [in the military] I didn't have anyone to really depend on. I had to be on my own, and that gave me more self-responsibility, I guess."

Anna Tarryk claimed that the military radically changed her perspective on life: "It gave me the opportunity to become independent and to mature quickly. It widened my horizons as far as people are concerned—learning about other cultures and stuff like that." When asked whether there were any disadvantages in serving in the military, Tarryk replied, "Well, at first there were some disadvantages because when we [African American women] went in we were not totally respected. We had to fight the war on three fronts: first we had to fight segregation, second was the war, and third were the men."

Margaret Jones also remembers military service as affecting her life significantly in the same way as it influenced Anna Tarryk's: "It was good because I was from a small town and it broadened my horizons." Jones adds that she had always associated and socialized with white people. Growing up in Oberlin, Ohio, where she went to school with white children, she had neither known nor experienced overt acts of racism: "I had always been associated with white people as a matter of course in Oberlin. After I came in contact with the kind of white people I came in contact with in the Army, I had to realize that I had seen only one side, that I had not seen all there was to see." Growing up in Oberlin, for Jones, was like "being in a cocoon. You were not aware of the prejudices that existed outside." But when she entered the military, Jones continues, "then I realized that it [racial prejudice] did exist, and that I had to learn how to live with it, or learn how to combat it."

Among the intangible rewards of military service, former members of the 6888th mention the opportunity to travel both within the United States and to countries they had previously only read about in books. During their travels members of the 6888th met African American women from different regions, as well as Europeans in England and France. Almost all of the interviewees stated that serving overseas during World War II was exciting, adventurous, and overall a fulfilling experience. Many said that their experience increased their knowledge of European culture. Dorothy Johnson, for example, had graduated with a degree in literature from Spelman College before joining the WAC. She found that her stay in France gave her the opportunity to visit the homes of many world-renowned writers:

Rouen was a rather bucolic town. It was a mecca for French seventeenth- and eighteenth-century writers. It was a place where Greek theater went on in the fifteenth, sixteenth, and seventeenth centuries. It was a place of culture. Flaubert's father was a doctor at the very hospital that I was admitted to when I suffered an intestinal flu, and his family lived in that hospital. I never dreamed that I would be treated in the very hospital that Flaubert's father once worked [in].

Elizabeth Eastman also appreciates the travel she did while on active duty and refers to it as educational: "I wouldn't have been in those different countries if I hadn't been in the service. . . . A lot of people have not had that experience in life."

Dorothy Jones was thrilled with the experience of traveling to Europe during the war: "Coming from as poor a family as I came from, even if Dad had been making a whole lot more money than he was, we still would have been poor with the number of mouths he had to feed. How was I ever going to get to Europe? I made the most of it!" Jones had an opportunity to attend Biarritz American University in France for six months while she was overseas: "Biarritz is a major resort town, and the military took it over during the war. The purpose of the school was for GIs to get a head start on going back to school before returning to the United States. I got college credit for the courses I took at Biarritz when we returned home."

Margaret Jackson, a schoolteacher before she joined the military and after she returned to civilian society, stated that although the military did not dramatically change her life financially, "it was a pleasant experience. Naturally any service in the military would have its moments of pain and happiness, but basically it was an enlightening, a broadening experience that I certainly would repeat." Elaine Bennett similarly describes the military as "both good and bad":

It was good and yet it was bad because you were just indoctrinated [into the military way of doing things without regard for your personal beliefs or desires], and as a result, time is the most important thing to me. Even after all these years . . . I met people [while in service] that I cherish, I developed some of the most beautiful friendships, and it's just like a sorority. They become sisters. They become very, very close to you. Whatever your problems are belong to them, and vice versa. I met some beautiful people in the service, and their friendships are everlasting.

Educational and Occupational Benefits

For the first time in any war, the Selective Service Act included a provision that guaranteed reemployment rights to all veterans who had left civilian jobs to enter the military. In addition, on 22 June 1944 President Roosevelt signed the GI Bill of Rights into law, providing educational benefits for military veterans. The final education title provided one year of education for ninety days of service and an additional period of education beyond the first year equal to the time the veteran spent on active duty. Educational funding, however, was not to exceed four years. The educational benefit package included payment of all fees, tuition, books, and supplies up to a maximum of $500 per school year, plus a monthly subsistence allowance while the veteran was enrolled in school.[20] These benefits were available to members of the Women's Army Corps; some members of the 6888th took advantage of them immediately after they left the military.

According to a study by Elder and associates, age of entry into the military strongly determined how much the service was perceived as a turning point in male veterans' lives.[21] These observers found that men age twenty-one and younger were more likely to view their military service as positively influencing social independence, educational benefits, and their relationships with their parents. Although there is no evidence that military service helped members of the 6888th to get along better with their parents, we know that age did not affect their inclination to perceive the military as positively influencing their independence. Nor was age a factor in determining the likelihood that the women would use military educational benefits in subsequent years. As indicated above, Leonard and Tarryk declared that the military gave them a greater sense of social independence. Leonard was twenty-one years old when she entered the military; Tarryk was twenty-eight.

On the other hand, several former 6888th members were in their late teens and early twenties when they cashed in on the GI

Bill of Rights. And some of the women were well into their thirties when they used the GI Bill for their college education. For many 6888th members, educational opportunities were the most significant gain from military service. Education in itself was regarded very highly by many African American women during World War II. Having been deprived of formal education for so many years, African Americans placed a high premium on college degrees.

Dorothy Johnson, who entered the military when she was in her late twenties, recalls, "We all were eligible for the GI Bill of Rights, and when I got out I went immediately to graduate school to get my degree in library science. The Bill paid for my graduate education." Allie Davis also praises the GI Bill. After leaving the military she received both her B.A. and M.A. degrees from Georgia State University. She went on to teach elementary school and retired after thirty-seven years.

Similarly, after serving on active duty for nineteen months, Willie Whiting used the GI Bill to assist her with her law school expenses. She worked as a secretary while attending law school: "Christmastime I worked in the post office; you could always make some extra bucks there." Just before graduating from law school, Whiting worked in her uncle's law firm in Chicago. She reports:

Six or eight months before I graduated law school, my uncle learned he had tuberculosis. (Incidentally, I worked for a certified public accountant during that period; most of the time I was in law school.) And so he [my uncle] decided that if I would give up working for Washington, Fidlan, and McKeeba [the accounting firm], I could come into his office and work until he completed the surgery that they [his doctors] had anticipated for him. And that's what I did. And he was out for about nine months. And during that period of time very few of his clients knew he was ill. I always take such pride in saying that because, whether he appreciated it or not, I thought I did an excellent job in handling his office and saving his practice. And he lived twenty-five years after that. I think I served him well. . . . By the time he came back, I had passed the bar and I was a lawyer. He had promised me some of his business when he got out of the hospital and was able to go back into the office and work. In the meantime I had gotten married. . . . I can't pinpoint the time. I had become unhappy because he [my uncle] never made good on his promise. So I left him and became an executive secretary for the NAACP for about two years. From there I became a city attorney, corporation counsel; and from there I went to the state's attorney's office for about four or five years. I spent a short stint in the U.S. Attorney's office. All of these are prosecutorial positions. Then I became a magistrate. That's what the lowest rung of the judiciary was called at that time. I've been here ever since.

Charity Adams Earley used the GI Bill to return to Ohio State University. She was discharged from the military on 26 March 1946, three months after her promotion to lieutenant colonel. Earley completed her master's degree, which she had begun before joining the military. She married in August 1949 and continued graduate studies in Europe. "I not only used the GI Bill at Ohio State University, but I married a man who was in medical school in Switzerland and I worked on a doctorate at the University of Zurich in Switzerland." Earley subsequently worked for a year as the registration officer for the Veterans Administration in Cleveland and later became dean of student personnel services at Tennessee A&I and at Georgia College.

Mattie Allen also went to college shortly after she returned to the United States: "After I moved to California I went to Compton College. I got a degree, and . . . I was very much satisfied with myself until 1965. That's when I had an operation at the VA hospital and they paralyzed one whole side of my body." Allen was told that she would live approximately five years. "And here, twenty-seven years later, I'm still living to tell it." Allen, now retired, celebrates life: "You know everybody says that it's my attitude, because I love to travel. The more I travel, the more I want to travel. I've been around the world twice, and a lot of places three or four times, and I've been on twenty-five cruises."

Some women benefited both educationally and occupationally as a result of their military service. Enid Clark, for instance, went to work as soon as she returned to civilian society:

I worked at school for a while. I became a dental nurse, and I did a few other things. I was connected with Tufts University when I was doing the dental nursing course, and it was about a year, but at that time in '46, dental nurses weren't paid very much, and you're on your feet all day. I decided I didn't need that, and that I would rather go back to secretarial work.

Clark worked as a school clerk for a short while, "and then I became principal secretary. I was promoted to principal secretary after the person holding the position before me left." Clark was promoted again and relocated to the central administrative office: "I went downtown to the administrative office and I became a secretary to three assistant superintendents [at three different times]." Determined to advance her career even further, she states, "Rather than retiring from my last secretarial position, I went to a community college . . . and I became a credentials technician."

Similarly, Virginia Frazier recalls, "I finished my business school training and went to work for the government again because there was a rule . . . that you're not to be put off of your job because you went into the service." Frazier later married a man who had been stationed in France while she was assigned to the 6888th; they had eight children together. Reflecting on her work as an accountant at the Sharpe Army Depot for thirty years, Frazier says, "You know, veterans have a lot of advantages. I have taken advantage of the GI Bill. I completed my education using the GI Bill. Both of us [she and her husband] were veterans, and I'm now living in San Jose in a home we bought under the GI Bill."

Anna Tarryk used the GI Bill to study elementary education at Temple University for a few years, but she left to work as an account clerk for the Veterans Administration. There she was advanced to a teaching position and remained until she retired:

"When I first left the military I did volunteer work at the Mental Reception Center, and I also did volunteer work at the Children's Hospital. I worked in accounting; and then I left that job to go into a teaching status at the Veterans Administration until I retired."

Elaine Bennett went back to college and completed a bachelor of science degree: "When I came out of the service and went back north, I worked for the Veterans Administration. I was there for a couple of years in loan guarantees. . . . I used my GI Bill to get a degree in business administration."

Mildred Dupee Leonard used the GI Bill to earn her master's degree in education: "When I came out of the military I went back to school. I worked for the women's division of the police department. During my maternity leave I had short stints with the welfare department. Then I went from the police department into teaching and stayed in teaching." Leonard was a high school counselor at Detroit's Northwestern High School when she retired. She had completed her undergraduate studies before going into the military, but she had never worked: "I felt that when I came out of the military I was really prepared to work."

Noel Campbell Mitchell attended graduate school on the GI Bill at Columbia University and received a master of science degree in 1948:

I came home in '46 and I went to Columbia Teachers College and got my masters in food and nutrition. That was my major in college. And then I went to Brigham Hospital in Boston to do a year's internship. And then I came back to Tuskegee and I worked for the VA Hospital for twenty-seven years. And I've been retired since 1980. . . . I got married after I came back to Tuskegee, after I finished my internship. I have two grown sons and two granddaughters.

Mitchell was appointed staff dietitian at Tuskegee Veterans Hospital in 1949, two years before she married. When I asked her whether the military had helped her to advance educationally and occupationally, she replied,

Yes, because I would not have had the money to go to graduate school and to do my internship. That was the best GI Bill they [the military] ever had. They paid for everything we had and gave us a stipend. I was at Columbia for two years and one year at Brigham Hospital in Boston, and I never had to pay one penny for it."

Even some of the women who did not take advantage of the GI Bill attribute their occupational mobility to their military service. This mobility was the primary benefit of service for Christine Stone Pinkney. She had worked for the War Department as an assistant messenger for six months before going into the military: "When I came back they held my job for me, but I didn't want to keep that job." Pinkney took a civil service examination for clerks and was placed in a clerical position at the Census Bureau. She worked in the geography division for nine years before moving to a position with the Food and Drug Administration; she retired thirty-five years later. Pinkney credits her civil service jobs to her service in the Women's Army Corps.

Paralleling Pinkney's experience was that of Vernelle Davis, who retired after twenty-six years with the Department of Health. Davis believes her veteran status helped her to get the job. Evelyn Fray also speaks of the preferential treatment she received for being a veteran when she was hired by the Veterans Administration and later by the U.S. Post Office. Fray recalls, "When other people were being laid off, I got veteran's preference." Similarly, occupational mobility was the main benefit for Frances Johnson. Before joining the WAC Johnson worked in a food factory. After completing her military tour of duty she used the GI Bill to complete a course in clerk typing. She subsequently worked as a hospital ward clerk for thirty-one years.

Marriage

For some members of the 6888th, military service played an important role in mate selection. Several women mentioned that they had married shortly after they were discharged from the military. A few members met their future spouses while on active duty and view the service as leading to marriage. Cleopatra Cohn, for example, met her future husband while she was stationed in Rouen; they married and started a family shortly after Cohn left the military. When their oldest child was almost ready to finish high school, Cohn began working as a clerk in a post office. She says, "I applied [for the position], and I got military preference." Cohn emphasizes marriage as "the very best thing that ever happened" to her: "I was fortunate enough to get a very good husband, and children, and family life." Military service also helped Cohn to "learn to live with people" and "to deal with adverse situations."

Gladys Carter also married after she completed her term of service and worked for the War Department for a short time:

That was in Washington, D.C., which is my husband's home. . . . I was the first Wac to come back and finish at Virginia State, I think. My degree was an A.B. I was a sociology major. Then we moved back to New York. Tank [Carter's husband] got his degree in health and physical administration. We lived in Yonkers. He worked in a factory, in Phelps Dodge in Yonkers. And he got up early in the morning and he went down to Columbia University . . . and I was a housewife. Tank got his master's degree at Columbia. . . . I had the two children, of course. Then he got a call through Columbia to go up to Hudson, New York, to interview for a job at a state facility for delinquent youngsters.

Carter and her husband moved up to Hudson. She eventually found a teaching position, went back to school, and received a master's degree in education from the State University of New York at Albany.

Gertrude LaVigne remained in the Army for eight years after World War II. When she returned to the United States, she recalls, "Many of the women in our unit were discharged, and many of us were reassigned to Camp Stoneman, California, to be assigned as a unit to Japan." These women, however, were never sent to Japan, but remained at Camp Stoneman "in postal, clerical, and hospital work." During the mid-1950s, when the WAC opened the officers' ranks to active-duty enlisted women, LaVigne became a second lieutenant, assigned to Fort Lewis, Washington, as an administrative assistant. LaVigne met her husband (Leon La-Vigne) while she was on active duty at Camp Stoneman, and they were married in 1948. In 1953 her husband was stationed in Korea. She requested a transfer to Korea through Japan, but was denied:

August 31, 1953 was the date of my release from the WAC. . . . My sister and I drove to Cincinnati, Ohio, where I lived with her and tried to get a compassionate transfer to Japan to visit my husband as a civilian dependent. While awaiting word I worked with the Red Cross and the Department of Schools. I also joined the reserve unit in Fort Thomas, Kentucky, where I served until my husband returned from Korea in 1954. My husband was transferred to Washington, D.C., in the spring of '57 to attend medical training school at Walter Reed Army Hospital. I went to American University, taking premed [courses] from fall 1956 through May 1957. At this time Leon [LaVigne's husband] was transferred overseas to Germany. We drove to my family's home in Addyston, Ohio (sixteen to twenty miles west of Cincinnati), where Leon, Jr., and I awaited orders to join him in Germany. In Germany I attended the University of Maryland. . . . I took Red Cross training classes and worked in the office while we were there. I helped to organize a preschool nursery school, which my children attended. I was also a member of the board, and I worked in the church as a Sunday school teacher and altar chairman. We adopted two of our children there (brown babies).

When I asked LaVigne whether she thought the military had helped her to advance educationally or occupationally, she replied, "Definitely. I'm one of those profound course takers. I haven't done anything in the last year . . . since my husband died, but I always take courses. I have over 500 credits [but] no degree because I got out of service and traveled with my husband." LaVigne worked part time mostly in youth activities.

Odessa Marshall left the military in November 1945 and married five months later. While rearing nine children, Marshall went back to school and completed a nursing degree. Her GI benefits had expired by the time she returned to college, so she had to pay for her education herself. She worked as a nurse for twenty-eight years before retiring. Elaine Bennett married when she left the military. Allie Davis married while she was in the service at Fort Benning, Georgia. Ruth Wright, when asked how military service had changed her life, replied:

One big thing [that resulted from my military service] is my husband, I can tell you that. I think as women we were exposed to, and this sounds sort of peculiar, but this [my time in service] was the first time, other than college, that I had been exposed to so many black men and women. When you live in a little village that's isolated and you're so protected, you really don't know there's a world out there.

Military Service as a Turning Point

Although many of the interviewees learned valuable lessons in the military and some advanced educationally and occupationally, fewer felt that their lives had taken a new direction as a result of their military service. Elder, Gimble, and Ivie define subjective turning points as the "perceptions of life transitions in which the individual takes on new sets of roles, enters fresh relations with a new set of people, and acquires a new self conception." [22] Although most of the women interviewed for this book perceived military service as a positive experience, fewer perceived it as a turning point in their lives. Members who had career aspirations when they left the military that were never fulfilled tended not to view the military in this way. As mentioned above, Ruth Hammond and Gladys Anderson both had frustrated occupational aspirations when they returned to the civilian world and stated that the military was not an avenue of upward mobility for them.

Likewise, members who had career goals before entering the military and fulfilled those goals after military service did not regard their service as a turning point. Most of the women in this study who had completed college before entering the military or who used their GI Bill when they returned to civilian society, or both, were college bound before they entered. For them military service represented less a turning point than a means of continuing to develop along the path they had already begun.

Battalion Commander Charity Adams Earley, for example, had received a letter of invitation to join the Women's Army Auxiliary Corps while she was enrolled in graduate school at Ohio State University. As mentioned earlier, she postponed completing her master's degree to enter the military. When she returned to the civilian world, she continued her life from the point at which she had left:

Well, I don't think it [military service] helped me educationally in terms of going to school and finishing my master's. I was already three-quarters of the way done with my master's, so I had two quarters to complete when I returned [to civilian society]. So it didn't help me in that sense. As far as an occupation was concerned, I was an educator before I went into service and have been connected to the school practically all of my life. I came out of service in March and finished the requirements for my Masters. I went later to Georgia State College. I was dean of students there.

Whiting, who was only in her teens when she joined the military, expresses a sentiment similar to Earley's. She stated that she knew she wanted to go to law school before she entered service and that military service represented a means to that end. When asked whether the military had changed her life, Whiting replied that military service did not change her goal of attending law school, so in that sense it was not a turning point. Still she acknowledges that the GI Bill provided her with the funds necessary to pursue her education:

There would have been no way for me to have gone further in my education without the GI Bill. . . . I don't think it has ever hurt me to have been a veteran. I had never flaunted it, but I certainly have never denied it. And I have said on more than one occasion I feel certain that the probability of my becoming a lawyer would have been a lot thinner had I not had the support of the GI Bill.

When I asked Dorothy Johnson if military service had been a turning point in her life, she replied:

Not really. I think I would have pursued my educational career even if I had not been in the military. . . . Maybe the discipline might have helped to some extent. But when I went into the military I was in my twenties, which meant that I had pretty much formed my philosophy. I was not a kid. . . . I really don't think that it [military service] had much to do with my life. It was an experience that I enjoyed and reveled in while I was there, and when it was over, I don't think it had much influence.

Still, Johnson recognizes the benefits she received from the GI Bill: "It [military service] made it easier for me to pursue my education, since I got my education financed by the government. . . . This house that I'm in now, I received a lesser interest rate because I had been in the military."

These cases are similar in that each of these women knew where she wanted to go in life, but they are not identical. Earley was in her early twenties when she was recruited to train as an officer in the Women's Army Auxiliary Corps. She had already begun graduate studies at Ohio State University and took a leave of absence to serve her country. After service, she picked up her life where she left off. Whiting, on the other hand, entered the Women's Army Corps with the intention of using the GI Bill when she returned to the civilian world. She was still in her teens and aspired to be a lawyer before, during and after military service. Johnson, who had completed her undergraduate studies, was in her late twenties and wanted to see the world. For Earley and Johnson the interruption that accompanied military service was like a moratorium in their lives. For Whiting it was a stepping-stone toward a goal.

Some former members of the 6888th hardly knew where they were going in life. Although they aspired to elevate their social and economic standing, they were not sure how they would do it. Members who were uncertain about their future before entering service and who could use the GI Bill or secure gainful employment when they reentered civilian life were more likely to view military service as a turning point. For these women the military provided a bridging environment to a more tolerant postwar society. Mary Daniels Williams, for example, was able to make dramatic changes in her social and economic status as a result of her military service. As described in chapter 1, Williams joined the Women's Army Corps because she recognized that she "was going nowhere fast" in the civilian world. She was influenced to join by her recruiter's assurance that she would be able to complete her formal education. Following up on her educational plans when she returned home from the military, she attended Cincinnati's Hughes High School and completed her General Equivalency Diploma (GED).

Determined to elevate her social status when the war was over, Williams declares, "I knew what I wanted, and I knew that I was never gonna scrub another floor." Using the GI Bill, Williams went on to earn her bachelor's degree from Salmon P. Chase College: "I went to day school and night school and summer school, and completed 126 credit hours and got the degree. I was in a hurry." She went on to work as a secretary before advancing to a professional position at the Hamilton County Welfare Department in Cincinnati: "I started off as a clerk, and then I was a secretary. Then I went on to become a supervisor, and then from there I was transferred upstairs and became a caseworker." She had to take additional college courses at the University of Cincinnati to qualify as a caseworker. "I had to go back to school to take Sociology 101. I had to learn what it took to get the job I wanted, and when I did, I went back to school. I worked very hard, I watched and memorized everything I could, and I started moving case work through the welfare department." Williams retired from the Hamilton County Welfare Department after more than twenty years of service, "I made my way to social worker/ case worker, and I was very well paid." Williams's testimony is one of the success stories of an African American woman who was able to change her life as a result of serving in the military during World War II.

Some 6888th members stayed in the military for a short time after they returned to the United States from Europe, and after being discharged worked in a civilian capacity. Bernice Thomas remained on active duty until 1948 and then joined the Army Reserves. She was assigned to Camp Bowman, which was located in Pittsburg, California, when she returned to the United States: "There we [African American Wacs] met a lot of segregation. There were white Wacs there, but they had all of the black Wacs on one side of the post—on the outside of the post, really. We had all of our facilities over where we lived. There was nothing there but us and the gophers." From Camp Bowman Thomas went to Fort Ord: "This is where we met a lot of opposition; they [white military personnel] did not want us there."

Thomas was discharged from the service in California and decided to stay there: "I stayed with some friends in Oakland, and I applied for a job in the Presidio, a military installation in San Francisco." After a great deal of dispute about hiring a black woman, Thomas was engaged to fill a clerical position at the Presidio: "I was accepted but I was completely ignored. I was seated in front of a typewriter and no one would talk to me. The other help in the office were all white, and they wouldn't give me anything to do. And if they did give me something, it would be just like throwing a dog a bone." Thomas later was reassigned to another office: "I eventually got assigned to work for a very nice officer, and he gave me a real job. I moved over to Oakland, and I started working in the Army Reserves." Thomas also had joined the Army Reserves, which gave her additional civil service points; and she was able to retire with a sizable pension: "I do believe that the Army was a turning point for me and my life because I know that I would never have been able to buy a home other than under the GI Bill. And I would never have had the other benefits that I have derived from being in the military, such as a civil service job."

Other members of the 6888th either remained in the military when they returned to the United States from Europe or left for a short time, returned to active duty, and retired from the military several years later. Some of the women I interviewed made a career of the military and viewed service as a change in the direction and quality of their lives. Blanche Scott, for example, stayed in the military and retired in 1965 as a major. She perceives the military as a turning point in her life because it offered her financial stability:

I did not have a job, nor did I know of one in civilian life when I came back [from overseas]. I went over to the Pentagon on my own and tried to find a job in the military—I went up and down the halls. I stopped in an office with Wacs [in it] and a young lady told me that Gen. B. O. Davis, Sr., had asked for some Wac officers out at Lockburn Air Force Base; and she told me that if I could get a letter from him stating that he would accept me, she would put me on orders to Lockburn Air Force Base.

Scott wrote to General Davis, explaining that she was looking for a job, and requested a letter of acceptance from him: "He answered the letter and said he would accept me." She credits her successful military career to Gen. Benjamin O. Davis, Sr.: "I went to Lockburn, and that's how I stayed in the Army, because B. O. Davis, Sr., said he would accept me. . . . And I stayed in twelve years, eight months, and twenty-eight days before getting out."

Scott says she used the GI Bill after she retired from military service. She worked at Fort Leonardwood in Missouri until 1972 and then left to go back to school: "That's why I quit when I did, because my [GI Bill] eligibility would have run out. I had been out of school for thirty-five years, and the University of Colorado accepted all of my credits from Howard University; and that's where I got a degree in sociology." In addition to financial stability, Scott credits the military for changing the course of her life in another way, "I was somewhat shy, and I'm still that, but it [the military] gave me a sense of confidence for myself. . . . I was just thinking the other day, if I didn't have military training I don't know whether I'd still be here."

Margaret Barnes Jones also views military service as a turning point in her life. She retired from active duty in 1965. "The 6888th went to Europe in '45; we came back before 1946. I went right to school; and then I was in reserve status and was ordered back to active duty in 1949 and went to Fort Lee, Virginia, where I trained troops." Jones credits her military service for her willingness to give so freely of herself: "I have more of a sense of responsibility to my fellow men. I feel that having seen the big picture, I know what's going on; I know what needs to be done. Anybody who's ever been in the Army loves peace. You know that because that's what you fight for. Peace is your ultimate goal. And the well-being of your fellow man. These are the things that are important." Since Jones has retired from the military, she has been very active in civic affairs:

I worked with the Armed Forces Association in the Pentagon. It's a volunteer organization. We have a file of every military post in the world: Army, Air Force, Navy, Marines, Coast Guard. On every military post in the world we provide information for military personnel who are being transferred to another post. Information about commissaries, nearest hospitals, those kinds of things. If they [military personnel] have a handicapped child and want to know if there's a school that will accommodate that child; if there's a place where a wife can work; if a family can accompany a soldier some places, that's the kind of information we have. I also do volunteer work at other organizations like Black Women United; I also work with children in homeless shelters.

When I asked Jones whether she thought her military experience would have been different if she had been of European descent, she replied,

Well, first of all I would have gotten different assignments. I probably would have gotten an assignment that would have put me in a better position to advance. I stayed a captain for ten years because of one man that I worked for. One white lieutenant colonel that I worked for who was just impossible. I think he was a psychopath, to tell you the truth. Be that as it may, I know, had I been white, I would not have been put in the position I was in. He [the lieutenant colonel] would not have regarded me the way he did. He would have probably written efficiency reports so that I would have gotten promoted after the first two years there [under his command]. But those are the kinds of things black women were confronted with. Of course it would have been different had I been white. It was the same for black men in the military during that time.

Dorothy Bartlett retired from the military after twenty-one years of service. Unlike Jones, however, she was not eager to advance in rank while she was in the military: "My commanding officer wanted me to be a first sergeant because I was older than most of them [women in military] that were in there at that time. But she [the commanding officer] was very disgusted with me because I didn't want it [the rank of first sergeant]. I told her that I didn't want it because it was the best way to lose friends, and I had too many friends. In 1975 I retired." Bartlett is proud that she owns her own home, is able to lease part of her home, and does not have to worry about financial security because of her military retirement. She declares, "Between my social security and Army pension, I can live without headaches."

Margaret Barbour is another former member of the 6888th who made military service a career. She entered the Army Air Corps in May 1944 and completed six weeks of basic training program at Fort Des Moines, Iowa, before working as a glider pilot records clerk at Maxton Air Force Base. She was later assigned to the 6888th, completed her tour of duty, and was discharged from the military in 1946, only to return to active duty the following year. She retired from the Air Force as a master sergeant twenty-seven years later.

I went in in March of '44, and retired in April of '72, but I had a year's break. I was trained as an administrative clerk in Des Moines. I went to Maxton Air Force Base in North Carolina. I was keeping records for the glider pilots; I was the only Black in the office. I only had a problem with one guy. He never said anything to me, but one day he came in and I had my coat hanging on the rack, and he didn't want to hang his coat by mine, so he went to one of the sergeants there and asked him to get me to move my coat. And the sergeant asked the guy, "What's wrong with you?" And they just let [that incident] pass. That was the only racial incident I ever had. I don't let things like that bother me because I can close my mind to it.

Barbour was a supervisor of mail clerks when she was assigned overseas with the 6888th. She mentions that the work itself was not challenging "because it was relatively easy to do. All you were doing was checking the file against the name to make sure the person was there and if the address had changed, readdress it." When Barbour returned to the United States, she was discharged from the military:

I got out of service because I was sick. My stomach was out of whack from eating that food. So I got out and I stayed out a year; and then I reenlisted with my same rank of Staff Sergeant. I came back to Lockburn Air Force Base. When I first went into service, I was in the Army Air Corps; when the Air Force came into being, I transferred over. I started off working in a headquarters admission center. They tried to give me a hard time, so they transferred me out of there, and I went into supply, repairs, and utilities, keeping track of the boys' supplies like white gloves and toilet tissues and making sure that everything was intact. They had to do something with me, and that's what I did while I was there, and then Lockburn closed and I moved up to Wright Patterson Air Force Base in Ohio. And there I was doing the same thing. At that time, you know, they [military officials] didn't really want to give women any authority if they could get around it. So I was in repairs and utilities there, and I went into training instructor, and I got a promotion to teach.

Barbour describes her tour of military service as a struggle for advancement, in which she prevailed. She takes great pride in having completed eight military schools during her career: Army Clerks School, Supply Management Staff Officer Course, Electronic Data Processing Standardized Supply Course, OJT (On the Job Training) Trainer Supervisor Course, OJT Administrator Course, Senior NCO Academy, Primary Management Course, and Supply System Management Course. She also was recognized for some of her accomplishments and received several meritorious awards, including the World War II Victory Medal, the Air Force

1. Members of the 6888th at the eastern Port of Embarkation dressed in field uniform, before sailing overseas. From left to right: (kneeling) Pvt. Genevieve Marshall of Washington, D.C., Pfc. Lillie Harrison of Washington, D.C., (standing) Pvt. Frances Chappell of South Boston, Va., Tech. 5 Amelia Akers of Roanoke, Va., Tech. 4 Alice Allison of Wytheville, Va., Pfc. Olive Dedeaux of Washington, D.C., Pfc. Margaret Barbour of Yorktown, Va., and Cpl. Susan Crabtree of Washington, D.C. February 1945. Courtesy of the WAC Museum, Fort McClellan, Ala.

2. Members of the 6888th at the eastern Port of Embarkation before sailing overseas in February 1945. From left to right: (seated) Tech. 5 Doris L. Paige of Ocean Springs, Mass., and Pvt. Elouise A. Pinkney of Brunswick, Ga., (standing) Pfc. Ruth L. Gaddy of Charlotte, N.C., Tech. 5 Lottie S. Mills of New York, Pvt. Lillian Battle of Tuskegee, Ala., and Pfc. Mary F. Davis of Atlanta, Ga. Courtesy of the WAC Museum, Fort McClellan, Ala.

3. Enlisted women in front of WAC Detachment No. 2 at Fort Dix, New Jersey. From the personal collection of Anna Tarryk.

4. Col. Oveta Hobby talking things over with three enlisted women at the eastern Port of Embarkation before their sailing for England. From left to right: Pfc. Aleese J. Robinson of Philadelphia, Colonel Hobby, Pfc. Catherine Lee of Greenville, Tex., and Pfc. Elizabeth M. McNair of New Haven, Conn. February 1945. Courtesy of the WAC Museum, Fort McClellan, Ala.

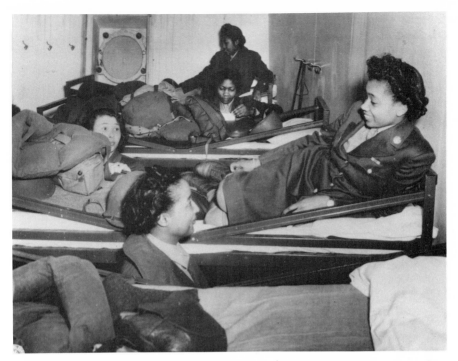

5. Members of the 6888th preparing to sail overseas from the eastern Port of Embarkation. Courtesy of the WAC Museum, Fort McClellan, Ala.

6. Lt. Gen. John C. H. Lee and Maj. Charity Adams, Birmingham, England. From the personal collection of Gladys O. Anderson.

7. Members of the 6888th standing in formation in front of the King Edward School, Birmingham, England. RG111, SC200585-S, National Archives.

8. Members of the 6888th cleaning their quarters at the King Edward School in Birmingham, England. RG111, SC257463, National Archives.

Above: 9. The mess hall of the 6888th in Birmingham, England. RG111, SC200790, National Archives.

Right: 10. Switchboard Operator Pfc. Vernese C. Hayes of Weldon, N.C., 6888th Central Postal Directory Battalion, Birmingham, England. Courtesy of WAC Foundation, Fort McClellan, Ala.

Left: 11. Sgt. Fannie Little (left) and Cpl. Virginia Lane making wastebaskets out of cardboard boxes at the King Edward School, Birmingham, England, February 1945. From the personal collection of Virginia Lane Frazier.

12. Maj. Charity Adams (front) inspecting members of the 6888th in Birmingham, England. U.S. Army Photograph RG111, SC200791, National Archives.

13. Company D of the 6888th, commanded by 1st Lt. Violet W. Hill, marching on the parade field in Birmingham, England. From the personal collection of Gladys O. Anderson.

14. The 6888th Central Postal Directory Battalion marching in Birmingham, England. Courtesy of the WAC Museum, Fort McClellan, Ala.

15. The 6888th Central Postal Directory Battalion standing at parade rest on parade field in Birmingham, England. From the personal collection of Bernice Thomas.

16. The 6888th Central Postal Directory Battalion standing at parade rest on parade field in Birmingham, England. From the personal collection of Bernice Thomas.

17. A quartet of men of the 452nd Antiaircraft Artillery Aircraft Warning Battalion singing on the Hour of Charm program given by the 6888th in Rouen, France. From left to right: Pfc. Alton Hawkins, Pfc. Henry Winston, Sgt. Melverse Mack, and Cpl. Rubin Sands. RG111, SC209960, National Archives.

18. Lt. Elfreda LeBeau, post exchange officer, serving Coca Cola to Maj. Charity Adams at the grand opening of the 6888th new snack bar in Rouen, France. RG111, SC209179, National Archives.

19. Rouen, France. Chaplain William T. Green reading the benediction at the marriage ceremony of Pfc. Florence Al Collins, postal clerk of the 6888th, and Cpl. William A. Johnson of the 1696th Labor Supervision Company. This was the first African American military couple to be married in the European Theater of Operations. RG111, SC210939, National Archives.

20. The 6888th Central Postal Directory Battalion, in Rouen, France, marching in a parade in honor of Joan of Arc following a ceremony at the market place where she was burned at the stake. RG111, SC26441, National Archives.

21. Maggie Chestang, one of the basketball players of the 6888th, sitting on an Army jeep at the 6888th motor pool in Rouen, France. From the personal collection of Gladys O. Anderson.

22. Members of the 6888th holding mess kits just before mealtime in Rouen, France. From the personal collection of Gladys O. Anderson.

23. Front gate entrance to the 6888th living and work quarters in Rouen, France. From the personal collection of Gladys O. Anderson.

24. Four members of the 6888th on a ship in France. From the personal collection of Gladys O. Anderson.

25. Two members of the 6888th on the rooftop of the enlisted women's barracks in Rouen, France. From the personal collection of Bernice Thomas.

26. Members of the 6888th sorting mail in France with French civilian employees. RG111, SC337995-5, National Archives.

27. The 6888th Central Postal Directory Battalion marching in a parade in Rouen, France. From the personal collection of Gladys O. Anderson.

28. Pvt. Ruth L. James on guard duty at an open house for the 6888th in Rouen, France, May 1945. Hundreds of soldiers attended. Courtesy of the WAC Museum, Fort McClellan, Ala.

29. Members of the 6888th taking part in a ceremony in Rouen, France, celebrating Joan of Arc Day, May 1945. From the personal collection of Gladys O. Anderson.

30. Members of the 6888th attending a dance sponsored by the 549th Engineer Company in France on 8 July 1945. Courtesy of the WAC Museum, Fort McClellan, Ala.

When I asked her how she spends her time, Barbour replied:

ong to a lot of organizations. I'm with the Tuskegee Airmen, and
ith the WAC Veterans Association. Every month we go out to the
tals and give patients a little party, and they're very happy. We call
the birthday boys. Whoever has a birthday gets a cupcake with a
on it, and they're just as happy [as can be]. And I do a lot of
ng; always to a convention or something somewhere. I'm with
senior groups. If something is going on that I want to be involved

ainly the military was a turning point in the lives of women
cided to make a career of it. Of necessity, military career-
k on new roles, entered relationships with new sets of
and acquired new self-concepts based in part on their
roles. Like Barbour, military careerists sometimes com-
veral military schools while on active duty, which gave
opportunity to advance not only in knowledge, but also

all of the women interviewed for this book acknowl-
itive influences military service had on their lives. The
most often described by members of the 6888th corres-
th eight of the ten reasons military service was viewed
g point in Elders, Gimble, and Ivie's Oakland/Berkeley
men and husbands.[23] For example, members of the
ntioned maturity, independence, altered view of life, a
, travel/adventure, marriage, education, and occupa-
among the positive consequences that military ser-
their lives. Despite the setbacks described by some of
embers of the 6888th, most of the women I inter-
that their military experiences were well worth the
were able to make educational and occupational
ook pleasure simply in having had the military ex-

31. Two members of the 6888th, while stationed in Paris, visiting a family in
Lucerne, Switzerland, at Christmas, 1945. From the personal collection of
Gladys O. Anderson.

32. Last wave of 6888th members to return to the United States in March 1946.
From the personal collection of Gladys O. Anderson.

33. Nine former members of the 6888th returned to England and France in April 1981. Three of them pose with Councillor Joseph Bailey, the lord mayor of Birmingham, England. From left to right: Dorothy Bartlett, Councillor Joseph Bailey, Essie Woods, and Lavinia Johnson. From the personal collection of Dorothy Bartlett.

34. Former members of the 6888th at a biennial reunion held in New York City, 1988. From the personal collection of Gladys Carter.

Good Conduct Medal, the Army Good Co[
Oak Leaf Clusters, the Air Force Commer[
ropean-African Middle Eastern Service M[
standing Unit Award, the National Def[
Air Force Longevity Service Award wit[
Clusters, and the American Campaign M[

Like Jones and Bartlett, Barbour st[
enough to experience racial integratio[
to serve overseas again before retiring[

While I was still at Wright Pat [Wright F[
to Hillfield, Utah, for supply training sy[
to other bases to be trained on the syste[
guy and two white guys [and myself]. [
Force Base, and I was still in trainin[
came back to the States. I requested[
sent me to Fort Snellen, Minnesota[
didn't even unpack my bags becaus[
was still doing the same thing, tra[
Andrews, and I was at Andrews[
over to Bowling, almost across[
three years.

Like many other people w[
Barbour identified with th[
remembered a comment m[
for her while she was in th[
have liked for me to hav[
said, I'm not pushing yo[
that's all." Barbour said[
employment in a store f[
want to work as a civ[
long time, you know,[
stuff. Salespeople wo[
be taking care of bus[
career of military[
largely by her milit[

W[
I be[
I'm [
hosp[
them [
dolla[
travel[
severa[
in, I go[

Cert[
who de[
ists too[
people,[
military[
pleted s[
them an[
in rank.

Nearly[
edged pos[
influences[
ponded w[
as a turnin[
sample of[
6888th mer[
break in lif[
tional caree[
vice had on[
the former r[
viewed state[
time. Some[
gains; others[
perience.

31. Two members of the 6888th, while stationed in Paris, visiting a family in Lucerne, Switzerland, at Christmas, 1945. From the personal collection of Gladys O. Anderson.

32. Last wave of 6888th members to return to the United States in March 1946. From the personal collection of Gladys O. Anderson.

33. Nine former members of the 6888th returned to England and France in April 1981. Three of them pose with Councillor Joseph Bailey, the lord mayor of Birmingham, England. From left to right: Dorothy Bartlett, Councillor Joseph Bailey, Essie Woods, and Lavinia Johnson. From the personal collection of Dorothy Bartlett.

34. Former members of the 6888th at a biennial reunion held in New York City, 1988. From the personal collection of Gladys Carter.

Good Conduct Medal, the Army Good Conduct Medal with two Oak Leaf Clusters, the Air Force Commendation Medal, the European-African Middle Eastern Service Medal, the Air Force Outstanding Unit Award, the National Defense Service Award, the Air Force Longevity Service Award with two Bronze Oak Leaf Clusters, and the American Campaign Medal.

Like Jones and Bartlett, Barbour stayed in the military long enough to experience racial integration. She had the opportunity to serve overseas again before retiring:

While I was still at Wright Pat [Wright Patterson Air Force Base] I went to Hillfield, Utah, for supply training system. They used to send people to other bases to be trained on the system. There were four of us, a black guy and two white guys [and myself]. From there I went to Newflyn Air Force Base, and I was still in training management procedures. Then I came back to the States. I requested Andrews Air Force Base but they sent me to Fort Snellen, Minnesota. . . . I only stayed there a month. I didn't even unpack my bags because I didn't intend to stay there. And I was still doing the same thing, training and stuff. And then I came to Andrews, and I was at Andrews fifteen years. I moved from Andrews over to Bowling, almost across the street, and I was at Bowling for three years.

Like many other people who make a career of military service, Barbour identified with the military way of doing things. She remembered a comment made by a civilian woman who worked for her while she was in the military: "She told me she would not have liked for me to have been her master if she was a slave. I said, I'm not pushing you; I expect you to get everything done, that's all." Barbour said that when she left the military she tried employment in a store for a while before deciding that she did not want to work as a civilian: "After you've been in the service a long time, you know, it's hard to get used to this lackadaisical stuff. Salespeople would stand around and talk when they should be taking care of business." Like most of the women who made a career of military service, Barbour's self-concept was shaped largely by her military training.

When I asked her how she spends her time, Barbour replied:

I belong to a lot of organizations. I'm with the Tuskegee Airmen, and I'm with the WAC Veterans Association. Every month we go out to the hospitals and give patients a little party, and they're very happy. We call them the birthday boys. Whoever has a birthday gets a cupcake with a dollar on it, and they're just as happy [as can be]. And I do a lot of traveling; always to a convention or something somewhere. I'm with several senior groups. If something is going on that I want to be involved in, I go.

Certainly the military was a turning point in the lives of women who decided to make a career of it. Of necessity, military careerists took on new roles, entered relationships with new sets of people, and acquired new self-concepts based in part on their military roles. Like Barbour, military careerists sometimes completed several military schools while on active duty, which gave them an opportunity to advance not only in knowledge, but also in rank.

Nearly all of the women interviewed for this book acknowledged positive influences military service had on their lives. The influences most often described by members of the 6888th corresponded with eight of the ten reasons military service was viewed as a turning point in Elders, Gimble, and Ivie's Oakland/Berkeley sample of men and husbands.[23] For example, members of the 6888th mentioned maturity, independence, altered view of life, a break in life, travel/adventure, marriage, education, and occupational career among the positive consequences that military service had on their lives. Despite the setbacks described by some of the former members of the 6888th, most of the women I interviewed stated that their military experiences were well worth the time. Some were able to make educational and occupational gains; others took pleasure simply in having had the military experience.

7

★ ★ ★

Cohesion, Conflict, and Phenomenology

My final analysis of the 6888th Central Postal Directory Battalion is informed by three important sociological theories: social cohesion, social conflict, and phenomenology. Social cohesion has always been of interest to military scholars because of its consequences for unit performance. Although few studies have focused on the social cohesion of support units during World War II (and none on female military units), many factors have been found to influence morale, cohesion, and esprit de corps among combat personnel. Some of these findings are not directly applicable to support units such as the 6888th, but other, more general findings are.

Social conflict has a unifying function and helped to produce and solidify solidarity among members of the 6888th. As discussed below, the sociopolitical struggle that led to the formation of the 6888th also served as a catalyst for the group's performance.

While stationed in Europe members of the 6888th were able to shape their reality by challenging racial discrimination and gender norms in a way that was not possible in the United States. I explain this fact by employing concepts of phenomenology.[1] My analysis draws from contemporary sociologists, such as Peter Berger and Thomas Luckmann, Erving Goffman, and Dorothy Smith, who have applied phenomenology to the study of everyday life.[2] Patricia Hill Collins's use of epistemology in her study of "the subjugated knowledge of a Black women's standpoint" is consistent with the phenomenological approach used here.[3] The last section of this chapter illustrates changes in the representation of African American women in the military over the last half century.

Factors Influencing Social Cohesion

A cohesive unit is an effective one that supports trust, teamwork, and commitment and protects its members against breakdown caused by stress. As mentioned earlier, vertical cohesion describes the bonding between superiors and subordinates. Horizontal cohesion describes the bonding between peers.

While noncombatant units do not experience physical, social, and emotional deprivation to the same extent as units directly involved in combat, they do encounter hardship. For the most part, members of the 6888th did not fear physical destruction while they were stationed in Europe. Even so, these women sometimes were confronted directly by the horrors of war. For example, many women were terrified when the *Ile de France* was engaged by German U-boats. Similarly, when the unit arrived in England in January 1945, fighting was still going on in Europe. Several women recalled dreadful air raids and blackouts during their stay in England. Dorothy Dailey Jones remembers an occasion when a black male unit in England was almost totally destroyed:

About forty miles from where we [the 6888th] were stationed there was a unit of [black] engineers. They were the target of the air raid, and the camp was really in bad shape. And that incident really brought it home to me. These were actual human beings, some of whom I had met. We were vulnerable like everybody else. When the sirens went off, we had to black out too.

Remembering another bombing incident, Jones says, "I was still stationed in Birmingham and had a friend in London, a young English woman I had met. I had visited her and her family a couple of times and was scheduled to visit them this particular weekend. So I went to their house and nobody was there. The entire block had been demolished. I never heard from her again."

The 6888th, however, did not experience high death rates, extreme food shortages, or a severe lack of health care, as did men in combat. Their clothing, although not always sized properly, was always adequate. What, then, were the day-to-day social and environmental stresses confronting members of the unit? In examining the working, living, and social conditions of the 6888th, it becomes clear that the unit experienced considerable stress. Some of the strains in performing their job were associated with war; others stemmed from racial and gender attitudes that prevailed in the United States and had followed them to Europe.

One stress associated with war was limited work space, which forced mail clerks to work rotating eight-hour shifts. Some of the women remembered that it was very difficult to become acclimated to a rotating shift. As Anderson states, "They [the commanders of the 6888th] had shift changes, and that was the hardest part to adjust to. One week you had the morning shift and you would have to adjust to sleeping [so you could work the morning shift]. When you had almost adjusted, then you'd have to go to another shift, and that was a hard thing to do; but we managed."

Another stress was the lack of adequate heat in the workplace. Work areas were so cold that the women worked in their ski pants and field jackets. Also, lighting was poor in England because windows were painted black for war-related blackouts. Many of the women said they suffered eyestrain as a result of the poorly lit work areas. The austere living facilities were still another source of stress, especially in Birmingham where living quarters were poorly heated and hot water was scarce.

Perhaps the most potentially demoralizing strain experienced by members of the 6888th was discrimination based on their ascribed characteristics of race and gender. They served during an era in which African American women in uniform could be beaten unmercifully by police in the South if they sat in a "white only" section of a train station. All of the 6888th members whom I interviewed recalled incidents of racial discrimination while they were in the military, many of which have already been discussed. Gladys Carter, for example, spoke of an episode she experienced while the 6888th was being fitted for new uniforms at Fort Ogle-thorpe. Similarly, Charity Adams Earley took a stand against racism in Red Cross facilities. And the unit's basketball team was denied the opportunity to compete for places on the All-Star team because "racially mixed teams" went against the War Department's racial segregation policy. As for gender discrimination, some women stated that male soldiers sometimes treated them as though they were sex objects.

Members of the 6888th remained unified in the face of stress. What was it about their military experience that pulled them together? One measure of cohesion commonly used during World War II was job satisfaction. Among the many factors influencing the job satisfaction and hence the cohesion of combat units was "elite status."[4] Stouffer and his associates, in comparing the morale of combat flying personnel in the Army Air Corps with that of ground forces, found that flying personnel tended to be more satisfied with their combat assignment and expressed greater pride in their military organization than did the ground troops. Three of the reasons given for this greater satisfaction were that flying personnel (1) were volunteers, (2) were terminated from combat duty when they had completed a specified number of combat missions (in contrast to the ground forces, who could expect their combat duty to continue as long as they met the minimum physical requirements); and (3) were able to take pride in their elite status. Similarly, volunteerism, the temporary nature of the assignment, and elite status played an important role in shaping the morale of the women in this study.

All of the members of the 6888th were volunteers. They all were able to rotate back to the United States after a specified period of time on active duty, and they were often placed on a pedestal by the Europeans they came in contact with. Both the British and the French treated members of the 6888th with the respect denied them in the United States. Indeed, they were treated as members of an elite group; they were a novelty in the eyes of Europeans, most of whom had never met black women before. A few of the women stated that Europeans were amazed at the variation in the skin color and style of dress among black women from the United States. Although members of the 6888th sometimes were reminded of the dehumanizing effects of racial discrimination by white American soldiers and by the discriminatory policies of the War Department, citizens of Britain and France neutralized these acts of racism by treating the women with dignity and respect. All of the women I interviewed have fond memories of the friendliness of the British and French people they knew while in Europe. Not only were members of the 6888th entertained at public establishments, they were also welcomed into private homes. British newspapers wrote laudatory comments about members of the unit and spoke highly of them in public gatherings.

Political, ideological, and cultural gestures also help to explain cohesion among 6888th members. While primary group relations are a central factor in explaining the performance of combat troops, secondary symbols are paramount in explaining performance of noncombatant units such as those Women's Army Corps units stationed overseas during World War II. Shils and Janowitz, for example, found that the central element holding together the Wehrmacht (German Army) under stressful circumstances was not so much the acceptance of political, ideological, and cultural gestures, which they regarded as secondary symbols, but rather the fact that a soldier's unit could function as a primary group, fulfilling the soldier's basic organic needs, supplying him with affection, and providing a sense of power.[5] I assert that secondary symbols offer more of an explanation for the performance of noncombatant, WAC units such as the 6888th because such units were generally not deprived of organic needs, as were combat units.

Members of the 6888th were indeed motivated by a grand cause. Living and working on a race- and gender-segregated military installation in Europe was not a central issue for some members of the unit. Certainly they did not view themselves as an inferior unit in any way, and nothing in the interviews suggests that they wished to be racially integrated at that time. All of the interviewees spoke about the 6888th with a great deal of pride; their unit had a very special mission, not only for the War Department but for the "Negro race." Janyce Stovall Taylor refers to political, ideological, and cultural symbols as being the driving force for the members of the unit to excel.

We were a select group, and we knew that they [the War Department] picked the eight hundred and fifty-some of us to go [overseas] because we were among the best enlisted personnel. We were the best, and when I say best I don't mean the smartest or anything like that . . . it's just a feeling that we had. We were continually told that only the best black Wacs were going overseas, and that the eyes of the world were upon us. We were the first black Wacs to go overseas, and I suppose it was drilled into us . . . and we never intended to let an officer, or anybody, fail. We never wanted anyone to say that those black Wacs messed up when they were overseas.

Similarly, remembering the unit members' pride in their appearance, Virginia Lane Frazier states, "One thing about us—they [the battalion leaders] made us be very neat and trim. You never saw any sloppy-looking black Wac. Nobody ever broke the rule. We all looked good." Margaret Jackson also recalls that the battalion held firmly to its pride. Remembering that negative newspaper articles occasionally were written about the 6888th, Jackson says,

We read articles, by Caucasian females, especially, who did not seem to want to admit the commendable work being done by a black unit. You must remember that we were the first all-black unit of females to have gone abroad, and for some reason it seemed to me, to most of us who would discuss the matter, that they were just not willing to admit our success. But we didn't worry about that.

Cohesion, however, does not always mean that the unit advances the interest of the larger institution. Tamotsu Shibutani found that the performance of a Japanese American unit in World War II was poor although the integrity of the unit was quite high. Shibutani reached the following conclusion, among others: If a leader is defined by the unit as someone who is concerned with the members' well-being, the members will sacrifice for him or her. Conversely, if a leader is defined as someone who is not thus concerned, the members will not sacrifice for him or her.[6] Hence, another reason why members of the 6888th fulfilled their mission of redirecting mail under stressful conditions, and did so cooperatively, was effective leadership on the part of the battalion's officers.

As the testimonies illustrate, the leaders of the 6888th behaved so as to demonstrate commitment to strengthening the unit. Some of the women said that the officers showed a genuine interest in the personal and professional welfare of all the battalion members. We learn from Shibutani that these elements of leadership are essential if subordinates are to be willing to work hard, strive to improve their skills, and commit themselves to the mission. The battalion commander, Major Charity Adams, was indeed committed to providing the resources her troops needed to perform their mission successfully.

Major Adams was also committed to providing the women with items for their personal needs: "With the support of Maj. Margaret Philpot, ETO WAC Director, and others, we acquired the items we needed, including straightening combs, marcel irons, special gas burners, and customer chairs."[7] These objects, used for grooming hair, were not usually provided for military units. Yet, because of special sensitivity on the part of the battalion commander, members of the 6888th were able to maintain their personal appearance with little difficulty.

Still, Major Adams realized that her success as a battalion commander depended on the cooperation of all of the women in her unit: "You cannot promote yourself; the people under you are the ones who move you up." The unit member's willingness to cooperate and to make the necessary sacrifices to get the job done are largely attributable to effective leadership on the part of the officers.

Another reason for the bond among 6888th members is that the unit was self-sustaining; members depended on each other for support services. Unlike other WAC battalions that served in Europe, the 6888th was not attached to a male unit and consequently did more than perform its primary mission of redirecting mail. Although the unit was homogeneous in terms of race and gender, members of the battalion entered the military from different regions of the United States and with varied work experiences, skills, and levels of education. This heterogeneity allowed the unit to function as a complex organization, relying on its member's diverse skills and talents. Together the members possessed the resources necessary to function efficiently and effectively as an independent organization within the military institution. This combination of diverse work experiences, various levels of education, different geographical origins, and interdependence also helps to explain the group's unity.

In sum, all indications are that the 6888th was a cohesive unit. There were no serious disciplinary problems among group members, as in the demoralized unit described by Shibutani. On the contrary, members of the 6888th reportedly broke previous records for redistributing mail in Europe. Unit members also were recognized for being well-groomed. Outside inspectors reported that the unit's quarters were well maintained.[8] These are indicators of cooperation, teamwork, and high morale. All of the women interviewed for this study claim that the 6888th was united in its efforts to perform its mission of redirecting mail, as well as in its struggle to overcome racism and sexism.

Social Conflict and Group Solidarity

Collectively, African American organizations were the driving force in the War Department's decision to deploy African American Wacs overseas. On one side of a metaphorical negotiating table were the War Department and white officials, who upheld the traditional norms of the institution; on the other side were the National Association for the Advancement of Colored People, the National Council of Negro Women, and representatives of black publications such as the *Pittsburgh Courier, Chicago Defender,* and *The Crisis.*[9] The overriding ethos for these African American reformists was that all American citizens, regardless of race or gender, should be afforded the opportunity to participate in national defense at all levels. Sometimes religious organizations such as the Young Women's Christian Association supported these struggles for racial equality. Through the efforts of these groups, the War Department conceded and directed military officials of the European Theater of Operations to requisition black Wacs. Only then were eight hundred African American Wacs requisitioned to set up half of a central postal directory.[10]

An important point for the present discussion is that the initial conflict surrounding the 6888th was "realistic" (directed toward an end) and was resolved after the unit was deployed to Europe.[11] This struggle largely concerned who would be permitted to participate in the war effort overseas and under what conditions. Unlike the first contingent of white Waacs that went overseas to England in July 1943, African American Wacs were not authorized to serve in the European Theater of Operations until the War Department acquiesced to sociopolitical pressures. Hence, it was conflict that led to this initial change. This observation is consistent with the following proposition of social conflict theory:

Where conflict is merely a means determined by a superior purpose, there is no reason to restrict or even avoid it, provided that it can be replaced by other measures which have the same promise of success. Where, on the other hand, it is exclusively determined by subjective feelings, where there are inner energies which can be satisfied only through fight, its substitution by other means is impossible.[12]

Thus, the conflict about deploying African American Wacs overseas was resolved once the 6888th was formed. The 6888th emerged as a result of "realistic" conflict, a means to an end and probably would not have emerged without it.

This initial conflict over the deployment of African American Wacs was also integrative in the sense that it fostered cooperation between two opposing groups: the War Department and the African American reformists. This point is also expressed in the following proposition of conflict theory:

Conflict acts as a stimulus for establishing new rules, norms, and institutions, thus serving as an agent of socialization for both contending parties. . . . As a stimulus for the creation and modification of norms, conflict makes the readjustment of relationships to changed conditions possible.[13]

The conflict about whether African American Wacs would serve overseas did not violate the fundamental principles of the United States; on the contrary, the struggle for racial equality was consistent with the American ideal of democracy. Because of the general agreement about the value of democracy, there was room for compromise between the War Department and black activists. The compromise was that African American women would be deployed overseas, but they would be required to serve in a race- and gender-segregated unit.

As a consequence of the political debate, and because the very establishment of the 6888th modified the traditional norms of the military institution, the unit was under constant scrutiny.

Sometimes the target of racial or gender hostility, the 6888th was subjected to various external pressures. External pressures, however, helped to unify the battalion by establishing boundaries between its members and antagonistic groups. As Georg Simmel states,

On the one hand, the group as a whole may enter into an antagonistic relation with a power outside of it, and it is because of this that the tightening of the relations among its members and the intensification of its unity, in consciousness and in action, occur.[14]

Therefore, dissension about the participation of African American women in the WAAC/WAC in general, and about the deployment of African American Wacs overseas in particular, helped to bind members of the 6888th.

All of the unit's members were able to identify with race and gender oppression; consequently they had created a sanctuary, protecting each other from the harsh effects of racism and sexism. Whether these pressures where structural, such as the Jim Crow laws dictating that African Americans were to use separate public facilities, or personal, such as the harassment by some white American soldiers of members of the 6888th in a British pub, they created a strong bond among the battalion members. This was demonstrated not only by the members' determination to break previous records in redirecting mail, but also by their determination to excel in other activities such as marching, performing in the theater, participating in sports, or taking college classes in their free time. They consciously performed each of their tasks with unshakable pride.

The members' united front against race and gender discrimination is portrayed throughout this book. Civil rights were byproducts of the these women's successful struggles. When members of the 6888th perceived that their human rights were being violated, they took action to facilitate change. On the one hand, the struggle for racial equality explains the group solidarity found among members of the 6888th. On the other hand, solidarity helps to

explain the conflicts in which members of the 6888th were engaged: "When a particular definition of reality comes to be
attached to a concrete power interest, it may be called an ideology.
. . . Every group engaged in social conflict requires solidarity.
Ideologies generate solidarity." [15]

Reconstructing Reality

Another way of viewing the solidarity among members of the
6888th is in terms of their ideas. A basic proposition posited by
proponents of phenomenology is that human thought arises from
a social context; thus reality is socially constructed. Supporters of
this approach seek to analyze the processes by which reality is
constructed in everyday life. Further, and significant to the present
discussion, they recognize that this process contains an element
of power.

Not everyone in society participates in the construction of
thought. As Dorothy Smith states,

The making and dissemination of the forms of thought we make use
of to think about ourselves and our society are part of the relations of
ruling and hence originate in positions of power. These positions of
power are occupied by men exclusively, which means that our forms
of thought put together a view of the world from a place women do
not occupy. [16]

In agreement with this view, Berger and Luckmann assert, "He
who has the bigger stick has the better chance of imposing his
definitions of reality." [17] Patricia Hill Collins, characterizing the
peculiar form of domination imposed on African American
women, distinguishes between domination with affection and
domination without affection,

Domination may be either cruel and exploitative with no affection or
may be exploitative yet coexist with affection. The former produces the
victim—in this case, the Black woman as "mule" whose labor has
been exploited. In contrast, the combination of dominance and affection

produces the pet, the individual who is subordinate but whose survival depends on the whims of the more powerful. . . . African American women simultaneously embody the coexistence of the victim and the pet, with survival often linked to the ability to be appropriately subordinate as victims or pets.[18]

When these propositions are applied to an analysis of the statements and archival documents reviewed here, it is clear that African American women were subjugated and subordinated to the white male power structure that existed in every American institution, and especially in the Army. It is also clear that although some of the African American Wacs were "victims" and expected to do the most menial work without regard for their skills or credentials, others (including many of the officers) were treated as "pets."

Members of the 6888th reconstructed their reality when they were deployed to Europe. The difference between the social environment of the United States and that which existed in Britain and France in the 1940s is central in analyzing the process of this reconstruction. For most of the women in this study, for example, Jim Crow laws were the norm in the United States before their service, during their military service, and for a short period after World War II, when many of them returned to the civilian world.[19] All institutions have what Berger and Luckmann call "recipe knowledge," that which "supplies the institutionally appropriate rules of conduct."[20] The norms of reciprocity between white Americans and black Americans were such that the latter were relegated a position of inferiority. This was manifested in all American institutions: labor institutions reserved the least desirable jobs for African Americans, medical institutions administered the poorest health care to African Americans, educational institutions reserved the poorest facilities for African Americans. In an effort to survive, African Americans were forced to adhere to the standards of role performance by deferring to white Americans. As one glaring example of African Americans' subordination, black adults were expected to address white children as "Miss" and "Mister," while white children addressed black adults by their first names.

As reflected in the historical documents and in the testimonies of former members of the 6888th, many African Americans challenged the dominant viewpoint of the 1940s, establishing alternative definitions of their personal identities and their appropriate social roles. These challenges were displayed in the military in the form of protest. For example, a number of African American Wacs protested malassignments in military occupations. While a few were victorious, many were labeled as deviants and viewed as posing a threat to the institutional order as it was; often they resigned, were court-martialed, or were forced into submission.

The African American Wacs who were deployed to Europe found a society that supported their ideology of racial equality; this support, in turn, encouraged them to challenge the American system of domination more often and with greater intensity. In the words of Berger and Luckmann, "It is one thing to have some individuals around, even if they band together as a minority group, who cannot or will not abide by an institutional rule. It is quite another thing to meet an entire society that has never heard of this rule, and that nevertheless seems to get along very well without it." [21]

Racial discrimination did not exist in England and France as it did in the United States. After receiving so many distorted images of African Americans from white American soldiers stationed in Europe, British people began to investigate those allegations. Several of my interviewees said that British people invited them to their homes and asked them to remain after midnight to see whether Blacks had tails.[22] Elsie Oliver recalls, "Children would ask us, 'Is it true that in your country they [white people] keep you people [black people] outside while they are eating?', and I said, 'whatever you read is true.' "

The role of African American Wacs in Europe during World War II was radically different from their role in civilian society and at duty stations in the United States, where a well-defined split labor market existed: the lowest, most undesirable jobs were filled by African American women.[23] In Europe all of the powerful positions in the battalion were filled by African American women. The 6888th consisted of approximately 850 women, all of African descent. All of the occupational positions, from a menial task such as "KP" (kitchen police) to the most prestigious role, battalion commander, were held by black women. Because the unit was segregated, the battalion's living quarters, eating facilities, motor pool, military police, administrative staff, and so on, were composed exclusively of African American women. This was a radical departure from an environment where practically all of the powerful positions were held by men of European descent. Being a self-contained WAC battalion in Europe, the 6888th had what Berger and Luckmann call a "plausibility structure," one in which they could reconstruct their reality, redefine their roles, and circumvent relations with outsiders (individuals who would attempt to subordinate them because of race or gender).

Major Adams, for example, while stationed in Birmingham encouraged the women under her command to boycott the American Red Cross's hotel in protest of that organization's racial segregation.[24] Yet her active stand against racial segregation in Europe contrasted oddly with the passive position she took when she was assigned to the WAC Training Center. As stated in chapter 3, Major Adams replied to allegations of racial discrimination in several facilities at Fort Des Moines and in the classroom with the declaration that she had found no racial discrimination as a result of her investigation.[25] When she was free from the direct rule of a white male commandant, however, Major Adams could take a more active position against racial inequality. She was the battalion commander of her unit, and thus had the liberty that was not available to her at Fort Des Moines because her reality had changed.

Although most of the women interviewed for this study viewed the resocialization process in basic training as different from what they had known, and even sometimes as challenging, they most often remembered their life-altering experiences in England and France. The royal treatment members of the 6888th describe receiving from the British not only boosted their morale, but also enhanced the self-concept of individual members. Bertha Solomon Walker says, "We realized that we had self-worth, a right to be proud and dignified. We wanted people abroad to know that we were proud to be black women, and carried ourselves as such."[26] In Europe they were no longer treated as second-class citizens. Through this experience members of the 6888th gained a new perspective on themselves. Many of the respondents had greater expectations of themselves when they left the military than when they entered the service.

How Far We've Come, How Far We've Got to Go

Some of the African American women who remained in the military after the war missed the camaraderie they had experienced in the 6888th. Frustrated by the marginal status they acquired in desegregated units, some African American women said that in some respects, they preferred serving in a race- and gender- segregated unit. Bernice Thomas recalls the discomfort experienced by African American women when the Army was first desegregated:

When the Army was desegregated, a lot of the women [who had previously served in the 6888th] were sorry. They felt better and more comfortable with just being all Afro-Americans. They didn't care about being integrated. Some of my friends said when they got up in the mornings, when we were all together, before the integration . . . they would put on their radios, they would be dancing and singing, and just having a good time. Whereas they felt that when we were integrated they couldn't do that. And another thing that some of my friends were concerned about was that when they straightened their hair, or washed their hair, they didn't want the white girls to see them. . . . You know, we've always had this thing about hair, and that was one thing that annoyed them. . . . It's just like when I was in Harlem. I never knew that I was culturally deprived until someone came into Harlem and told me I was culturally deprived. I was very happy in my little ghetto in Harlem.

Solidarity among African American Wacs began to unravel during the early period of racial desegregation of the armed forces. Changing the focus to white Wacs, desegregation forced black Wacs to either conform to the dominant rule (behave in a way deemed appropriate by white superordinates) or suppress their behavior (be silenced). In the process, the African American Wac, in relation to her white counterpart, was often deprived socially, politically, and culturally; she was expected to fit the Eurocentric image (in regard to religious orientation, style of dress, taste in music, hair style, cuisine, and so on) that dominated all American institutions.

This feeling of powerlessness on the part of African American Wacs has been assuaged in more recent years as racial and gender integration has become more of a reality in the armed services. When asked "What do you think would be most surprising to women serving in the armed services today about your experience on active duty?" (see Item 36, Appendix B), several former members of the 6888th replied as Edith Tyrell did: "Well, the way I look at it, today they've got it made. They're not segregated, and they can probably move up [in rank] faster." Indeed, the armed forces today are not only racially integrated but also integrated by gender. In more recent years the armed services have expanded their boundaries, allowing women to compete for all military occupations except those involving direct combat.

The number of African American women serving in the military declined sharply after World War II, as did the number of military women in general. In December 1946 the strength of the Women's Army Corps had fallen to 9,655; it did not exceed 12,000 again until 1970, when the number of women in the armed services began to soar.[27] Table 4 shows the drop in the number of black Wacs from 2,532 in 1943 to 319 in 1947. Also shown in table 4

Table 4. African American Women in the Army from 1943 to 1993

Year	Number of Officers	Number of Enlisted	Total Number	Percent of All Women in the Army
1943	65	2,467	2,532	5.7
1947	9	310	319	3.9
1951	30	1,015	1,045	8.7
1955	29	954	983	11.4
1959	27	1,015	1,042	12.1
1973	56	3,184	3,240	18.2
1977	236	11,293	11,529	23.7
1981	1,144	27,185	28,329	38.7
1985	1,872	28,979	30,851	39.3
1989	2,236	34,855	37,091	43.3
1993	2,048	28,819	30,867	43.9

SOURCES: Mattie Treadwell, *The Women's Army Corps*, 777; Bettie Morden, *The Women's Army Corps 1945-1978*, 409-410, 415; Defense Manpower Data Center, Washington, D.C.
NOTE: There were no statistics maintained on black personnel from 1961-1971.

is that from 1970 to 1989 the number of African American women in the Army has been continually increasing.

In the 1970s, for the first time in American history, the percentage of African American women on active duty increased more rapidly than that of white women (the percentage of African American men also increased rapidly). While the number of women on active duty in general increased threefold from 1973 to 1979 the percentage of African American women increased fivefold.[28] This unprecedented expansion in the representation of African American women is in stark contrast to the underrepresentation of African American women in the military during and immediately following World War II (see table 4). In 1943 African American women comprised 5.7 percent of all women in the Army; by 1993 their percentage had soared to 43.9 percent. Major factors leading to this expansion were the end of the draft and the subsequent decline in the participation rate of middle-class white males. With the onset of the all-volunteer force in 1975, military organizations began to heavily recruit minorities and women in an effort to help meet personnel goals. This was especially true in 1979, when the Army fell short of its manpower objective.[29]

It appears that efforts to expand opportunities for African

American women in the military during World War II were not in vain. Today, as in the World War II period, there is a heavy concentration of African American women in the U.S. Army. Over the last decade, however, the proportion of black enlisted women in the Army has decreased as their proportion has increased in the Navy. Current data support Edith Tyrell's assumption that African American women are making rank more rapidly. While the percentage of African American women in lower pay grades (E1-E4; private through corporal) is declining, it is increasing at higher pay grades (E5-E8; sergeant through master sergeant). The percentage of African American women in pay grades O1-O3 (second lieutenant through captain) has been relatively stable (at 5 or 6 percent) over the years, but representation has increased among O4s (majors) from 0.2 percent in 1980 to 1.0 percent in 1990 and has remained at that level.

The expansion of military personnel boundaries to include African American women reflects both conflict and collective action. Examples in this book illustrate that African American women sometimes succeeded in their struggle for equal rights. When these acts of resistance were successful, the result was often a redefinition of norms. African American women's entry into the Army during World War II and their subsequent deployment to the European Theater of Operations marked a significant breakthrough in their opportunities to serve in the military. The disproportionately large numbers of African American women in the armed services suggests that the military offers them greater employment opportunities than do institutions in the civilian sector.

Still, the overrepresentation of African Americans in the military has raised some ethical and political concerns. One concern is that the disproportionately large black participation in the military would discourage white participation. Some people have argued that as the number of black military personnel increases, the number of whites may be expected to decrease.[30] Because of this country's ambivalent attitudes toward African Americans, social groups such as organizations, neighborhoods, and schools have been devalued erroneously when the proportion of African Americans increases. This was not the case, however, with the U.S. military, which had begun to lose white male enrollment even before the number of African Americans increased. The increased enrollment of African Americans was an effect and not a cause of the refusal of white middle-class men to serve on active duty. During the 1970s and 1980s African Americans in general, and African American women in particular, were joining the military in disproportionately large numbers because they were doing a job that other segments of the population did not want to do.

On the other hand, some observers espouse the counterargument that the overrepresentation of African Americans in the American armed forces is not a cause for alarm, but should be applauded because it is a superior alternative to being unemployed and homeless. Several arguments supporting the overrepresentation of African Americans in the military followed this line of reasoning in the 1970s and 1980s.[31] Although these views appeared to advocate sound remedies to unemployment in the short term, they neglected the fundamental issue of choice. Should unemployment be the only choice open to African Americans in general and African American women in particular, other than enlisting in the American armed services? What we are witnessing is too few career options available to African American women in the civilian sector. Given the recent efforts of the services (especially the Army) to reduce personnel, it is unlikely that the military will continue to be a career opportunity for a disproportionately large number of African American women.

★ ★ ★

Epilogue

They're fantastic! They're breaking all of the rules; they have their lonnnggg cigarettes, their drinks; and they're talking about not being able to walk but they still do everything. They really have a fantastic spirit.

—Lorraine West

Birmingham Revisited

In April 1981 a few former members of the 6888th took a nostalgic trip back to England and France. In Birmingham they were greeted by the lord mayor, Councillor Joseph Bailey, who gave a reception in their honor. After having lunch with city officials, they were given a tour of Birmingham. Essie Woods declares, "We were treated royally. . . . They rolled out the red carpet for us; we just weren't expecting all that."[1] The women were also met by British diplomats in London; the events they attended are described in a newspaper article: "They lunched with Lord Mayor Colonel Sir Ronald Gardner-Thorpe and Brigadier Director Anne Fields, the head of the Women's Royal Army Corps in London. Later they dined with Edwina Coven, Deputy Chairman Magistrate of London and member of the Court of Common Council.[2] Dorothy Bartlett reports that they also visited France on their trip: "In a few words it was lovely, and I enjoyed it. We went not only to England, but we went also to France while we were there. Everyone was lovely to us." Lavinia Johnson recalls:

We were very well received and welcomed. In England we had a wonderful time. We visited the old King Edward School in Birmingham where we were once billeted, and they really received us very well. We went to Paris—we didn't get to Rouen, where we were also stationed, but we did go to Paris, and we had a very nice time there. They had planned a wonderful guided tour of the city. We had time to shop, and we had time to take a boat ride down the Seine.

Reuniting

Today, fifty years after the unit was founded, many members of the 6888th stay in touch and participate in reunions. In 1979 Mary Rozier organized a reunion of all former members of the 6888th Central Postal Directory Battalion, which was held at Stouffer's Cincinnati Towers. In subsequent years many of the members participated, and continue to participate, in the Black WAAC-WAC Women in the Services Biennial Reunions. The fact that some of the unit's members continue to write each other and to attend reunions more than fifty years after the war suggests that the group indeed was cohesive.

The very first Black Wac Reunion was organized by a group of African American women veterans who had served in the military during and shortly after World War II and was held in Texas in 1981. Charity Adams Earley was the guest speaker of the sixth reunion, in New York City in 1988. Since the late 1980s these reunions have included African American women in the contemporary armed services. The meetings, which usually last four to eight days, begin with registration and an informal social hour. On the evening of the first day a welcoming reception is generally held. Each of the following days begins with a breakfast; the schedule usually includes time to discuss business, as well as several tours to major attractions of the city where the conference occurs. Each reunion features a formal banquet with a guest speaker and ends with a candlelight memorial service for the African American women veterans who have died since the last reunion.

I attended the eighth biennial reunion in Orlando, Florida, in September 1992. The reunion was scheduled for eight days: four days at the luxurious Stouffer Resort in Orlando and four aboard the cruise ship *Carnival*. The event began with the usual registration, including packets with mementos, a souvenir journal, knitted coasters, various advertisements, and several knick-knacks. The first evening ended with a jubilant welcoming reception, complete with a dance band.

On the following day, after breakfast in one of the restaurants at the hotel, we held a business meeting. I was introduced as a new member, having served in the military for six years in the 1970s, and as a professor doing research on the 6888th. After the meeting several former members of the 6888th approached the table where I sat and introduced themselves.

On the evening of the third day a formal banquet was held in one of the ballrooms at the hotel. The guest speaker was an African American woman who had just retired from the Army as a sergeant first class after twenty years of service. Brig. Gen. Clara L. Adams-Ender, a veteran of thirty-two years and the first woman to be awarded the Expert Field Medical Badge, also spoke.

The four days at the Stouffer ended with a candlelight memorial, during which one of the members played "Taps" on the harmonica. Another member read the names of fifty-three African American women veterans who had died, including the three black women who were killed in the line of duty during the Gulf War. Although some of us did not board the *Carnival* with the rest of the group, I received word that they had a wonderful time.

★ ★ ★

Appendix A

★ ★ ★

Interviewees

	Birthplace	Interviews by Author
Mattie Jackson Allen	Sycamore, Ill.	Fort McClellan, Ala., 30 May 1992
Gladys Thomas Anderson	Shreveport, La.	Fort McClellan, Ala., 14 May 1992
Margaret Barbour	Seaford, Va.	Los Angeles, 14 June 1992
Tessie O'Bryant Barr	Augusta, Ga.	Ecorse, Mich., 29 May 1992
Dorothy A. Gee Bartlett	Newark, N.J.	Detroit, 27 May 1992, 16 October 1994
Sadie Moore Belcher	Atlanta, Ga.	Mattapan, Mass., 12 January 1991
Elaine Smith Bennett	Madison, Fla.	Cambridge, Md., 30 May 1992
Dorothy Hutchins Carter	Portsmouth, Va.	Baltimore, 1 May 1994
Gladys Schuster Carter	Brooklyn, N.Y.	Orlando, Fla., 25 September 1992
Enid Clark	Boston, Mass.	Daly City, Calif., 27 May 1992

	Birthplace	Interviews by Author
Cleopatra Evans Cohn	Memphis, Tenn.	Tulsa, 25 July 1993
Allie Love Davis	Colbert, Okla.	Colbert, Okla., 28 March 1993
Sammye Trail Davis	Cottage Grove, Ala.	Los Angeles, 6, 12 June 1992
Vernelle Hannah Davis	Savannah, Ga.	Fort McClellan, Ala., 16 May 1992
Charity E. Adams Earley	Columbia, S.C.	Arlington, Va., 6, 10 June 1992
Elizabeth Patterson Eastman	Nashville, Tenn.	Los Angeles, 21 June 1992
Dorothy Ellis	Carver, Ill.	Chicago, 26 October 1994
Bernadine Frazier Flannagan	Key West, Fla.	New London, Conn., 31 October 1994
Evelyn Fray	Brooklyn, N.Y.	Jamaica, N.Y., 23 March 1993
Virginia Lane Frazier	Minneapolis, Minn.	San Jose, Calif., 30 March, 29 July 1993
Ruth Hammond	Louisville, Ky.	Roxbury, Mass., 12 January 1991
Margaret Jackson	Selma, Ala.	Washington, D.C., 9 July 1993
Dorothy Johnson	Dubbin, Ga.	Orlando, Fla., 11 July 1993
Frances Pickett Johnson	St. Louis, Mo.	New Orleans, 25 October 1992
Lavinia Lowery Johnson	Sterling, Kans.	Fort McClellan, Ala., 14 May 1992; Detroit, 16 October 1994
Dorothy Dailey Jones	Richmond, Va.	Sommerville, Mass., 30 October 1994

	Birthplace	Interviews by Author
Margaret Barnes Jones	Oberlin, Ohio	Alexandria, Va., 30 May 1992; Orlando, Fla., 16, 25 September 1992
Gertrude Cruse LaVigne	Jacksonville, Ala.	Anchorage, 23 January 1991
Mildred Dupee Leonard	Charleston, W.V.	Detroit, 3 June 1992
Odessa Taylor Marshall	Stanton, Tenn.	Los Angeles, 6 June 1992
Mary McBride	Chicago, Ill.	Chicago, 8 May 1992
Lucille Johnson McJimpsey	Washington, D.C.	Washington, D.C., 22 February 1991
A. Noel Campbell Mitchell	Tuskegee, Ala.	Tuskegee, Ala., 12 January 1991, 30 January, 2 February 1992
Elsie Oliver	Burkeville, Va.	Boston, 1 April 1991, 12 November 1993
Christine Stone Pinkney	Washington, D.C.	Washington, D.C., 2 June 1992
Ardella Pitts	Augusta, Ga.	Washington, D.C., 22 May 1992
Mary Crawford Ragland	Atlanta, Ga.	Washington, D.C., 19 August 1993
Myrtle Rhoden	New York, N.Y.	Orlando, Fla., 25 September 1992; Charlotte, N.C., 12 November 1993
Mary Rozier	Danville, Ky.	Cincinnati, 18 January 1991
Blanche Scott	Boydton, Va.	Alexandria, Va., 19 January 1991

	Birthplace	Interviews by Author
Kitty Bowden Smith	Hampton, Va.	South Bend, Ind., 22 February 1991
Anna M. Tarryk	Brooklyn, N.Y.	Philadelphia, 19 July 1993
Janyce Stovall Taylor	Philadelphia, Pa.	Philadelphia, 3 March 1993
Bernice Thomas	New York, N.Y.	Berkeley, Calif., 30 July 1993
Edith Armstrong Tyrell	New York, N.Y.	St. Albans, N.Y., 3 June 1992
Ruth Wade	Jackson, Tenn.	Detroit, 6 July 1993
Johnnie Walton	Hempsted, Tex.	Hempsted, Tex., 19 July 1993
Willie Whiting	Chicago, Ill.	Chicago, 6 May 1992
Mary Daniels Williams	Cleveland, Ohio	Cincinnati, 18 January 1991, 19 June 1993
Essie O'Bryant Woods	Augusta, Ga.	Detroit, 3 June 1992
Ruth Jefferson Wright	Yellow Springs, Ohio	Orlando, Fla., 26 September 1992

★ ★ ★

Appendix B

★ ★ ★

Survey of Members of the 6888th Central Postal Directory Battalion*

Veteran's Name _____

Date of Birth _____ .

Rank & Position Held with 6888th _____

_____

Current Address _____

_____

Telephone Number _____

Today's Date _____

Questions for Women Who Served in the 6888th

Let's Talk about Your Life before Military Service

1. Would you briefly describe your life before you entered the military? For example:

   a. Where were you born? _____

   b. Did you live with your biological parents or other relatives when you were a child? _____

   c. How many brothers and sisters did you have? _____

---

*This survey was prepared by Dr. Brenda L. Moore, Department of Sociology, State University of New York at Buffalo, Buffalo, N.Y. 14260. The information received from respondents will be used only for the study of women in the military.

    d. What type of work did your parents do? _____

_____

    e. Would you describe your family as being closely knit?_____;
       Please explain: _____

_____

    f. Where did you live before entering the military and what was life
      like for a young woman of African descent there? _____

_____

    g. How many years of education did you complete before going into
      the military? _____

    h. What was your occupation before going into the military? _____
    i. Did you receive special training for the work you did before
      joining the military? _____

    j. What was your marital status when you entered the military? ___
    k. Additional comments: _____

_____

2. What were some of the reasons that you joined the military?

_____

3. How old were you when you went into the military? _____

4. Where were you inducted into the military? _____

5. What years were you on active duty? _____

6. Did you marry while you were on active duty? _____

7. Did you have any dependents other than yourself while you were on
   active _____

8. Where did you go for basic training? _____

9. After basic training were you trained in a specific military occupation? _____ If yes, which occupational field were you trained
   in _____
   and where _____

10. Describe your experiences at your basic training station and at your
    advanced training station. For example:
    a. To what extent were active duty women separated from active

duty men (did they house, socialize, eat and work in separate facilities)? _____

   b. To what extent were active duty black women separated from active duty white women (did they house, socialize, eat, and work in separate facilities)? _____

   c. Additional comments: _____

11. Where was your permanent duty station after military training?

_____

12. What occupation were you assigned to at your permanent duty station? _____

13. Briefly describe your experiences at your permanent duty station. For example:

   a. To what extent were active duty women separated from active duty men (did they house, socialize, eat, and work in separate facilities)? _____

   b. To what extent were active duty black women separated from active duty white women (did they house, socialize, eat, and work in separate facilities)? _____

   c. Additional comments: _____

14. Did you personally experience racial or gender discrimination in the military? _____ If the answer is yes, then describe how you were discriminated against and how you coped with discrimination.

_____

Let's Talk about Your Experiences with the Six-Triple-Eight

15. Describe the training that the group received to prepare for overseas duty. _____

_____

16. How were you treated by white United States military personnel when you were in England and France during the war?

_____

17. How were you treated by African American men in uniform when you were overseas during World War II? _____

18. How were you treated by the British and the French while you were overseas during World War II? _____

19. What social activities were available to members of the 6888th; did you take advantage of those activities? _____
_____

20. What are some of the things that you and your friends overseas shared in common? _____
_____

21. Briefly describe the type of work you did when you were assigned to the 6888th. _____
_____

22. What were some of the difficulties, if any, in carrying out the assigned duties of the 6888th? _____
_____

23. What was morale like among the members of the 6888th? _____
If morale was high, then what kinds of things did members of the 6888th do to keep their spirits high? _____
_____

24. Were rewards, such as promotions, and punishments, such as dismissals, distributed fairly within the 6888th Battalion? _____
Please explain. _____

25. In your opinion, how did the 6888th perform as a unit? _____

26. Do you have a scrap book of your military experiences while you were assigned to the 6888th? _____ If yes, may I make arrangements to look at it? _____

Let's Discuss What It Was Like When You Reentered the Civilian World

27. Did your military service help you to advance educationally and/or occupationally? _____ Please explain. _____
_____

28. Have you received a college degree and/or vocational certificate since you left the military? _____ What is your highest level of education? _____

29. a. What were some of the jobs you held when you were discharged from the Army? _____

    b. If you are not currently employed, what was the title of your most recent job? _____

    c. Briefly describe what type of work you did. _____

    _____

30. Have you participated in any form of community service or volunteer work since you left the military? _____

31. Do you feel that your military experience was a turning point in your life? _____ If yes, how? _____
What were some [other] turning points in your life? _____

    _____

32. What are (were) some personal benefits from being a former military person? _____

33. What are (were) some personal disadvantages for having served in the United States military? _____

34. Do you think that your service experience would have been different had you been of European descent? _____ Please explain.

    _____

35. Were training experiences in the military helpful in your subsequent work career? _____

36. What do you think would be most surprising to women serving in the armed services today about your experience on active duty?

    _____

37. What does citizenship mean to you? _____

38. Have you ever had a reunion with women of the 6888th? _____

39. Over the years have you received G.I. benefits for education? _____
Did you earn a degree with G.I. benefits? _____

40. Over the years have you received G.I. benefits for buying a house?

    _____

41. Over the years have you received G.I. benefits for health care? _____
42. Considering the most influential events in your life, where would you place military service as an influence on the person you are now? [least influential = 1, most influential = 10] _____
43. Do you have any problems today that are due to your military service such as nightmares, depression, nervousness, and the like?

_____

44. Are you willing to speak candidly about sexual orientation among unit members? _____ If yes,
    a. Were there lesbians in the unit? _____ If yes,
    b. Was there any tension in the unit due to the presence of lesbians?
    c. Were lesbians treated unfairly because of their sexual orientation? _____
    d. Was the mission of the 6888th impaired because of the presence of lesbians? _____

★ ★ ★

Appendix C

★ ★ ★

Roster Containing Names, Ranks, and Serial Numbers of 742 6888th Members

Compiled from SO #89 (3/30/45), SO #18 (5/30/45), and SO #84 (10/12/45), Personnel Records Office, St. Louis, Mo.

Officers (31)

*MAJ Charity E. Adams, L201378
*CAPT Abbie N. Campbell, L402518
CAPT Mildred E. Carter, L115021
CAPT Vera A. Harrison, L500024
CAPT Mary F. Kearney, L125005
*1ST LT Margaret F. Barnes, L500995
1ST LT Doris N. Cable, L500022
1ST LT Willa Cherry, L600718
*1ST LT Mildred V. Dupee, L500418
1ST LT Fannie A. Griffin, L200109
1ST LT Bernice G. Henderson, L501504
1ST LT Violet Hill, L600015

ST LT Catherine G. Landry, L303726
*1ST LT Blanche L. Scott, L303576
1ST LT Dorothy H. Scott, L600932
1ST LT Corrie S. Sherard, L402006
1ST LT Ella B. Tatum, L800726
1ST LT Vashti B. Tonkins, L308032
1ST LT Julia H. Williams, L402781
2ND LT Hazel E. Craddock, L702373
2ND LT Lillian Duncan, L402584
2ND LT Alice E. Edwards, L900401
2ND LT Bertie M. Edwards, L204945
2ND LT Vivian N. Elzie, L304676
2ND LT Frances Flatts, L201378

Note: Only forty-two of the interviewees are listed in this roster. Their names are designated by an asterisk (*).

219

2ND LT Merceedees A. Jordan,
  L200271
2ND LT Elfreda S. LeBeau, L801480
2ND LT Calonia V. Powell,
  L801525

2ND LT Julia A. Rich, L3108863
2ND LT Gussye D. Stewart,
  L1000500
2ND LT Aubrey A. Stokes,
  L1000267

Enlisted (711)

M Sgt Tommie Berry, A701216
1st Sgt Cleopatra Daniels, A402507
T Sgt Mary Buster, A306772
S Sgt Catherine Brown, A1000026
S Sgt Juanita Goodloe, A802450
S Sgt Marseleana Goodwin,
  A202561
S Sgt Norene Harris, A501428
S Sgt Jerreli Lawrence, A801977
S Sgt Annie Lawson, A804644
S Sgt Fannie Little, A411035
S Sgt Ruby McClung, A821203
S Sgt Ina McRae, A201008
S Sgt Gertrude Rose, A202729
*S Sgt Elaine Smith, A407644
S Sgt Amanda Thomas, A504193
S Sgt Birdie Tillman, A805807
S Sgt Eunice Williams, A30546
Tec 3 Mattie Garrett, A200465
Sgt Dolores Browne, A125448
Sgt Gladys Brumfield, A402493
Sgt Lillian Butterfield, A221376
Sgt Gladys Clayton, A400889
Sgt Rhode Daniel, A305985
Sgt Liddie Duncan, A805258
Sgt Mary Ebo, A216143
Sgt Erma Fifer, A610839
Sgt Dolores Gray, A310877
Sgt Gertrude Hall, A1000577
Sgt Rosa Harris, A405639

*Sgt Mattie Jackson, A1000778
Sgt Anne Johnson, A400401
Sgt Cecelia Kelly, A303728
Sgt Catherine King, A305097
Sgt Marion Lawrence, A308639
Sgt Lucille Lewis, A809804
Sgt Vivian Mazyck, A401149
Sgt Ruby McClung, A811203
Sgt Stella Patillo, A305004
Sgt Louisa Penny, A308725
Sgt Annie Reed, A409015
Sgt Bernyce Scott, A504567
Sgt Sallie Smith, A505286
Sgt Pettie Smith, A701698
Sgt Vernie Smith, A706540
Sgt Dorothy Tabb, A811417
*Sgt Bernice Thomas, A207239
Sgt Marcell Wilson, A308685
Sgt Alice Woodson, A514090
Sgt Ruth Wyatt, A504247
Sgt Vivian Young, A302520
Tec4 Alice Allison, A309816
Tec4 Annetta Batiste, A801376
Tec4 Addie Campbell, A412031
Tec4 Mamie Doss, A602952
Tec4 Mercelene Fairgood, A402896
Tec4 Marilyn Gill, A501492
Tec4 Creadell Haley, A600988
Tec4 Minnie Lackey, A401593
Tec4 Maggie Latta, A405509

Tec4 Edith Linzey, A220147
Tec4 Ethel Loving, A202800
Tec4 Evelyn Martin, A217520
Tec4 Alma Minter, A1000171
Tec4 Mattie Moorhead, A900530
Tec4 Lucia Pitts, A611207
Tec4 Bessie Robinson, A203485
Tec4 Florence Scales, A708141
Tec4 Myke Smith, A309576
Tec4 Rose Stuart, A810379
*Tec4 Odessa Taylor, A700125
Cpl Love Anderson, A310893
Cpl Bernice A. Augustine, A201979
Cpl Lena Bell, A311607
Cpl Theresa Bell, A804902
Cpl Jennetta Blythe, A501724
Cpl Alberta O'Bradley, A703466
Cpl Lucille Brooks, A407036
Cpl Marjorie Brown, A205281
Cpl Theodore Bryant, A203273
Cpl Irma Campbell, A1000142
Cpl Irene Carr, A308711
Cpl Edith Carter, A225360
Cpl Virgie Caywood, A811464
Cpl Alberta Coleman, A521353
Cpl Susan Crabtree, A1000523
Cpl Bennye Daniels, A514024
Cpl Elizabeth DeWitt, A506395
Cpl Daisy Dinkins, A1000448
Cpl Blanche Logan, A502315
Cpl Lorener Ford, A125926
Cpl Jessie Godboldte, A311412
Cpl Martha Goddard, A402423
Cpl Flora Grace, A401833
*Cpl Ruth Hammond, A521686
Cpl Constance Hernandez, A116907
Cpl Louise Heyward, A1000989
Cpl Florine Hill, A402424

Cpl Dorothy Howard, A801979
Cpl Madelyn Hudgins, A607157
Cpl Edna Jackson, A201374
Cpl Jewell Jackson, A805611
Cpl Mary Jackson, A303164
*Cpl Ruth Jefferson, A521463
Cpl Hazel Jennings, A308435
Cpl Willie Jewett, A802393
Cpl Willene Johnson, A221001
*Cpl Virginia Lane, A1000261
Cpl Marion Mackey, A400874
Cpl Eddye Maddox, A603277
Cpl Charlotte McCullum, A813214
Cpl Pearline McKell, A700480
Cpl Elizabeth Moore, A315627
Cpl Jennie Moton, A308787
Cpl Mable Nevels, A703222
Cpl Lucie Ownes, A203130
Cpl Alma Philpot, A318880
*Cpl Frances Pickett, A805093
Cpl Elouise Pinkney A407085
Cpl Louise Reid, A206104
Cpl Ruth Riddick, A308441
Cpl Florida Robey, A810448
Cpl Gertrude Sessoms, A700152
Cpl Dannie Singleton, A400894
Cpl Callie Smith, A202929
*Cpl Christine Stone, A1000731
Cpl Helen Streibling, A300075
Cpl Jennie Turner, A314000
*Cpl Johnnie Walton, A810521
Cpl Clara Webb, A514056
Cpl Lauretta Wray, A225408
Tec5 Henrietta Adam, A521739
Tec5 Amelia Akers, A309794
Tec5 Luvenia Allen, A409654
Tec5 Novella Auls, A408560
Tec5 Adeline Bell, A311275

Tec5 Betty Bowen, A605088
Tec5 Annie Braceful, A600761
Tec5 Ora Bragg, A900714
Tec5 Ruth Brown, A801836
Tec5 Edna Burton, A400907
Tec5 Gloria Carr, A605072
Tec5 Beverly Carrington, A117157
Tec5 Dare Charlet, A804888
Tec5 Florence Cole, A802390
Tec5 Madeleine Coleman, A201548
Tec5 Dorothy Cox, A701277
*Tec5 Gertrude Cruse, A501299
*Tec5 Mary Daniels, A501161
Tec5 Millie Dunn, A400399
Tec5 Evelyn Eiland, A610840
Tec5 Isabella Evans, A303948
Tec5 Vernice Evans, A811139
Tec5 Bessie Foster, A409162
Tec5 Christel George, A402897
Tec5 Arena Glover, A305354
Tec5 Cecilia Goldsby, A605196
Tec5 Helen Gould, A1000848
Tec5 Marie Hairston, A521700
Tec5 Nellie Harmon, A506477
Tec5 Velma Hayes, A504876
Tec5 Loraine Hinton, A610838
Tec5 Luella Holbert, A705166
Tec5 Helen Holmes, A309965
Tec5 Ernestine Hughes, A802081
*Tec5 Dorothy Hutchins, A308501
Tec5 Emma Jacobs, A811603
Tec5 Frances Jefferson, A308941
Tec5 Catherine Johnson, A506741
Tec5 Martha Johnson, A805133
Tec5 Elaine Jones, A304692
Tec5 Annie Lawson, A804664
Tec5 Katherine Lee, A308604
Tec5 Ruth Lottier, A504401

Tec5 Jeanette Martin, A506038
Tec5 Geneva McRae, A203795
Tec5 Mary Medley, A309573
Tec5 Lottie Mills, A204214
Tec5 Mary Monroe, A300355
Tec5 Mildred Montgomery,
   A810483
Tec5 Mary Moody, A202979
Tec5 Jeanetta Moorhead, A402782
Tec5 Georgiana Morton, A220573
Tec5 Ruby O'Brien, A903999
*Tec5 Essie O'Bryant, A407096
Tec5 Mablyne Ortiz, A800447
Tec5 Doris Paige, A401672
*Tec5 Elizabeth Patterson, A604947
Tec5 Golda Patton, A701697
Tec5 Jewel Rettig, A802395
*Tec5 Myrtle Rhoden, A202597
Tec5 Velma Riddick, A205575
Tec5 Beulah Robinson, A204490
Tec5 Hazel Russell, A500240
Tec5 Edna Sanders, A205891
Tec5 Lerah Saunders, A521731
Tec5 Annett Simmons, A801309
Tec5 Henrie Smith, A407083
Tec5 Mary Smith, A403402
Tec5 Thelma Smith, A500774
Tec5 Doris Stewart, A200575
Tec5 Viola Suarez, A900467
Tec5 Fannie Talbert, A1001102
Tec5 Georgia Tivis, A701225
Tec5 Mary Walker, A205855
Tec5 Hazel Washington, A701334
Tec5 Lelia Watkins, A500624
Tec5 Essie Watts, A411037
Tec5 Shirley Wearye, A605051
Tec5 Theada Woddle, A708110
Tec5 Leola Wheat, A402221

Tec5 Valma White, A801043
Tec5 Allie Williams, A805882
Tec5 Dorothy Williams, A306833
Tec5 Bessie Willis, A602989
Tec5 Levonia Woodward, A602177
Tec5 Edna Zeigler, A805860
Pfc Bettie Albert, A610214
Pfc Sallie Alexander, A410759
Pfc Dorothy Allen, A308648
Pfc Hazel Allen, A807863
Pfc Margie Amis, A204283
Pfc Margaret Anderson, A204577
Pfc Velma Arkward, A221522
Pfc Ella Armstrong, A607647
Pfc Mary Artist, A311186
Pfc Gladys Avant, A221561
Pfc Alva Bacote, A1000600
Pfc Myrtle Baker, A403253
Pfc Mary Bankston, A207949
*Pfc Margaret Barbour, A315589
Pfc Elizabeth Barker, A405619
Pfc Crinne Barksdale, A409653
Pfc Geraldine Beaumont, A606275
Pfc Laura Bias, A135193
Pfc Bridget Bivens, A514180
*Pfc Kitty Bowden, A308745
Pfc Hettie Boyce, A504245
Pfc Herlene Bradsher, A407171
Pfc Phyllis Branch, A200736
Pfc Lillie Bratcher, A308458
Pfc Emma Brock, A501807
Pfc Dorothy Brown, A412535
Pfc Susie Brown, A505144
Pfc Vivian Brown, A507110
Pfc Louise Bruce, A409668
Pfc Vyvyanne Bugg, A312834
Pfc Annie Burrell, A409668
Pfc Lillian Cabbell, A204633

Pfc Marcella Canty, A207184
Pfc Arlethea Cawthorne, A521851
Pfc Frances Cephas, A1009347
Pfc Freddie Chinn, A819002
*Pfc Enid Clark, A1000952
Pfc Elizabeth Colbert, A803272
Pfc Arjean Conner, A610312
Pfc Elizabeth Cornwell, A311028
Pfc Beatrice Cosey, A406704
Pfc Anna Couch, A603173
Pfc Minnie Cross, A521978
Pfc Violet Dabney, A310456
*Pfc Dorothy Dailey, A117722
Pfc Ruth Daniels, A204472
Pfc Elsie Dannals, A307560
Pfc Naomi Davenport, A306939
Pfc Elizabeth Davis, A408712
Pfc Ella Davis, A811060
Pfc Mary Davis, A406379
Pfc Gladys Debman, A221879
Pfc Olive Dedeaux, A1000147
Pfc Addie Demby, A310444
Pfc Rosa Diggs, A308775
Pfc Alyce Dixon, A1000656
Pfc Harriett Douglas, A205741
Pfc Althea Dunn, A804601
Pfc Sophie Easterling, A401673
Pfc Marguerite Ellis, A810420
Pfc Edith Ellison, A1001455
Pfc Marian Elzie, A305924
*Pfc Cleopatra Evans, A403197
Pfc Ophelia Ewings, A306782
Pfc Jennie Fayson, A408149
Pfc Beula Fant, A705471
Pfc Jessie Faulk, A406090
Pfc Annie Finley, A303039
Pfc Vivian Fitzsimmons, A505111
Pfc Edna Fletcher, A401547

*Pfc Evelyn Fray, A206538
*Pfc Bernadine Frazier, A125431
Pfc Polly Frazier, A917880
Pfc Jacqueline Fuller, A604673
Pfc Winona Fuller, A604888
Pfc Ruth Gaddy, A400088
Pfc Edith Gaskill, A1000367
Pfc Sarah Gary, A1000429
Pfc Mildred Gates, A607776
Pfc Marie Gillisslee, A202680
Pfc Elsie Givens, A1000020
Pfc Hester Givens, A221304
Pfc Bernice Grant, A297786
Pfc Callie Grant, A6107748
Pfc Mattie Gray, A403338
Pfc Thelma Green, A310349
Pfc Irene Greene, A408557
Pfc Mary Greens, A205981
Pfc Mattie Griffin, A800974
Pfc Annie Grimes, A811184
Pfc Marion Grundy, A305363
Pfc Lucile Hairston, A405620
Pfc Dolly Hall, A205722
Pfc Jesse Hall, A901239
Pfc Margaret Hampton, A696002
*Pfc Vernelle Hannah, A407033
Pfc Audrey Harris, A1305527
Pfc Julia Harris, A221773
Pfc Lillie Harrison, A303982
Pfc Mabel Haskin, A409005
Pfc Vivian Hayden, A501458
Pfc Vernese Hayes, A410583
Pfc Helen Henderson, A308796
Pfc Geraldine Herndon, A703144
Pfc Mary Hill, A809835
Pfc Mildred Hooper, A808517
Pfc Willie House, A412955
Pfc Bernice Hugger, A605548

Pfc Sadie Huff, A406308
Pfc Cora Hurston, A406225
Pfc Anna Jackson, A701376
Pfc Ella Jackson, A810117
Pfc Elvire Jackson, A1000990
Pfc Marion Jackson, A125674
Pfc Novella Jackson, A401308
Pfc Ruth Jacobs, A1001395
Pfc Evangeline Jeffrey, A203159
Pfc Hessie Johnson, A310404
Pfc Philista Johnson, A611639
Pfc Lillian Jones, A202784
Pfc Elizabeth Lamb, A407776
Pfc Juanita Lane, A608852
Pfc Catherine Lee, A810279
Pfc Hattie Lee, A203958
Pfc Theodosia Lee, A803132
Pfc Evelyn LeSuerer, A318533
Pfc Bernice Lewis, A312253
Pfc Ruby Lipscomb, A401267
Pfc Sarah Longmire, A521979
Pfc Evelyn Lozi, A207180
Pfc Grace Lucas, A307019
Pfc Mary Maniece, A402777
Pfc Annie Mason, A407038
Pfc Vashti Matthews, A302920
Pfc Emily Mays, A204867
Pfc Maggie McClenton, A804028
Pfc Bette McDonald, A605566
Pfc Vernell McMillan, A221057
Pfc Elizabeth McNair, A125632
Pfc Julia McNeal, A301348
Pfc Susie Middlebrooks, A412646
Pfc Hylda Miller, A1000782
Pfc Ophelia Mills, A810308
Pfc Lethelma Moore, A604416
Pfc Marion Moore, A801481
Pfc Norma Moore, A206981

Pfc Beatrice Morris, A204172
Pfc Mamie Lewis, A202986
Pfc Mary McClain, A813227
Pfc Almota Morrison, A804648
Pfc Carrie Nelson, A501380
Pfc Normal Niblet, A805260
Pfc Emily Noisette, A302872
Pfc Hazel Norman, A506207
Pfc Helen Norris, A605047
*Pfc Tessie O'Bryant, A407021
Pfc Evelena Odell, A703242
Pfc Thelma O'Kelly, A1001355
*Pfc Elsie Oliver, A117381
Pfc Essie O'Riley, A807606
Pfc Theodore Palmer, A202000
Pfc Kate Pate, A810164
Pfc Willa Perkins, A601171
Pfc Ethel Philyaw, A302778
Pfc Lucille Poindexter, A521317
Pfc Duray Prestwood, A521080
Pfc Thelma Purdy, A319699
Pfc Florence Radcliff, A605656
Pfc Farlene Reeves, A207542
Pfc Dorothy Reid, A1000946
Pfc Elouise Rice, A407279
Pfc Cora Richardson, A811661
Pfc Winnie Richardson, A801651
Pfc Dorothy Ringer, A505452
Pfc Aleese Robinson, A311249
Pfc Juanita Rogers, A318864
Pfc Mary Rose, A403399
Pfc Grace Ruffin, A308291
Pfc Girtie Seddler, A409004
Pfc Edna Samples, A604677
Pfc Lillian Showell, A217546
Pfc Minnie Sibbie, A409071
Pfc Margaret Simmons, A1001127
Pfc Helen S. Simmons, A708115

Pfc Rosalie Simmons, A405739
Pfc Virginia Singleton, A506412
Pfc Ann Smalls, A207665
Pfc Erma Smith, A810417
Pfc Florita Smith, A411097
Pfc Lucille Smith, A204208
Pfc Mabel Sneed, A805545
Pfc Hattie Steele, A521918
*Pfc Janyce Stovall, A311077
Pfc Naomi Studdard, A206953
Pfc Effie Sutton, A405546
Pfc Sarah Tabb, A521348
Pfc Menthie Talbert, A813215
*Pfc Anna Tarryk, A125895
Pfc Lyria Tate, A811276
Pfc Ermene Taylor, A407072
Pfc Sarah Taylor, A308723
*Pfc Gladys Thomas, A608577
Pfc Hazel Threadgill, A701597
Pfc Cordelia Tolliver, A514307
*Pfc Sammye Trail, A409883
Pfc Alva Truatt, A1000255
Pfc Bessie Turner, A406098
Pfc Marion Van Orkey, A221340
Pfc Alberta Washington, A504033
Pfc Malinda Washington, A804956
Pfc Lilla Waters, A507112
Pfc Virginia Watkins, A521293
Pfc Esther Wells, A522232
*Pfc Willie Whiting, A609042
Pfc Artelya Whitley, A115835
Pfc Emma Wilson, A319040
Pfc Annie Wimberley, A401591
Pfc Ethel Wingo, A405912
Pfc Heather Withers, A221374
Pfc Helen Wood, A201746
Pfc Hilda Wood, A318747
Pfc Myrtle Wright, A808174

Pfc Margaret Young, A702639
Pvt Leona Abrams, A817065
Pvt Blanche Albritton, A812117
Pvt Lubertha Alexander, A410498
Pvt Earnestine Allen, A309100
Pvt Joyce Anderson, A130460
Pvt Rose Anderson, A811668
Pvt Edith Armistad, A202252
Pvt Sylvia Armstrong, A407097
Pvt Bernice Axam, A222566
Pvt Lucille Balloon, A412327
Pvt Louisa Balls, A318786
Pvt Mary Barlow, A130463
Pvt Agnes Barnes, A1000466
Pvt Wilma Barnes, A905021
Pvt Dorothy Bartlett, A209505
Pvt Edna Bastin, A319166
Pvt Arleatha Battle, A1001683
Pvt Lillian Battle, A135413
Pvt Mamie Beard, A608837
Pvt Pearl Bennett, A504232
Pvt Carolyn Berry, A319130
Pvt Dorothy Birkhead, A225321
Pvt Clarice Blackett, A209569
Pvt Virginia Blake, A203037
Pvt Willamae Boatwright, A222610
Pvt Ruth Beggues, A401499
Pvt Bessie Booker, A807813
Pvt Erma Brady, A613036
Pvt Odessa Brake, A315527
Pvt Claudia Braxton, A507577
Pvt Eugenia Brown, A303409
Pvt Izona Brown, A812074
Pvt Lila Burt, A615436
Pvt Anna Bybee, A507784
Pvt Gladys Carter, A308602
Pvt Charlotte Cartwright, A311548
Pvt Effie Chambers, A409110

Pvt Frances Chappell, A314080
Pvt Maggie Chestang, A903245
Pvt Lela Cleggett, A409263
Pvt Mary Coleman, A308954
Pvt Willie Coleman, A408790
Pvt Gladys Collier, A926463
Pvt Arthurine Collins, A611757
Pvt Carmen Collins, A209638
Pvt Florence Collins, A311269
Pvt Charlot Conrad, A310869
*Pvt Mary Crawford, A225827
Pvt Annie Crawl, A413040
Pvt Catherine Crump, A312841
Pvt Pearl Cumberbatch, A205784
Pvt Ruthanna Cummings, A608642
Pvt Gladys Dailey, A714557
Pvt Dorothy Daniels, A905769
Pvt Ella Davis, A811060
Pvt Eula Davis, A308988
Pvt Lola Davis, A413042
Pvt Ursula Davis, A311010
Pvt Freda Dean, A1000988
Pvt Ruth Dean, A312394
Pvt Gwendolyn Deane, A208368
Pvt Emma DeFreese, A201844
Pvt Izetta Douglas, A202856
Pvt Thelma Duncan, A411316
Pvt Lula Edmonson, A514661
Pvt Carroll Edwards, A522201
Pvt Eva Edwards, A508247
Pvt Adele Evans, A603369
*Pvt Dorothy Ellis, A606296
Pvt Margaret Ellis, A805059
Pvt Helen English, A615046
Pvt Ruby Everette, A411285
Pvt Amy Fairweather, A208846
Pvt Jennie Fayson, A408149
Pvt Lora Ferguson, A304966

Pvt Jane Ferguson, A521932
Pvt Rebecca Ferguson, A208266
Pvt Ermantrude Finch, A208210
Pvt Alice Ford, A319117
Pvt Frances Poster, A926452
Pvt Rosetta Gaines, A611638
Pvt Phyllis Galloway, A1001317
Pvt Mamie Gammon, A522233
Pvt Crescenia Garcia, A208371
Pvt Anne Garrison, A309020
Pvt Sarah Gary, A1000428
Pvt Dorothy Gatliff, A507893
Pvt Eleanor Gibton, A303854
Pvt Sylvia Gillis, A222276
Pvt Virginia Glenn, A410934
Pvt Frances Gray, A414094
Pvt Dorothy Green, A508489
Pvt Irene Greene, A408557
Pvt Phyletus Greene, A413242
Pvt Evelina Griffin, A225699
Pvt Isabel Griffin, A401896
Pvt Hilda Griggs, A311758
Pvt Annie Grimes, A811184
Pvt Annie Grinter, A606660
Pvt Maetris Hairston, A612217
Pvt Jessie Hall, A901239
Pvt Bernice Hester, A606993
Pvt Rhoda Hibler, A615165
Pvt Catherine Hinton, A319219
Pvt Ada Holley, A225252
Pvt Wilhelmina Holmes, A403875
Pvt Marian Horace, A604902
Pvt Lima Howard, A611206
Pvt Sadie Huff, A406308
Pvt Indiana Hunt, A209371
Pvt Alice Hunter, A515338
Pvt Cora Hurston, A406225
Pvt Willie Irvin, A406744

Pvt Elvena Isaac, A206939
Pvt Dollie Jackson, A701570
Pvt Dorothy Jackson, A500627
Pvt Florida Jackson, A407716
Pvt Julia Jackson, A501259
Pvt Willie Jackson, A311588
Pvt Isofine Jacobs, A311127
Pvt Ruth Jamos, A209332
Pvt Emma Jenkins, A410591
Pvt Alease Johnson, A204234
Pvt Bebe Johnson, A201464
Pvt Eunice Johnson, A526708
Pvt Felicia Johnson, A412035
Pvt Johnita Johnson, A202410
Pvt Lauretta Johnson, A208676
*Pvt Lucille Johnson, A1001655
Pvt Oliva Johnson, A409096
Pvt Romay Johnson, A1000722
Pvt Thelma Johnson, A903098
Pvt Tommie Johnson, A130318
Pvt Dolores Johnston, A311118
Pvt Laura Jones, A320862
Pvt Leona Jones, A321035
Pvt Louise Jones, A609180
Pvt Lucille Jones, A813066
Pvt Mintha Jones, A709055
Pvt Nannie Jones, A405819
Pvt Adella King, A611782
Pvt Sybil King, A208046
Pvt Ilda League, A221794
Pvt William Lee, A205389
Pvt Ruth Lewis, A615407
Pvt Velma Lofty, A1001240
Pvt Leatha Loggins, A805657
Pvt Phyllis Long, A209599
Pvt Dorothy Lounds, A205941
Pvt Josie Lowe, A411268
Pvt Leatrice Lowe, A615084

*Pvt Lavinia Lowery, A701586
Pvt Wilma Lucas, A307020
Pvt Josephine Macklin, A515323
Pvt Cora Madison, A409806
Pvt Rosa Marsaw, A605919
Pvt Bernice Marsett, A310966
Pvt Genevieve Marshall, A1001636
Pvt Frances Martin, A522266
Pvt Mary Martin, A403249
Pvt Celestine Mathis, A617289
Pvt Doris Maxwell, A514766
Pvt Ruth Mays, A207904
*Pvt Mary McBride, A608878
Pvt Evelyn McDougal, A604900
Pvt Marie McKinney, A1001199
Pvt Martha McKnight, A809128
Pvt Eloise McNeeley, A201720
Pvt Katherine Metoyer, A507499
Pvt Delois Miller, A607935
Pvt Doretha Miller, A221100
Pvt Evelyn Miller, A522180
Pvt Phoebe Miller, A521695
Pvt Annie Moore, A320864
Pvt Doris Moore, A105236
Pvt Elizabeth Moraney, A307002
Pvt Sarah Morgan, A611949
Pvt Irene Morrow, A812046
Pvt Mary Nailor, A320605
Pvt Gladys O'Gilvie, A805369
Pvt Sarah Parker, A608259
Pvt Thelma Parker, A302881
Pvt Beulah Patten, A311201
Pvt Essie Penn, A810475
Pvt Nazimova Perry, A319403
Pvt Mildred Peterson, A809077
Pvt Monierah Petway, A308777
Pvt Helen Pinkett, A320710
*Pvt Ardella Pitts, A407223

Pvt Annie Pleasants, A309107
Pvt Lucy Pollitt, A302603
Pvt Carolyn Poole, A407090
Pvt Maude Poeter, A1001666
Pvt Josephine Powell, A205982
Pvt Margaret Powell, A507658
Pvt Dona Primus, A1001326
Pvt Minnie Quarles, A606504
Pvt Annie Reese, A120631
Pvt Minerva Revernal, A809671
Pvt Eddie Richards, A801729
Pvt Bette Richardson, A514347
Pvt Erma Rodriguez, A130219
Pvt Tommie Rookard, A504261
Pvt Louise Ross, A207818
Pvt Guthrie Rowland, A816904
Pvt Deloris Ruddock, A1001101
Pvt Margaret Sales, A615968
Pvt Nettie Saunders, A521836
Pvt Benita Schuster, A208161
Pvt Antoinette Scott, A308627
Pvt Clara Simon, A308549
Pvt Anjenettie Smith, A812015
Pvt Caroline Smith, A221563
Pvt Dolores Smith, A402633
Pvt Fannie Smith, A410750
Pvt Geneva Smith, A522391
Pvt Mary Smith, A615473
Pvt Rubye Smith, A522314
Pvt Ozie Smothers, A406786
Pvt Mable Sneed, A805515
Pvt Bertha Solomon, A507595
Pvt Naomi Stewart, A318562
Pvt Trenna Stokenberry, A812177
Pvt Rose Stone, A202936
Pvt Eleanor Sullivan, A318550
Pvt Gloria Sydner, A320905
Pvt Nispa Tankard, A208591

Pvt Maybell Tanner, A412039
Pvt Alonda Tapp, A709373
Pvt Gloria Taylor, A302941
Pvt Maude Taylor, A612225
Pvt Millie Taylor, A809227
Pvt Lydia Thornton, A918183
Pvt Edna Toolsie, A206163
Pvt Margoit Townsend, A311534
Pvt Catherine Turner, A225372
Pvt Bernice Underwood, A701040
Pvt Louise Usher, A508443
Pvt Lucy Ussery, A612152
Pvt Grace Vatrin, A606205
Pvt Elnora Wallace, A710944
Pvt Mary Walthall, A412715
Pvt Ruby Ward, A814008
Pvt Constance Wardell, A1001432
Pvt Laura Wardon, A508154
Pvt Doris Ware, A1001121
Pvt Cornelia Warfield, A300969
Pvt Lois Washington, A615286
Pvt Norma Watts, A208756
Pvt Constance Webb, A1001555

Pvt Grace Whyte, A1000951
Pvt Breda Williams, A221158
Pvt Dora Williams, A1001402
Pvt Estell Williams, A811419
Pvt LeMonthal Williams, A920035
Pvt Lettie Williams, A402048
Pvt Sarah Williams, A202695
Pvt Vertile Williams, A318924
Pvt Benevieve Williamson, A912383
Pvt Alberta Willis, A319476
Pvt Anna Wilson, A811273
Pvt Cecil Wilson, A701784
Pvt Eleanor Wilson, A318857
Pvt Clara Wilson, A320871
Pvt Mildred Wilson, A608853
Pvt Ruby Wilson, A317111
Pvt Dolly Woods, A514703
Pvt Johnnie Yerger, A604874
Pvt Dorothy Young, A201954
Pvt Evelyn Young, A811573
Pvt Mary Young, A305113
Pvt Mable Zemen, A819772

★ ★ ★

Notes

Notes to Chapter 1

1. Jesse Johnson, *Black Women in the Armed Forces: 1942–1974* (Hampton, Va.: Jesse Johnson, 1974), 47; Ulysses Lee, *United States Army in World War II: Special Studies: The Employment of Negro Troops* (Washington, D.C.: U.S. Government Printing Office, 1966), 5; U.S. Department of Defense, Office of the Assistant Deputy of Defense for Equal Opportunity and Safety Policy, *Black Americans in Defense of Our Nation* (Washington, D.C.: U.S. Government Printing Office, 1985), 98.

2. Lee, *Employment of Negro Troops*, 422.

3. Johnson, *Black Women in the Armed Forces*, 33.

4. D'Ann Campbell, *Women at War with America: Private Lives in a Patriotic Era* (Cambridge: Harvard University Press, 1984), 25.

5. Mildred McAfee Horton, "Recollections of Captain Mildred McAfee, USNR (Ret.)," in *WAVES Officers of World War II*, vol. 1 (Annapolis: U.S. Naval Institute, 1971), 46–48.

6. Ibid., 46–48.

7. Ibid., 41.

8. Johnson, *Black Women in the Armed Forces*, 48.

9. Among the magazines were *American, Cosmopolitan, Reader's Digest,* and *Saturday Evening Post.* See Maureen Honey, *Creating Rosie the Riveter: Class, Gender, and Propaganda during World War II* (Amherst: University of Massachusetts Press, 1984), 117–20; Mattie E.

Treadwell, *United States Army in World War II: Special Studies: The Women's Army Corps* (Washington, D.C.: U.S. Government Printing Office, 1954), 187.

10. Johnson, *Black Women in the Armed Forces,* 21.

11. See Appendix A for the places and dates of interviews with members of the 6888th Central Postal Directory Battalion. All quotations throughout the book for which sources are not indicated are taken from these interviews.

12. Allison Davis, Burleigh Gardner, and Mary Gardner, *Deep South* (Chicago: University of Chicago Press, 1941). There is a broad sociological literature that supports the fact that African Americans lagged behind European Americans during the World War II era. Many of the studies conducted during and just after the war were heavily theoretical. See, for example, Oliver C. Cox, *Caste, Class, and Race: A Study in Social Dynamics* (Garden City, N.Y.: Doubleday, 1948), 317–583; E. Franklin Frazier, *The Negro in the United States,* rev. ed. (New York: Macmillan, 1957); Gunnar Myrdal, *An American Dilemma: The Negro Problem and Modern Democracy* (New York: Harper, 1944). More recent studies on the topic attempt to explain previous existing theories through the use of historical and statistical data. For a discussion about the impact of the political economy on black-white relations, see William J. Wilson, *The Declining Significance of Race: Blacks and Changing American Institutions* (Chicago: University of Chicago Press, 1980). According to Wilson, racial conflict during the World War II era was influenced by the nature of an industrial economy. Also see Bart Landry, *The New Black Middle Class* (Berkeley: University of California Press, 1987); Stanley Lieberson, *A Piece of the Pie: Blacks and White Immigrants since 1880* (Berkeley: University of California Press, 1980). Lieberson analyzes the differential access Blacks and new white immigrant groups have had to the political and legal institutions, education, occupations, and housing. On pages 217–19 and 235 he produces statistical evidence illustrating that after the Civil War northern-born African American men and women were actually better educated than southern, central, and eastern European immigrants and were obtaining education faster than northern-born Whites with native parents. During World War I, however, northern Blacks' education began to deteriorate. Lieberson attributes this decline to an increase in the degree of black isolation

in northern city schools at the time when the isolation of new Europeans had decreased.

13. Treadwell, *Women's Army Corps,* 599.

14. Several programs under the National Youth Administration helped African American youths to continue their education. Thirteen percent of the enrollees of the NYA Out-of-School Program, which provided vocational training, were black. Sixty-four thousand black youths took advantage of the NYA student work program. See John Hope Franklin and Alfred A. Moss, Jr., *From Slavery to Freedom: A History of Negro Americans,* 6th ed. (New York: Knopf, 1988), 353.

15. At the time Bethune founded the National Council of Negro Women, it represented fourteen black women's organizations. Today, twenty-seven national organizations are affiliated with the NCNW, and there are two hundred local council sections throughout the United States. See "History of the National Council of Negro Women" in *The Guide to the Records of the National Council of Negro Women,* Bethune Museum and Archives, Washington, D.C.

16. Charity Adams Earley, *One Woman's Army: A Black Officer Remembers the WAC* (College Station: Texas A&M University Press, 1989), 121.

17. Dovey Johnson Roundtree was one of the forty African American women to attend the first Officer Candidate School at Fort Des Moines, Iowa. Roundtree had a reputation for standing up for racial equality. She often spoke with Bethune about race-related affairs in the WAC. Roundtree was stationed at Fort Des Moines when Margaret Barnes Jones called about the events at Camp Breckenridge.

18. Treadwell, *Women's Army Corps,* 545.

19. Gladys Carter is referring to an African American woman who protested against separate water fountains for "coloreds" and for "whites" by openly drinking from a fountain labeled "whites" in the southern United States. For details see: Ernest J. Gaines, *The Autobiography of Miss Jane Pittman* (New York: Dial, 1971).

Notes to Chapter 2

1. Richard H. Day, "Technological Change and the Sharecropper," *American Economic Review* 57 (June 1967): 429.

2. Perhaps the most serious race riots that occurred during the war

were the violence against "zoot suiters" (Mexican and Negro citizens) in Los Angeles and a race riot in Detroit for which President Roosevelt sent soldiers to patrol the city. Both riots occurred in June 1943.

3. The World War II era was not the only time in U.S. history when military and civilian occupations resembled each other. During the pre-Civil War era, the American military witnessed a period of what Samuel Huntington called "technicism," in which vocational skills for military personnel were stressed. We learn from Huntington that the emphasis on specialization by the American military derived from Jeffersonians, who drew no distinction between civilian and military skills. Nineteenth-century West Point graduates were in high demand by private employers, and many students entered the academy primarily to become scientists or engineers rather than Army officers. See Samuel Huntington, *The Soldier and the State* (Cambridge: Harvard University Press, 1957), 199.

4. Janowitz claimed that the conspicuous leaders in World War II were "exaggerations of the conflicting themes in the military profession." The themes to which Janowitz was referring were those of the hero, who was a warrior type, and the manager, who "maintained a position of effective authority." Janowitz categorized Dwight Eisenhower, Omar Bradley, H. H. Arnold, Walter Bedell Smith, William Leahy, and Ernest King as men "who reflected the technical and pragmatic dimensions of war making." On the other hand, he categorized Bull Halsey, George Patton, Jonathan Wainwright, James Doolittle, and Curtis LeMay as examples of heroic leaders. Douglas MacArthur, claimed Janowitz, "fused both roles, but . . . often performed as the heroic fighter." See Morris Janowitz, *The Professional Soldier* (New York: Free Press, 1971), 21, 154.

5. Ulysses Lee, *United States Army in World War II: Special Studies: The Employment of Negro Troops* (Washington, D.C.: U.S. Government Printing Office, 1966), 5, 703; Martin Binkin, Mark Eitelberg, Alvin Schexnider, and Marvin Smith, *Blacks and the Military* (Washington, D.C.: Brookings Institution, 1982), 17.

6. Mady W. Segal, "Women in the Military: Research and Policy Issues," *Youth and Society* 10, no. 2 (December 1978): 102; Mattie E. Treadwell, *United States Army in World War II: Special Studies: The Women's Army Corps* (Washington, D.C.: U.S. Government Printing Office, 1954), 6.

7. Treadwell, *Women's Army Corps*, 231.

8. During World War II Blacks made up approximately 4 percent (167,000) of the Navy and 2.5 percent (17,000) of the Marine Corps. Only 3 percent of the Army combat positions were filled by black men. The greatest majority of Blacks were assigned to services such as quartermaster, engineer, and transportation corps. See Binkin et al., *Blacks and the Military*, 20, 24.

9. There are different accounts of how many women served in the WAAC/WAC during World War II. In *Black Women in the Armed Forces: 1942–1974* (Hampton, Va.: Jesse Johnson, 1974), 15, Jesse Johnson estimated that 150,000 women served in the WAAC/WAC during the war years and that approximately 6,500 were black. D'Ann Campbell, in *Women at War with America: Private Lives in a Patriotic Era* (Cambridge: Harvard University Press, 1984), 253, stated that 140,000 Wacs served during World War II.

10. Stanley Lieberson, *A Piece of the Pie: Blacks and White Immigrants since 1880* (Berkeley: University of California Press, 1980); Gunnar Myrdal, *An American Dilemma: The Negro Problem and Modern Democracy* (New York: Harper, 1944); William J. Wilson, *The Declining Significance of Race: Blacks and Changing American Institutions* (Chicago: University of Chicago Press, 1980).

11. Brenda L. Moore, "Serving with a Dual Mission: African American Women in World War II," *National Journal of Sociology* 7, no. 1 (1993): 34. According to Bettina Aptheker, "Hundreds if not thousands of white people participated in the torture and killing of one or two individuals. Souvenirs in the form of body parts, pieces of rope and clothing were often taken by members of the mob." See Bettina Aptheker, *Woman's Legacy: Essays on Race, Sex, and Class in American History* (Amherst: University of Massachusetts Press, 1982), 60, 61. Also see Alfreda M. Duster, ed., *Crusade for Justice: The Autobiography of Ida B. Wells* (Chicago: University of Chicago Press, 1970), 69–71, 84–85, 126, 128, 129, 138–39, 148, 149, 154, 182, 186, 187, 195, 196, 252, 266, 267, 284, 299.

12. John Hope Franklin and Alfred A, Moss, Jr., *From Slavery to Freedom: A History of Negro Americans,* 6th ed. (New York: Knopf, 1988); John A. Garraty, *The American Nation: A History of the United States since 1865,* vol. 2, 3rd ed. (New York: Harper and Row, 1975).

13. Lee, *Employment of Negro Troops,* 52.

14. Some people argue that African Americans' gains in war produc-

tion during World War II were not as great as during World War I because large numbers of white women were available to work and because powerful Whites resisted black migration to the North. See Myrdal, *An American Dilemma*. The failure to allow Blacks full participation in war production sparked a scheduled march on Washington organized by A. Phillip Randolph in 1941. The march was called off when President Roosevelt agreed to issue an executive order forbidding racial discrimination in war industries. Executive Order 8802, the Fair Employment Practices Order, was signed by the president on 25 June 1941.

15. Lee, *Employment of Negro Troops*, 54. Lee mentions several organizations, including the Civilian Conservation Corps (CCC), a major youth training program that was developed during the Great Depression as a relief program for unemployed youths; the National Youth Administration (NYA), an organization that trained mechanics and technical specialists; and the Civil Aeronautics Authority (CAA), which provided students with pilot training in cooperation with colleges and private airfields.

16. For a complete discussion of the War Department's post-World War I plans to mobilize black manpower, see Lee, *Employment of Negro Troops*, 21–50.

17. Ibid., 73. The legislation stipulated that "any person, regardless of race or color, between the ages of 18 and 36, shall be afforded an opportunity to volunteer for induction into the land or naval forces." In addition there was be no discrimination against any person on account of race or color.

18. Lee, *Employment of Negro Troops*, 76.

19. *The Crisis: A Record of the Darker Races*, 49, no. 2 (February 1942): 47.

20. Lee, *Employment of Negro Troops*, 98–99.

21. Ibid., 97, 100–101.

22. Ibid., 107–10.

23. Ibid., 211.

24. African American Waacs normally commanded African American WAAC troops. In one isolated case, however, a Negro Waac officer commanded a white WAAC platoon. The *Louisville Defender* published an article on 27 February 1943 entitled, "Negro Waac Commands White Platoon." The article stated that Third Officer Ann M. Clark of Ken-

tucky was the first black officer being assigned to duty with an all- white company (Fourth Company, Third Regiment at Fort Des Moines). The article is accompanied by a picture of Third Officer Clark; her physical appearance is that of a white woman. She received her B.A. degree from Kentucky State College at Frankfurt in 1941 and she was a member of Delta Theta Sorority. Unfortunately I have not been able to obtain any further information about this event.

25. Lee, *Employment of Negro Troops,* 17.

26. Lee Nichols, *Breakthrough on the Color Front* (New York: Random House, 1954), 32.

27. Lee, *Employment of Negro Troops,* 429.

28. Ibid., 433.

29. African Americans' negative sentiments toward their participation in World War II are documented in a speech given by Edward E. Strong, national secretary of the National Negro Congress, at the Eastern Seaboard Conference on the Problems of the War and the Negro People, 10 April 1943 in New York City. The document is part of the Schomburg Collection at the Schomburg Center for Research in Black Culture, New York City.

30. This is obvious when we consider that approximately 694,500 African American men served in the Army during World War II during their peak strength in June 1944, as compared with the 99,288 peak strength of Wacs in April 1945. See Lee, *Employment of Negro Troops,* 416; Treadwell, *Women's Army Corps,* 765.

31. Lee, *Employment of Negro Troops,* 423.

32. According to Treadwell, the bill introduced in December 1917 was returned to the House Military Affairs Committee by the secretary of war. The Navy, on the other hand, enlisted nearly thirteen thousand women in the Navy and Marine Corps during World War I, with the same status as men. See Treadwell, *Women's Army Corps,* 8.

33. In 1918 the House of Representatives passed the Nineteenth Amendment; the Senate passed it the following year; in 1920 the amendment became part of the Constitution.

34. Treadwell, *Women's Army Corps,* 12–14.

35. Ibid., 18, 19.

36. Ibid., 24.

37. Michael J. Lyons, *World War II: A Short History* (Englewood Cliffs, N.J.: Prentice Hall, 1994), 147.

38. Treadwell, *Women's Army Corps,* 45.

39. The age limits were changed to 20 and 50 in July 1943. See Treadwell, *Women's Army Corps,* 57, 220.

40. Ibid., 58–59.

41. Myra Marx Ferree and Beth C. Hess, *Controversy and Coalition: The New Feminist Movement* (Boston: Twayne, 1985), 2.

42. Sherna B. Gluck, *Rosie the Riveter Revisited: Women, the War, and Social Change* (Boston: Twayne, 1987).

43. Treadwell, *Women's Army Corps,* 29.

44. "Excerpts from the Remarks of Mrs. Emily Newell Blair on the Occasion of Her First Address as Chief of the Women's Interests Section, War Department Bureau of Public Relations, to the Advisory Council of the Section, Monday June 15, [1943] Washington D.C.," Records of the National Council of Negro Women, series 5, box 37, folder 522, Bethune Museum and Archives, Washington, D.C.

45. "Résumé of the Meeting of the Advisory Council on June 15 [1943] at the War Department," Records of the NCNW, series 5, box 37, folder 522, Bethune Museum and Archives.

46. Meyer Zald and John McCarthy, *Social Movements in an Organizational Society* (New Brunswick, N.J.: Transaction Books, 1987), 20.

47. Treadwell, *Women's Army Corps,* 75.

48. "Report of Meeting Held on October 28, 1942 on Invitation of Miss Mary E. Woolley," Records of the NCNW, series 5, box 38, folder 535, Bethune Museum and Archives.

49. Ibid.

50. "Report on the Work of the Women's Interests Section in Connection with the Advisory Council, June 1942 to June 1943," Washington, D.C., 25 June 1943, Records of the NCNW, series 5, box 37, folder 526, Bethune Museum and Archives.

51. "Advisory Council to the Women's Interests Section, War Department Meeting held June 25, 1943, Mayflower Hotel, Washington, D.C. (Summary of remarks)," Records of the NCNW, series 5, box 37, folder 526, Bethune Museum and Archives.

52. Ibid.

53. Ibid.

54. Ibid.

55. "War Department Bureau of Public Relations, Women's Interests Section of Publications Branch, Bulletin of Information, January 1944,"

Records of the NCNW, series 5, box 37, folder 523, Bethune Museum and Archives.

56. "Report of Civilian Advisory Committee," Second Service Command Civilian Advisory Committee, Women's Army Corps, 16 December 1944, Records of the NCNW, series 5, box 37, folder 523, Bethune Museum and Archives.

57. "Third Service Command WAC Civilian Advisory Committee," Records of the NCNW, series 5, box 37, folder 523, Bethune Museum and Archives.

58. "Report of Civilian Advisory Committee, Ninth Service Command," Records of the NCNW, series 5, box 37, folder 523, Bethune Museum and Archives.

59. Letter, Mrs. Oswald B. Lord, national chairman, National Civilian Advisory Committee, Women's Army Corps, February 1945, Records of the NCNW, series 5, box 37, folder 523, Bethune Museum and Archives.

60. "Second Service Command Civilian Advisory Committee," Women's Army Corps, Bulletin no. 14, 13 November 1945, Records of the NCNW, series 5, box 37, folder 523, Bethune Museum and Archives.

61. "Report of Genevieve Forbes Herrick," February 1946, Records of the NCNW, series 5, box 37, folder 523, Bethune Museum and Archives.

62. Ibid.

63. Ibid.

64. Ibid.

65. Ibid.

Notes to Chapter 3

1. The most acclaimed African American woman to help lead black slaves into freedom was Harriet Tubman. She is said to have escaped from slavery herself as well as leading her parents, children, sisters, and others out of slavery. See John Hope Franklin and Alfred A. Moss, Jr., *From Slavery to Freedom: A History of Negro Americans,* 6th ed. (New York: Knopf, 1988), 171–72; Mary Frances Berry and John W. Blassingame, *Long Memory: The Black Experience in America* (New York: Oxford University Press, 1982). Ida B. Wells is often cited as a principal person to launch an international campaign against lynching, the bar-

baric act of torturing and murdering black men who had been accused, usually falsely, of raping white women. See Alfreda M. Duster, ed., *Crusade for Justice: The Autobiography of Ida B. Wells* (Chicago: University of Chicago Press, 1970).

2. Angela Y. Davis, *Women, Race, and Class* (New York: Random House, 1981), 37.

3. Barbara S. Deckard, *The Women's Movement: Political, Socioeconomic, and Psychological Issues* (New York: Harper and Row, 1983), 254.

4. The names of black women leaders include Sara Parker Remond, Sarah Mapps Douglass, Letetia Still, and the Forten sisters (Margaretta, Harriet, and Sarah). See Bettina Aptheker, *Woman's Legacy: Essays on Race, Sex, and Class in American History* (Amherst: University of Massachusetts Press, 1982), 19.

5. Susan B. Anthony and Elizabeth Cady Stanton, both longtime activists for human rights and cofounders of the American Equal Rights Association along with Frederick Douglass, for the purpose of unifying abolitionists and feminists, did not support the Fifteenth Amendment because it did not extend the vote to women. The division in the early feminist movement over this amendment is cited in the literature as marking an end to cooperation between the black and the women's liberation movements. See Aptheker, *Woman's Legacy,* 11; Paula Giddings, *When and Where I Enter: The Impact of Black Women on Race and Sex in America* (New York: Bantam, 1984), 65.

6. Deckard, *The Women's Movement,* 256.

7. Duster, *Crusade for Justice;* Giddings, *When and Where I Enter.*

8. See Duster, *Crusade for Justice;* Giddings, *When and Where I Enter.*

9. Letter to Mary McLeod Bethune from Emily Newell Blair, 24 June 1942, Records of the National Council of Negro Women, series 5, box 37, folder 522, Bethune Museum and Archives, Washington, D.C.

10. Letter to Mary McLeod Bethune from Margaret S. Banister, organization director of the Women's Interests Section, Publication Branch, dated 13 January 1943; also letter from Bethune to Banister dated 25 January 1943, Records of NCNW, series 5, box 37, folder 526, Bethune Museum and Archives.

11. Letter to Mary McLeod Bethune from Emily Newell Blair, 12

February 1943, Records of NCNW, series 5, box 38, folder 535, Bethune Museum and Archives.

12. Mary McLeod Bethune, "A Century of Progress of Negro Women," an address delivered to the Chicago Women's Federation on 30 June 1933, reprinted in Gerda Lerner, ed., *Black Women in White America: A Documentary History* (New York: Vintage, 1972), 579–84.

13. See letter to Mary McLeod Bethune from Emily Newell Blair, Chief, Women's Interests Section, Publication Branch, dated 12 February 1943; also Bethune's letter to Blair dated 22 March 1943, Records of NCNW, series 5, box 38, folder 535, Bethune Museum and Archives.

14. Document of National Council of Negro Women, 16 August 1943, RG 165, Army G-1 WAC Decimal File 1942–46 250.3–291.2, box #50, National Archives, Washington, D.C.

15. Ibid.

16. Mattie E. Treadwell, *United States Army in World War II: Special Studies: The Women's Army Corps* (Washington, D.C.: U.S. Government Printing Office, 1954), 594.

17. Ibid., 318–21.

18. Martha S. Putney, *When the Nation Was in Need: Blacks in the Women's Army Corps during World War II* (Metuchen, N.J.: Scarecrow Press, 1992), 14–16.

19. Ibid., 102.

20. Ibid., 6.

21. *Michigan Chronicle*, "Woman of the Week," 19 December 1942.

22. Correspondence of Mrs. E. P. Trezevant to WAAC headquarters, 29 May 1942, 7 June 1942, War Department's replies to Trezevant, 3 June 1942, 10 June 1942, Trezevant's letter to Mary McLeod Bethune, 7 June 1942, Bethune's letter to Oveta Culp Hobby, 17 June 1942, Hobby's reply to Bethune, 19 June 1942, Hobby's 19 June 1942 letter to Trezevant stating that she did not hear of Trezevant's complaint of discrimination until all of the applicants had been processed and that there was nothing she could do about it at that time. Also see Western Union telegram dated 28 May 1942, sent to Hobby by Earl G. Davis, president of the Winston-Salem Youth Council of the NAACP, complaining that the local recruiting officer, Sergeant Stephenson, refused to accept applications from Negro women. Also see Hobby's reply by telegram dated 29 May 1942 stating that Sergeant Stephenson would

correct his mistake and accept applications from Negro applicants. Also see letter dated 29 May 1942 to Attorney William H. Hastie, civilian aide on Negro affairs to the secretary of war, by G. F. Porter, secretary of the Dallas Branch, NAACP, alleging that the local recruiting station in Dallas was discriminating against Negro applicants. All items are in RG 165, Army G-1 WAC file 291.21, box #50, National Archives.

23. Western Union to Oveta Hobby from Earl Davis, 28 May 1942, telegram to Earl Davis from Oveta Hobby, 29 May 1942, letter to Oveta Hobby from P. L. Prattis, executive editor of the *Pittsburgh Courier,* 28 May 1942, letter to P. L. Prattis from Oveta Hobby, 3 June 1942, letter to Attorney William H. Hastie, civilian aide to the secretary of war, from G. F. Porter, secretary of the Dallas Branch, NAACP, 29 May 1942, letter to Col. William F. Pearson, adjutant general, WAAC, from William Hastie, 6 July 1942, letter to William Hastie from Col. William Pearson, 8 July 1942, RG 165, Army G-1 WAC file 291.21, box #49, National Archives.

24. Letter to U.S. Army Recruiting Corps from Mrs. E. P. Trezevant, 29 May 1942, letter to Trezevant from W. H. Nealing, 3 June 1942, letter to Oveta Culp Hobby from Trezevant, 7 June 1942, letter to Trezevant from William F. Pearson, 10 June 1942, letter to Mrs. Mary McLeod Bethune from Trezevant, 7 June 1942, letter to Hobby from Bethune, 17 June 1942, letter to Bethune from Hobby, 19 June 1942, RG 165, Army G-1 WAC file 291.21, box #49, National Archives.

25. Dovey Roundtree, interview by author, Washington, D.C., 30 January 1991.

26. Noel Campbell Mitchell, unpublished memoirs, Tuskegee, Ala.

27. Memo, Major Tasker, GSC, to Colonel Hobby, director of WAAC, 14 May 1942, RG 165, Army G-1 WAC file 291.2, box #49, National Archives.

28. Treadwell, *Women's Army Corps,* 71.

29. *Chicago Defender,* 1 August 1942, 6.

30. See, for example, Charity Adams Earley, *One Woman's Army: A Black Officer Remembers the WAC* (College Station: Texas A&M University Press, 1989).

31. News release document, Records of the NCNW, series 5, box 38, folder 535, Bethune Museum and Archives.

32. Letter to Col. Don C. Faith, 28 July 1942, letter to E. J. Adams,

3 August 1942, RG 165, Army G-1 WAC file 291.21, box #49, National Archives.

33. Memorandum to Colonel Tasker from Harry McAlpin, 25 August 1942, letter to McAlpin from J. Noel Macy, 8 September 1942, RG 165, SPWA file 291.21, National Archives.

34. Ibid.

35. Report to Mary McLeod Bethune from Charles P. Howard, 26 August 1942, RG 165, SPWA file 291.21, National Archives.

36. Ibid.

37. Memorandum for War Department, Bureau of Public Relations (Attention Lt. Col. David Page), 17 September 1942, RG 165, National Archives.

38. Putney, *When the Nation Was in Need,* 155.

39. The proportion of black officers of the WAAC declined steadily each quarter. By December 1945 black women made up only 1.8 percent of the officers and 4.1 percent of the enlisted women.

40. By contrast, the highest-ranking African American man in the Army at the time was Brig. Gen. Benjamin O. Davis.

41. For statistics on WAAC/WAC strength by rank see Treadwell, *Women's Army Corps,* 776.

42. Putney, *When the Nation Was in Need,* 130–31.

43. Earley, *One Woman's Army,* 107–8, 126.

44. Ibid., 107–8.

45. Ibid., 45, 46.

46. Ibid., 60.

47. Ibid., 47.

48. Treadwell, *Women's Army Corps,* 635.

49. "Colored WAAC Units with D. C. Officers Arrive in Arizona," *Washington Star,* December 1942.

50. Earley states that Lt. Aubrey Stokes was her assistant. See Earley, *One Woman's Army,* 98. Stokes was later assigned to the 6888th as the company officer of Company A.

51. "Memorandum for the Assistant Chief of Staff, G-1, Policy Regarding Colored Personnel in WAAC," RG 165, G-1 WAC file 291.21, National Archives.

52. Letter to Colonel Faith from Edwin Embree, 23 September 1942, RG 165, SPWA file 291.21, National Archives.

53. Letter to Eleanor Roosevelt from Viola A. McAtee, 30 September 1942, RG 165, SPWA file 291.21, National Archives.

54. Letter to Col. Don C. Faith from S. Joe Brown, 27 October 1942, RG 165, SPWA file 291.21, National Archives.

55. Dorothy Dailey Jones, videotaped conference, William Joiner Center for the Study of Peace, University of Massachusetts, Boston, March 1990.

56. Ibid.

57. Letter from Emily Hickman to Oveta Culp Hobby, 14 October 1942, letter from Lt. Col. J. Noel Macy to Hickman, 23 October 1942, letter from Hickman to Henry L. Stimson, 15 December 1942, letter from Hobby to Hickman, 1 January 1943, RG 165, SPWA file 291.21, National Archives.

58. Morris J. MacGregor, *Integration of the Armed Forces, 1940– 1965* (Washington, D.C.: U.S. Government Printing Office, 1981), 51.

59. Letter to Walter White from Mary McLeod Bethune, 4 November 1942, Records of NCNW, series 5, box 38, folder 535, Bethune Museum and Archives.

60. "Mrs. Bethune Denies She Asked for Jim Crow Waacs," *Washington Tribune*, 21 November 1942, 108.

61. Treadwell, *Women's Army Corps*, 591.

62. Letter to John D. Ewing from John McCormack, 17 April 1943, RG 165, SPWA file 291.21, National Archives.

63. Letter to John C. McCormack from Oveta Culp Hobby, 7 May 1943, RG 165, SPWA file 291.21, National Archives.

64. "The Facts Regarding Segregation and Discrimination against the Negro in the Armed Forces," 14 June 1943, Records of the NCNW, series 5, box 8, folder 139, Bethune Museum and Archives.

65. Letter to Florence Murray from Gretchen Thorp, 7 August 1943, RG 165, SPWA file 291.2, National Archives.

66. Charity Earley speaks about her multiple military occupation at Fort Des Moines as consisting largely of assignments that no one else wanted. See Earley, *One Woman's Army*, 98.

67. Letter to Harriet West from Lula Jones Garrett, 4 February 1944, list of grievances, 4 February 1944, memorandum to Captain McCarthy for Colonel Brown, 7 February 1944, memorandum to Colonel Brown from Captain McCarthy, no date, memorandum to Lieutenant Lee from Treadwell, no date, memorandum to Colonel Brown from Major West,

no date, letter to commanding general, seventh service command, through deputy chief of staff for service commands, from WAC director Oveta Culp Hobby, 7 February 1944, First Indorsement from WAC Director, 15 February 1944, Second Indorsement from Col. F. U. McCoskrie, Third Indorsement signed M. S. B., 9 March 1944, RG 165, SPWA file 291.2, National Archives.

68. Letter to Bethune from Rice, 16 August 1944, Records of the NCNW, series 5, box 37, folder 523, Bethune Museum and Archives.

69. *Amsterdam-Star News,* 25 July 1945.

70. Earley, *One Woman's Army,* 103.

71. "Disillusioned by Jim-Crow Washington Girl Quits WAC," *Washington Afro American,* 10 March 1945.

72. "4 Negro Wacs Convicted—NAACP Leader Calls It Fair," *New York Post,* 21 March 1945; "Army Court Convicts 4 Negro Wacs of Disobeying Superior," *Washington Post,* 21 March 1945; "3 Congressmen Ask Probe of Wac Trials," *Washington Post,* 23 March 1945.

73. Memorandum for the Director of Personnel, Army Service Forces: "Report of Protest on the Assignment of Negro WACs to Gardiner General Hospital, Chicago, Illinois," 6 April 1945, RG 165, SPWA file 291.1, National Archives.

74. Ibid. Also see Putney, *When the Nation Was in Need,* 39, 89–95.

75. Letter to Oveta C. Hobby from Mary McLeod Bethune, 14 August 1944, Records of the NCNW, series 5, box 37, folder 523, Bethune Museum and Archives. For more information about the Black WAC Band see Martha S. Putney, "The Women's Army Corps' Black Band: A Historical Note," in *Army History: The Professional Bulletin of Army History,* 20–94–5, no. 32 (Fall 1994): 7–13.

76. Harry McAlpin, "Turn Down Negro Wacs for Overseas Service," *Chicago Defender,* 5 February 1944, 5.

77. "Army Will Send Negro Waacs to England to Help Entertain Troops of Their Race," *New York Times,* 16 August 1942.

78. "WAACS May Go Abroad, Gen. Eisenhower Reveals," *Philadelphia Tribune,* 22 August 1942, 28.

79. "WAACS Abroad Perform Specific Military Duties," *Philadelphia Tribune,* 5 September 1942, 108.

80. Treadwell, *Women's Army Corps,* 599.

81. This conclusion is based on a report of an informal visit to the WAAC training camp (Fort Des Moines, Iowa) by Edwin R. Embree in

1942. According to Embree's report, "facilities for whites and colored were equal." Embree stated further that Negro Waacs made up a separate platoon. A special table had been assigned to "colored" girls in the officers' mess. This was a conspicuous form of segregation and was resented by black Waacs. It was recommended in the report that the separate table for Waacs in the officers' mess be done away with. See "Report of Informal Visit to Training Camp for WAAC'S, Des Moines, Iowa: Made By Edwin R. Embree in Company with W. W. Alexander," RG 165, Army G-1 WAC decimal file 1942–46 250.3–291.2, National Archives.

Notes to Chapter 4

1. St. Clair Drake and Horace R. Cayton, *Black Metropolis: A Study of Negro Life in a Northern City* (New York: Harper and Row, 1945), 438.

2. See Joseph Pierce, *Negro Business and Business Education, Their Present and Prospective Development* (Westport, Conn.: Negro University Press, 1971).

3. See E. Franklin Frazier, *The Negro in the United States,* rev. ed. (New York: Macmillan, 1957), 286; E. Franklin Frazier, "Occupational Classes among Negroes in Cities," *American Journal of Sociology* 35 (March 1930): 718–38.

4. Socioeconomic status in this study is determined by occupation, as categorized by the U.S. Census. Thus, the socioeconomic status of a member's family of origin is determined by the parent's occupation (or head of household's occupation if the respondent was not reared by her parents). The following nine broad occupational categories are used to determine socioeconomic status: professional, clerical, retail trade, service (excluding private household work), domestic (private household service workers), crafts, operatives, laborers, and farmers. The "other" category refers to unemployed persons, students, disabled persons, and so on.

5. Mattie E. Treadwell, *United States Army in World War II: Special Studies: The Women's Army Corps* (Washington, D.C.: U.S. Government Printing Office, 1954), 220.

6. Ibid., 599.

7. U.S. Department of Commerce, *Statistical Abstract of the United*

States 1989 (Washington, D.C.: U.S. Government Printing Office, 1989), table 211, 130.

8. "Things Talked About," *Birmingham Sunday Mercury*, February 1945.

9. Joan Capreol, "Bagpipes Play for Happy Women Whose Dreams Come True," press clipping, February 1945, War Department, RG 165, SPWA 291.1, National Archives, Washington, D.C.

10. *New York Amsterdam News*, "French Wacs Get New Commander," 9 February 1946.

11. Obituary of Mildred E. Davenport Carter, 18 October 1990, St. Cyprian's Episcopal Church, Roxbury, Massachusetts.

12. U.S. Department of Commerce, *Sixteenth Census of the United States: 1940* (Washington, D.C.: U.S. Government Printing Office, 1943), table 63, "Race of Employed Persons (Except on Public Emergency Work) and of Experienced Workers Seeking Work, by Occupation and Sex, for Regions: 1940," 91.

13. "Wacs in Postal Unit Praised for Efficiency," *Chicago Defender*, 14 April 1945, 15.

14. Jennie Moton's father succeeded Booker T. Washington as head of the Tuskegee Institute in Alabama. See "First Negro Wac Unit Overseas," *The Call and Post*, 20 January 1945.

15. The roster was compiled from Special Orders no. 89, 30 March 1945, Special Orders no. 18, 30 May 1945, and Special Orders no. 84, 12 November 1945, National Personnel Records Center, St. Louis.

16. Although the service commands do not correspond directly to the U.S. Bureau of the Census regions, they are a close approximation.

17. Charity Adams Earley, *One Woman's Army: A Black Officer Remembers the WAC* (College Station: Texas A&M University Press, 1989), 63.

18. Lucia M. Pitts, *One Negro WAC's Story* (Los Angeles: Lucia M. Pitts, 1968), 4.

19. Earley, *One Woman's Army*, 124.

20. Ibid., 130.

21. Ibid., 134.

22. Unpublished written statement by Gertrude LaVigne, 23 January 1991.

23. Letter to Sadie from Ollie, 13 February 1945, Benjamin O. Davis,

Sr., Papers, personal letters to wife written in ETO, 1 January-30 April 1945, Archives, U.S. Military History Institute, Carlisle Barracks, Pa.

24. Earley, *One Woman's Army,* 144.

Notes to Chapter 5

1. Edward B. Toles, "First Negro Wacs Reach Continent at French Town," *Chicago Defender,* 9 June 1945, 1, 6.

2. The following officers were part of the inspection team: Maj. Gen. Sir Eric Girwood of the British Army; Air Commodore Tom Howe, RAF; Col. C. C. Sibley, port commander; Maj. K. E. Campbell, PRO-ComZ; and Maj. H. Horak, PRD-SHAEF.

3. Edward B. Toles, "First Wacs Overseas Greeted in Britain," *Chicago Defender,* 27 February 1945, 5.

4. "Special Inspection, WAC Detachment, First Base Post Office APO 640," memorandum to Maj. Gen. Charles H. Bonesteel, chief, General Inspectorate Section, ETOUSA, APO 887, United States Army, from B. O. Davis, brigadier general, USA, 18 February 1945, Benjamin O. Davis, Sr., Papers, Archives, U.S. Army Military History Institute, Carlisle Barracks, Pa.

5. Lucia M. Pitts, *One Negro WAC's Story* (Los Angeles: Lucia M. Pitts, 1968), 8.

6. Inspection report to Maj. Gen. Charles H. Bonesteel, chief, General Inspectorate Section, ETOUSA, dated 18 February 1945, Benjamin O. Davis, Sr., Papers, Archives, U.S. Army Military History Institute, Carlisle Barracks, Pa.

7. Charity Adams Earley, *One Woman's Army: A Black Officer Remembers the WAC* (College Station: Texas A&M University Press, 1989), 148.

8. Pitts, *One Negro WAC's Story,* 14.

9. Edward B. Toles, "First Negro Wacs Reach Continent at French Town," *Chicago Defender,* 9 June 1945, 1, 6.

10. Pitts, *One Negro WAC's Story,* 15.

11. Earley, *One Woman's Army,* 198, 199.

12. "Only Overseas Negro WAC Section Home," *Army Times,* 16 March 1946.

13. "Things Talked About," *Birmingham Sunday Mercury,* February 1945.

14. Cynthia Enloe, *Bananas, Beaches, and Bases* (Berkeley: University of California Press, 1990), 70; Graham Smith, *When Jim Crow Met John Bull: Black American Soldiers in World War II Britain* (New York: St. Martin's, 1988), 20–36, 70.

15. G. Smith, *When Jim Crow Met John Bull,* 218.

16. Earley, *One Woman's Army,* 156.

17. Ibid., 201.

18. In France, meals were prepared for the battalion by prisoners of war.

19. Earley, *One Woman's Army,* 185.

20. Ibid., 190.

21. Max Weber, *The Theory of Social and Economic Organization,* (Glencoe, Ill: Free Press, 1947), 324–406.

22. Earley, *One Woman's Army,* 164.

23. Gertrude LaVigne, interview by author, Anchorage, 23 January 1991.

24. Frank Godden, "French Town Greets WAC Postal Unit," *Chicago Defender,* 23 June 1945, 15.

25. *Special Delivery,* 6888th Central Postal Directory Newsletter, 30 July 1945, vol. 1, no. 9, 1.

26. Earley, *One Woman's Army,* 187.

27. Mattie E. Treadwell, *United States Army in World War II: Special Studies: The Woman's Army Corps* (Washington, D.C.: U.S. Government Printing Office, 1954), 191–218.

28. I am referring specifically to events such as the Tailhook incident, which took place in the Navy and became a serious problem in 1991. See Timothy J. McNulty, "Scandal Forces Kelso to Retire," *Chicago Tribune,* 18 February 1994: 1, 11.

29. Earley, *One Woman's Army,* 181.

30. Louis Wirth, "Morale and Minority Groups," *American Journal of Sociology* 47, no. 3 (1941): 426.

31. Pitts, *One Negro WAC's Story,* 13.

32. I had an opportunity to visit the Normandy American Cemetery and Memorial during the D-Day celebration in June 1994, and I visited these women's grave sites.

33. Treadwell, *Women's Army Corps,* 600.

Notes to Chapter 6

1. Modell and others explored data in the literature for *The American Soldier* to determine how the hoped-for postwar world differed for Whites and for Blacks and how that world differed for black servicemen whose prior experience had differed from their military experience. See John Modell, Marc Goulden, and Sigurdur Magnusson, "World War II in the Lives of Black Americans: Some Findings and an Interpretation," *Journal of American History* 76, no. 3 (December 1989): 839–47.

2. Samuel Stouffer and his associates conducted a large-scale study in the Research Branch, Information and Education Division of the United States Army on the adjustment of American soldiers in World War II. See Samuel Stouffer, Arthur Lumsdaine, Marion Lumsdaine, Robin Williams, M. Brewster Smith, Irving Janis, Shirley Star, and Leonard Cottrell, Jr., *The American Soldier*, vol. 1, *Adjustment during Army Life* (Princeton, N.J.: Princeton University Press, 1949). Modell and coworkers examined questions in Surveys S-106 and S-144, which are now available at the Roper Center Archives at the University of Connecticut and at the Machine Readable Records Division of the National Archives. See Modell et al., "World War II in the Lives of Black Americans," 841.

3. Modell et al., "World War II in the Lives of Black Americans," 842.

4. Ibid.

5. During World War II approximately five million Americans migrated from farms to industrial centers. See Donald Bogue, *Principles of Demography* (New York: Wiley, 1969), 767.

6. Stouffer et al., *American Soldier*.

7. Edward Shils and Morris Janowitz, "Cohesion and Disintegration in the Wehrmacht," *Public Opinion Quarterly* 12 (Summer 1948): 280–315.

8. Gary Becker, *Human Capital* (Chicago: University of Chicago Press, 1975).

9. Glen H. Elder, Cynthia Gimble, and Rachel Ivie, "Turning Points in Life: The Case of Military Service and War," *Military Psychology* 3, no. 4 (1991): 215.

10. See Buncan Bailey and Thomas F. Cargill, "The Military Draft and Future Income," *Western Economic Journal* 7 (1969): 365–70;

W. Lee Hansen and Burton Weisbrod, "Economics of the Military Draft," *Quarterly Journal of Economics* 81 (1967): 395–421; Walter Y. Oi, "The Economic Cost of the Draft," *American Economic Review* 57 (1967): 39–62; Thomas D. Willett, "Another Cost of Conscription," *Western Economic Journal* 6 (1963): 425–27.

11. Irving G. Kattenbrink, "Military Service and Occupational Mobility," in *Selective Service and American Society,* ed. Roger Little (New York: Russell Sage Foundation, 1969); Sally Lopreato and Dudley Poston, "Differences in Earnings and Earnings Ability between Black Veterans and Nonveterans in the United States," *Social Science Quarterly* 57 (March 1977): 750–66; William M. Mason, "On the Socioeconomic Effects of Military Service," Ph.D. diss., University of Chicago, 1970).

12. Kattenbrink examined the intergenerational mobility of two groups of white males in New York State: former servicemen who had returned to the civilian community, and men who had not served in the military. See Kattenbrink, "Military Service and Occupational Mobility."

13. Mason compared the socioeconomic status of veterans with that of nonveterans. He found that the degree of education during and after service was influenced by the serviceperson's occupational status as well as by the length of time he spent on active duty. In addition, more significant differences existed between men of different rank than between men who did and did not serve. See Mason, "On the Socioeconomic Effects of Military Service."

14. These authors studied the connections between military service and status attainment in conjunction with the location of African and Mexican Americans in the civilian stratification system. The military creates a "bridging environment" (one that provides the conditions for upward mobility) by providing the individual with (1) a radical break from civilian life and kinship ties, thereby facilitating resocialization, (2) further education and on-the-job training, and (3) an increased capability to cope with and manipulate the large-scale organizational structures that typify the United States. See Harley Browning, Sally Lopreato, and Dudley Poston, "Income and Veterans Status: Variations among Mexican Americans, Blacks, and Anglos," *American Sociological Review* 38 (1973): 74–85. The authors adapted the definition of a bridging environment from Broom and Smith, who defined it as one that provides

the conditions and opportunities for movement from one occupation to another. See Leonard Broom and J. H. Smith, "Bridging Occupations," *British Journal of Sociology* 14 (December 1963): 321–34.

15. Lopreato and Poston, "Differences in Earnings and Earnings Ability between Black Veterans and Nonveterans in the United States."

16. Dudley Poston, "The Influence of Military Service on the Civilian Earning Patterns of Blacks, Mexican Americans, and Anglos," *Journal of Political and Military Sociology* 7 (1979): 71–88.

17. Fredland and Little found that skilled manual civilian training yielded significantly high premiums to those who received and used civilian training, but the premiums were not significant for skilled manual military training. See Eric Fredland and Roger Little, "Long Term Returns to Vocational Training: Evidence from Military Sources," *Journal of Human Resources* 15 (Winter 1980): 49–66.

18. Elder et al., "Turning Points," 217.

19. Ibid.

20. Keith W. Olson, *The G.I. Bill, the Veterans, and the Colleges* (Lexington: University Press of Kentucky, 1974), 17.

21. Elder et al., "Turning Points," 227.

22. Ibid., 217.

23. Elder, Gimble, and Ivie listed ten reasons military service was a turning point in lives of eighty-six men in the Oakland/Berkeley sample used in their study. In rank order the reasons were maturity, education, travel/adventure, independence, altered view of life, life disruption, met spouse, altered view of death, career, and leadership. See Elder et al., "Turning Points," 223.

Notes to Chapter 7

1. The study of phenomenology is rooted in the work of Edmund Husserl, who sought the essence of human knowledge and was not concerned with the objects of the empirical world. See Edmund Husserl, *Idea,* trans. W. Boyce-Gibson (New York: Macmillan, 1962); Edmund Husserl, *The Phenomenology of Internal Time-Consciousness,* ed. Martin Heidegger (Bloomington: Indiana University Press, 1964); Edmund Husserl, *Formal and Transcendental Logic,* trans. Dorion Cairns (The Hague: Martinus Nijhoff, 1969).

2. Peter Berger and Thomas Luckmann, *The Social Construction of Reality: A Treatise in the Sociology of Knowledge* (Garden City, N.Y.:

Anchor, 1967); Erving Goffman, *The Presentation of Self in Everyday Life* (New York: Doubleday/Anchor, 1959); Dorothy Smith, *The Everyday World as Problematic: A Feminist Sociology* (Boston: Northeastern University Press, 1987).

3. Patricia Hill Collins, *Black Feminist Thought: Knowledge, Consciousness, and the Politics of Empowerment* (New York: Routledge, 1991), 202.

4. Samuel Stouffer, Arthur Lumsdaine, Marion Lumsdaine, Robin Williams, M. Brewster Smith, Irving Janis, Shirley Star, and Leonard Cottrell, Jr., *The American Soldier* vol. 1, *Adjustment during Army Life* (Princeton: Princeton University Press, 1949).

5. Edward Shils and Morris Janowitz, "Cohesion and Disintegration in the Wehrmacht," *Public Opinion Quarterly* 12 (Summer 1948): 280–315.

6. Tamotsu Shibutani, *The Derelicts of K Company* (Berkeley: University of California Press, 1978).

7. Charity Adams Earley, *One Woman's Army: A Black Officer Remembers the WAC* (College Station: Texas A&M University Press, 1989), 145.

8. Mattie E. Treadwell, *The Women's Army Corps* (Washington, D.C.: U.S. Government Printing Office, 1954), 600.

9. Some black political groups urged Congress to write a protective nondiscriminatory clause in the WAAC bill to guarantee racial equality. Vowing that black Waacs would be treated equally and would not suffer discrimination because of their race, the War Department insisted that such a clause was unnecessary. Because of this promise, the dispute about the clause never developed into a major issue. Issues concerning the treatment of African American Waacs/Wacs surfaced periodically, however; as illustrated above, these issues were confronted by African American organizations unified for change. See Ulysses Lee, *The Employment of Negro Troops* (Washington, D.C.: U.S. Government Printing Office, 1966), 421–22.

10. Mattie Treadwell, *United States Army in World War II: Special Studies: The Women's Army Corps* (Washington, D.C.: U.S. Government Printing Office, 1954), 599.

11. Coser argues that conflicts that arise from frustration of specific demands within the relationship and from estimates of the participants' gains, and which are directed at the presumed frustrating object, can be

called realistic conflicts insofar as they are means toward a specific result. Nonrealistic conflicts, on the other hand, although still involving interaction between two or more persons, are not occasioned by the rival ends of the antagonists but by the need for release of tension by at least one of the parties. See Lewis Coser, *The Functions of Social Conflict* (New York: Free Press, 1956), 49.

12. Simmel, *Conflict,* 27–28.

13. Coser, *Functions of Social Conflict,* 128.

14. Simmel, *Conflict,* 91, 92.

15. Berger and Luckmann, *Social Construction of Reality,* 123, 124.

16. Smith, *Everyday World as Problematic,* 19.

17. Berger and Luckmann, *Social Construction of Reality,* 109.

18. Collins, *Black Feminist Thought,* 174.

19. Several women returned to the civilian sector in the mid to late 1940s; most public facilities in the South were not desegregated until after the civil rights movement of the 1960s.

20. Berger and Luckmann, *Social Construction of Reality,* 65.

21. Ibid., 108.

22. Myrtle Rhoden, interview by author; Mary Rozier, interview by author; Gertrude LaVigne, interview by author.

23. One of the central propositions of split (dual) labor market theory is that jobs can be divided into two groups, primary and secondary. Jobs in the primary sector offer more money and security, and otherwise are more desirable, than those of the secondary sector. Although the split (dual) labor market theory has many proponents, the study referenced for the present analysis is Suzanne Berger and Michael Piore, *Dualism and Discontinuity in Industrial Societies* (New York: Cambridge University Press, 1980).

24. Earley, *One Woman's Army,* 164, 165.

25. See chapter 3 for discussion about complaints made by Negro Wacs at Fort Des Moines in February 1944.

26. Bertha Solomon Walker, *Call and Post,* Cleveland, 9 June 1994, 1.

27. Bettie J. Morden, *The Women's Army Corps, 1945–5978* (Washington, D.C.: U.S. Government Printing Office, 1990), 28.

28. Edwin Dorn, *Who Defends America? Race, Sex, and Class in the Armed Forces* (Washington, D.C.: Joint Center for Political Studies, 1989), 46–48; Brenda L. Moore, "African American Women in the U.S.

Military," *Armed Forces and Society* 17, no.3 (Spring 1991): 363–65.

29. Curtis Gilroy, Robert Phillips, and John Blair, "The All-Volunteer Army: Fifteen Years Later," *Armed Forces and Society* 16, no. 3 (Spring 1990): 329–35.

30. Alvin Schexnider, "Symposium: Race and the United States Military," *Armed Forces and Society* 6, no. 4 (Summer 1980): 606–13.

31. Ronald Dellums, "Don't Slam the Door to Military," *Focus* 3, no. 8 (June 1975): 6; Alvin Schexnider, "Expectations from the Ranks: Representativeness and Systems," *American Behavioral Scientist* 19, no.5 (May/June 1976): 523–42; Alvin Schexnider and John S. Butler, "Race and the All-Volunteer System," *Armed Forces and Society* 2, no. 3 (May 1976): 421–32.

Notes to Chapter 8

1. "Tripping Down Memory Lane," *Birmingham Evening Mail*, 29 April 1981; Cassandra Spratling, "Hands across the Water Give a Warm Shake," *Detroit Free Press*, 12 May 1981.

2. Spratling, "Hands across the Water Give a Warm Shake."

★ ★ ★

Bibliography

Aptheker, Bettina. *Woman's Legacy: Essays on Race, Sex, and Class in American History*. Amherst: University of Massachusetts Press, 1982.

Bailey, Buncan, and Thomas F. Cargill. "The Military Draft and Future Income." *Western Economic Journal* 7, (1969): 365–70.

Becker, Gary. *Human Capital*. Chicago: University of Chicago Press, 1975.

Berger, Peter, and Thomas Luckmann. *The Social Construction of Reality: A Treatise in the Sociology of Knowledge*. Garden City, N.Y.: Anchor, 1967.

Berger, Suzanne, and Michael Piore. *Dualism and Discontinuity in Industrial Societies*. New York: Cambridge University Press, 1980.

Berry, Mary Frances, and John W. Blassingame. *Long Memory: The Black Experience in America*. New York: Oxford University Press, 1982.

Binkin, Martin, Mark Eitelberg, Alvin Schexnider, and Marvin Smith. *Blacks and the Military*. Washington, D.C.: Brookings Institution, 1982.

Bogue, Donald. *Principles of Demography*. New York: Wiley, 1969.

Broek, Jacobus ten. *The Anti-Slavery Origins of the Fourteenth Amendment*. Berkeley: University of California Press, 1951.

Broom, Leonard, and J. H. Smith. "Bridging Occupations." *British Journal of Sociology* 14 (December 1963): 321–34.

Browning, Harley, Sally Lopreato, and Dudley Poston. "Income and

Veterans Status: Variations among Mexican Americans, Blacks, and Anglos." *American Sociological Review* 38 (1973): 74–85.

Campbell, D'Ann. *Women at War with America: Private Lives in a Patriotic Era.* Cambridge: Harvard University Press, 1984.

Clark, Grenville. "National War Service Act Is Regarded as Essential." *New York Times,* 29 August 1943.

Clausen, John A. "Turning Points as a Life Course Concept." Paper presented at the annual meeting of the American Sociological Association, Washington, D.C., August 1990.

———. *American Lives: Looking Back at the Great Depression.* New York: Free Press, 1993.

Collins, Patricia Hill. *Black Feminist Thought: Knowledge, Consciousness, and the Politics of Empowerment.* New York: Routledge, 1991.

Coser, Lewis. *The Functions of Social Conflict.* New York: Free Press, 1956.

Cox, Oliver C. *Caste, Class, and Race: A Study in Social Dynamics.* Garden City, N.Y.: Doubleday, 1948.

Davis, Allison, Burleigh Gardner, and Mary Gardner. *Deep South.* Chicago: University of Chicago Press, 1941.

Davis, Angela Y. *Women, Race, and Class.* New York: Random House, 1981.

Day, Richard H. "Technological Change and the Sharecropper." *American Economic Review* 57 (June 1967): 427–29.

Deckard, Barbara S. *The Women's Movement: Political, Socioeconomic, and Psychological Issues.* New York: Harper and Row, 1983.

Dellums, Ronald. "Don't Slam the Door to Military." *Focus* 3, no. 8 (June 1975): 6.

Dorn, Edwin. *Who Defends America? Race, Sex, and Class in the Armed Forces.* Washington, D.C.: Joint Center for Political Studies, 1989.

Drake, St. Clair, and Horace R. Cayton. *Black Metropolis: A Study of Negro Life in a Northern City.* New York: Harper and Row, 1945.

Du Bois, W. E. B. "Close Ranks." *The Crisis: A Record of the Darker Races,* July 1918, 11.

Duster, Alfreda M., ed. *Crusade for Justice: The Autobiography of Ida B. Wells.* Chicago: University of Chicago Press, 1970.

Earley, Charity Adams. *One Woman's Army: A Black Officer Remembers the WAC.* College Station: Texas A&M University Press, 1989.

Elder, Glen H. "Military Times and Turning Points in Men's Lives." *Developmental Psychology* 22 (1986): 233–45.

Elder, Glen H., Cynthia Gimble, and Rachel Ivie. "Turning Points in Life: The Case of Military Service and War." *Military Psychology* 3, no. 4 (1991): 215–31.

Enloe, Cynthia. *Bananas, Beaches, and Bases.* Berkeley: University of California Press, 1990.

Ferree, Myra Marx, and Beth C. Hess. *Controversy and Coalition: The New Feminist Movement.* Boston: Twayne, 1985.

Foner, Jack. *Blacks and the Military in American History.* New York: Praeger, 1974.

Franklin, John Hope, and Alfred A. Moss, Jr. *From Slavery to Freedom: A History of Negro Americans.* 6th ed. New York: Knopf, 1988.

Frazier, E. Franklin. "Occupational Classes among Negroes in Cities" in *American Journal of Sociology* 35 (March 1930): 718–38.

———. *The Negro in the United States.* Rev. ed. New York: Macmillan, 1957.

Fredland, Eric, and Roger Little. "Long Term Returns to Vocational Training: Evidence from Military Sources." *Journal of Human Resources* 15 (Winter 1980): 49–66.

Gaines, Ernest J. *The Autobiography of Miss Jane Pittman.* New York: Dial, 1971.

Garraty, John A. *The American Nation: A History of the United States since 1865.* Vol. 2, 3rd ed. New York: Harper and Row, 1975.

Giddings, Paula. *When and Where I Enter: The Impact of Black Women on Race and Sex in America.* New York: Bantam, 1984.

Gilroy, Curtis, Robert Phillips, and John Blair. "The All-Volunteer Army: Fifteen Years Later." *Armed Forces and Society* 16, no. 3 (Spring 1990): 329–35.

Gluck, Sherna B. *Rosie the Riveter Revisited: Women, the War, and Social Change.* Boston: Twayne, 1987.

Goffman, Erving. *The Presentation of Self in Everyday Life.* New York: Doubleday/Anchor, 1959.

Goode, Erich. *Collective Behavior.* New York: Harcourt Brace Jovanovich, 1992.

Hansen, W. Lee, and Burton Weisbrod. "Economics of the Military Draft." *Quarterly Journal of Economics* 81 (1967): 395–421.

Hastings, T. J. "The Stanford-Terman Study Revisited: Postwar Emotional Health of World War II Veterans." *Military Psychology* 3 (1991): 201–14.

Hitler, Adolf. *Mein Kampf.* Boston: Houghton Mifflin, 1943.

Honey, Maureen. *Creating Rosie the Riveter: Class, Gender, and Propaganda during World War II.* Amherst: University of Massachusetts Press, 1984.

hooks, bell. *Feminist Theory from Margin to Center.* Boston: South End Press, 1984.

Hope, Richard. *Racial Strife in the U.S. Military.* New York: Praeger, 1979.

Horton, Mildred McAfee. "Recollections of Captain Mildred McAfee, USNR (Ret.)." In *WAVES Officers of World War II,* vol. 1. Annapolis: U.S. Naval Institute, 1971.

Huntington, Samuel. *The Soldier and the State.* Cambridge: Harvard University Press, 1957.

Husserl, Edmund. *Idea.* Translated by W. Boyce-Gibson. New York: Macmillan, 1962.

———. *The Phenomenology of Internal Time-Consciousness.* Edited by Martin Heidegger, translated by James Churchill. Bloomington: Indiana University Press, 1964.

———. *Formal and Transcendental Logic.* Translated by Dorion Cairns. The Hague: Martinus Nijhoff, 1969.

Janowitz, Morris. *The Professional Soldier.* New York: Free Press, 1971.

Johnson, Jesse. *Black Women in the Armed Forces: 1942–1974.* Hampton, Va.: Jesse Johnson, 1974.

Kanter, Rosabeth Moss. *Men and Women of the Corporation.* New York: Basic Books, 1977.

Karenga, Maulana. *Introduction to Black Studies.* Los Angeles: Kawaida, 1987.

Kattenbrink, Irvin G. "Military Service and Occupational Mobility." In *Selective Service and American Society,* edited by Roger Little. New York: Russell Sage Foundation, 1969.

Landry, Bart. *The New Black Middle Class.* Berkeley: University of California Press, 1987.

Lasky, A. Victor. "First Negro Wacs Overseas Reach U.K." *Stars and Stripes,* 14 February 1945.

Lee, Ulysses. *United States Army in World War II: Special Studies: The Employment of Negro Troops.* Washington, D.C.: U.S. Government Printing Office, 1966.

Lerner, Gerda, ed. *Black Women in White America: A Documentary History.* New York: Vintage, 1972.

Lieberson, Stanley. *A Piece of the Pie: Blacks and White Immigrants since 1880.* Berkeley: University of California Press, 1980.

Lopreato, Sally, and Dudley Poston. "Differences in Earnings and Earnings Ability between Black Veterans and Nonveterans in the United States." *Social Science Quarterly* 57 (March 1977): 750–66.

Lynd, Robert S., and Helen M. Lynd. *Middletown.* New York: Harcourt Brace, 1929.

Lyons, Michael J. *World War II: A Short History.* Englewood Cliffs, N.J.: Prentice Hall, 1994.

MacGregor, Morris J. *Integration of the Armed Forces, 1940–1965.* Washington, D.C.: U.S. Government Printing Office, 1981.

Mannheim, Karl. *Ideology and Utopia.* New York: Harcourt, Brace and World, 1936.

Marshall, T. H. *Class, Citizenship, and Social Development.* Chicago: University of Chicago Press, 1977.

Mason, William M. "On the Socioeconomic Effects of Military Service." Ph.D. diss, University of Chicago, 1970.

Modell, John, Marc Goulden, and Sigurdur Magnusson. "World War II in the Lives of Black Americans: Some Findings and an Interpretation." *Journal of American History* 76, no. 3 (December 1989): 839–47.

Moore, Brenda L. "African American Women in the U.S. Military." *Armed Forces and Society* 17, no. 3 (Spring 1991): 363–84.

———. "Serving with a Dual Mission: African American Women in World War II." *National Journal of Sociology* 7, no. 1 (1993): 1–42.

Morden, Bettie J. *The Women's Army Corps, 1945–5978.* Washington, D.C.: U.S. Government Printing Office, 1990.

Myrdal, Gunnar. *An American Dilemma: The Negro Problem and Modern Democracy.* New York: Harper, 1944.

Nichols, Lee. *Breakthrough on the Color Front.* New York: Random House, 1954.

Oi, Walter Y. "The Economic Cost of the Draft." *American Economic Review* 57 (1967): 39–62.

Olson, Keith W. *The G.I. Bill, the Veterans, and the Colleges.* Lexington: University Press of Kentucky, 1974.

Pierce, Joseph A. *Negro Business and Business Education, Their Present and Prospective Development.* Westport, Conn.: Negro Universities Press, 1971.

Pitts, Lucia M. *One Negro WAC's Story.* Los Angeles: Lucia M. Pitts, 1968.

Poston, Dudley. "The Influence of Military Service on the Civilian Earning Patterns of Blacks, Mexican Americans, and Anglos." *Journal of Political and Military Sociology* 7 (1979): 71–88.

Putney, Martha S. *When the Nation Was in Need: Blacks in the Women's Army Corps during World War II.* Metuchen, N.J: Scarecrow Press, 1992.

Schexnider, Alvin. "Expectations from the Ranks: Representativeness and Systems." *American Behavioral Scientist* 19, no. 5 (May/June 1976): 523–42.

———. "Symposium: Race and the United States Military." *Armed Forces and Society* 6, no. 4 (Summer 1980): 606–13.

Schexnider, Alvin, and John S. Butler. "Race and the All-Volunteer System." *Armed Forces and Society* 2, no. 3 (May 1976): 421–32.

Segal, Mady W. "Women in the Military: Research and Policy Issues." *Youth and Society* 10, no. 2 (December 1978): 101–26.

Shibutani, Tamotsu. *The Derelicts of K Company.* Berkeley: University of California Press, 1978.

Shils, Edward, and Morris Janowitz. "Cohesion and Disintegration in the Wehrmacht." *Public Opinion Quarterly* 12 (Summer 1948): 280–315.

Simmel, Georg. *Conflict.* Translated by Kurt Wolf. Glencoe, Ill.: Free Press, 1955.

Smith, Dorothy. *The Everyday World as Problematic: A Feminist Sociology.* Boston: Northeastern University Press, 1987.

Smith, Graham. *When Jim Crow Met John Bull: Black American Soldiers in World War II Britain.* New York: St. Martin's, 1988.

Spratling, Cassandra. "Hands across the Water Give a Warm Shake." *Detroit Free Press,* 12 May 1981.

Stouffer, Samuel, Arthur Lumsdaine, Marion Lumsdaine, Robin Williams, M. Brewster Smith, Irving Janis, Shirley Star, and Leonard Cottrell, Jr. *The American Soldier.* Vol. 1, *Adjustment during Army Life.* Vol. 2, *Combat and Its Aftermath.* Princeton, N.J.: Princeton University Press, 1949.

Treadwell, Mattie E. *United States Army in World War II: Special Studies: The Women's Army's Corps.* Washington, D.C.: U.S. Government Printing Office, 1954.

U.S. Department of Commerce. *Sixteenth Census of the United States: 1940.* Washington, D.C.: U.S. Government Printing Office, 1943.

———. *Statistical Abstract of the United States 1989.* Washington, D.C.: U.S. Government Printing Office, 1989.

U.S. Department of Defense. Office of the Assistant Deputy of Defense for Equal Opportunity and Safety Policy. *Black Americans in the Defense of Our Nation.* Washington, D.C.: U.S. Government Printing Office, 1985.

———. *Blacks in the Defense of Our Nation.* Washington, D.C.: U.S. Government Printing Office, 1991.

van den Berghe, Pierre L. *The Ethnic Phenomenon.* New York: Praeger, 1987.

Weber, Max. *The Theory of Social and Economic Organization.* Glencoe, Ill; Free Press, 1947.

Wells, Ida B. *Crusade for Justice: The Autobiography of Ida B. Wells.* Edited by Alfreda M. Duster. Chicago: University of Chicago Press, 1970.

Willett, Thomas D. "Another Cost of Conscription." *Western Economic Journal* 6 (1963): 425–27.

Wilson, William J. *The Declining Significance of Race: Blacks and Changing American Institutions.* Chicago: University of Chicago Press, 1980.

Wirth, Louis. "Morale and Minority Groups." *American Journal of Sociology* 47, no. 3 (1941): 415–33.

Zald, Meyer, and John McCarthy. *Social Movements in an Organizational Society.* New Brunswick, N.J.: Transaction Books, 1987.

★ ★ ★

Index

Jordan, Mercedes, 97
Julius Rosenwald Fund, 68

Kanter, Rosabeth, 24
Kattenbrink, Irving, 150–51, 251 n. 12
Kearney, Mary, 96
Kennedy, Vann B., 62, 63
King Edward School, 111–13, 115–56
Kitchen Police (KP), 72
Kronberg Castle, 46
Ku Klux Klan, 95

Lam, Dr. Elizabeth, 45
Landry, Bart, 232 n. 12
LaVigne, Gertrude Cruse, 8, 82, 98, 105, 107, 124, 126, 127, 146, 166–67, 189, 247 n. 22, 249 n. 23, 254 n. 22
Leadership: military, 25; 6888th, 129–33, 185
Lee, Gen. John C. H., 30, 109
Lee, Ulysses, 231 n. 1, 234 n. 5, 236 nn. 15, 17, 18, 20, 237 nn. 25, 26, 27, 31, 253 n. 9
Le Havre, 115
Leonard, Mildred Dupee, 72, 93, 97, 100, 105, 111, 157, 160, 164
Lerner, Gerda, 241 n. 12
Lesbians. *See* Homosexuals
Lieberson, Stanley, 232–33 n. 12, 235 n. 10
Little, Roger, 148, 251 n. 11, 252 n. 17
Living quarters. *See* Quarters, living
Lockburn Air Force Base, 173
Locket, Colonel, 18
Lopreato, Sally, 152, 251 n. 14, 252 n. 15
Lord, Mrs. Oswald B., 44, 239 n. 59
Lowe, Leatrice, 125–26
Luckman, Thomas, 190–93, 252 n. 2, 254 n. 15
Lumsdaine, Arthur, 250 n. 1, 253 n. 4
Lumsdaine, Marion, 250 n. 1, 253 n. 4
Lyons, Michael, 237 n. 37

MacGregor, Morris, 244 n. 58
Macy, Col. Noel, 62, 243 n. 33
Magnusson, Sigurdur, 145–46, 250 n. 1
Malassignments, 69; rebelling against, 78
Marcantonio, Congressman Vito, 78
Marine Corps, 1, 3

Marriage, 165–68
Marshall, Gen. George C., 33
Marshall, Odessa Taylor, 134, 155, 167
Mason-Dixon line, 58
Mason, William, 151–52, 251 n. 13
Maw, Governor Herbert, 43
Maxton Air Force Base, 175
McAlpin, Harry, 62, 243 n. 33, 245 n. 76
McAteea, Viola, 69, 244 n. 53
McBride, Mary, 100, 125–26, 134
McCarthy, John, 38, 238 n. 46
McCormack, John, 72, 73, 244 n. 63
McCoskrie, Col. F. U., 245 n. 67
McNulty, Timothy J., 249 n. 28
Mental alertness test, 57
Michigan Chronicle, 241 n. 21
Miles, Gen. Sherman, 78
Military Branch Personnel Division, 67
Military Reference Branch of the National Archives, 4
Military service: as bridging environment, 152–53, 171, 251–52 n. 14; as confirmation of citizenship, 9, 194; effects of, 144–78; intangible rewards of, 154–60; previous studies of effects of, 148–54; regional variation in effects of, 145; self-confidence as reward of, 156; tangible rewards of, 154–60; as turning point, 168–78, 250 n. 9, 252 n. 18
Miller, Capt. Mary, 112
Mitchell, Noel Campbell, 14, 17, 53, 58, 59, 60, 84, 91, 94, 96–99, 101, 103, 104, 109–10, 112, 140, 164, 242 n. 26
Modell, John, 145–46, 250 nn. 1, 3
Moore, Brenda L., 235 n. 11, 254 n. 28
Moore, Irma L., 69
Morale, 55, 70, 76, 78, 111, 139–43, 148, 187, 194
Morden, Bettie J., 254 n. 27
Moss, Alfred, 233–35, 239 n. 1
Moton, Jennie, 92, 247 n. 14
Motor convoy, 118
Murray, Florence, 73, 244 n. 65
Myrdal, Gunnar, 232 n. 12, 235 n. 9, 236 n. 14

Nash, Col. John, 79
National American Woman Suffrage Association (NAWSA), 51